W9-BNB-648

ABORTION
A Reference Handbook

ABORTION

A Reference Handbook

Marie Costa

CONTEMPORARY WORLD ISSUES

ABC-CLIO

Santa Barbara, California
Denver, Colorado
Oxford, England

Library of Congress Cataloging-in-Publication Data

Costa, Marie, 1951–
    Abortion : a reference handbook / Marie Costa
      p. cm. — (Contemporary world issues)
    Includes bibliographical references and index.
    1. Abortion—United States—Handbooks, manuals, etc.
  I. Title. II. Series.
  HQ767.5.U5C67 1991   363.4'6—dc20   91-15231

ISBN 0-87436-602-X (alk. paper)

98 97 96 95 94 93 92   10 9 8 7 6 5 4 3 2

ABC-CLIO, Inc.
130 Cremona Drive, P.O. Box 1911
Santa Barbara, California 93116-1911

This book is printed on acid-free paper ∞ .
Manufactured in the United States of America

This book is dedicated to my husband,
whose loving support made it possible

Contents

Introduction

ABORTION, A WORD ONCE RARELY SPOKEN OUT LOUD, has over the last three decades become synonymous with controversy and conflict. Many of those involved in the controversy seem to feel they are at war with an enemy that strikes at the heart of their values and beliefs, at the whole order by which they organize their lives. "We are pro," claims each camp, "and they are anti"—anti-baby, anti-woman, anti-family, anti-choice, anti-life, anti-everything we and the country stand for.

Participants in a debate such as this often hold the common belief that "if people really understood what this is all about, they would agree with us (and do what we want them to)." But this is not necessarily the case. People can understand one another and still disagree. A pregnant woman may understand that an abortion means the death of a living human being and still choose to abort. A "sidewalk counselor" may understand that continuing a pregnancy will disrupt or even devastate a woman's life and still urge her to have the baby. By the same token, a woman who always believed that if she got pregnant she would have an abortion may be unwilling to carry through with her plan, and a woman who has picketed an abortion clinic may find herself a patient at that very clinic. When the abstract becomes real and personal, what seemed clear and indisputable can become murky indeed. Yet each side continues to hurl its slogans and images at the other and at anyone in the vicinity, as if shouting louder and harder, telling the most poignant stories, or displaying the most riveting images will somehow convince everyone to see it their way.

Although abortion has been a source of conflict throughout history and all over the world, the battle as it is being fought in the United States today is distinctly American. Laurence Tribe (1990) compares American attitudes about abortion with those in more repressive societies such as Stalinist Russia, Nazi Germany, and Communist China. In these countries, he writes, "neither those advocating abortion nor those opposing it use the language of 'rights' that characterizes the abortion debate in the United States. Scant attention is paid either to the rights of the woman to have her child or to her right to terminate her pregnancy—or to any right of the fetus to be born. Rather, the conflict is structured almost wholly in terms of corporate groups, like the state and the family, and centers on the needs of and the duties owed to such groups" (p. 63).

But the United States was largely founded on the concept of rights, so that here even moral issues—and almost no one would disagree that abortion is a moral issue—are framed in the language of rights. Few issues, however, place such cherished and, in many minds, fundamental rights in direct conflict—the right to live versus the right to choose how to live, including whether or not to become a parent. Other rights, too, are involved in the struggle over abortion, such as the right to speak out versus the right to exercise a legal option. Values are also at issue in the American battle over abortion. Some see the conflict as one between traditional family values and self-expression and fulfillment, between Judeo-Christian ethics and the more amorphous "situational ethics," between selflessness and selfishness. Others see it as a conflict between those who would stop change and those who would pursue a vision of a new world.

Can such a conflict ever be resolved? Some, such as sociologist Kristin Luker, say no, because those holding "pro-choice" and "pro-life" opinions also hold world views that are diametrically opposed. Others believe a resolution is possible by adopting a compromise solution that would please neither side but that "most people" could live with—allowing abortions only in the first 12 weeks, for example, or only for specific reasons. Still others believe the issue will eventually become moot, as RU 486 or some other drug becomes readily available—if not in the near future, then in ten years, after the drug's patent expires and it becomes financially easier to introduce in the United States.

Perhaps in anticipation of this time, or simply through a realization that the old tactics have brought about a stalemate, significant changes are taking place on both sides. The battle for safe, legal abortion has expanded, in large part due to the efforts of women of color, into a call for full reproductive freedom, including the right to have, as well as not to have, children. Such a movement seeks access not only to contraceptives and safe abortion, but also to prenatal care, child care, and help for women and families. In the same way, many of those opposed to abortion have chosen to focus on making the alternatives more attractive and feasible, by providing housing, medical care, jobs, education help, financial assistance, parenting classes, and compassionate adoption services to women facing unplanned pregnancies.

The publicity given to the loud voices, the demonstrations, and the slogans obscures the fact that many people on both sides share a common goal: to make "choice" a reality where little choice existed before. In the past, a woman with an unwanted pregnancy usually "had no choice" but to continue being pregnant, often at the price of social disgrace. Then she "had no choice" but to relinquish her baby to strangers, to enter a too-hasty marriage, or to struggle as a single parent of a child branded as illegitimate. Today, thousands of women have abortions because they feel they "have no choice"—because they lack financial resources, family support, or a loving partner; because their education or their career is at stake; or because they have too much to cope with already. As Mary Cunningham Agee, founder of The Nurturing Network, says, "Both the 'pro-life' and 'pro-choice' movements—characterized most often by their emotionally-charged legislative battles, rhetorical debates and judgmental protests—often overlook the imminent needs of the woman about whom they are arguing." Agee believes that "there *does* exist, between the two groups, a *common ground* (not necessarily a 'middle' ground), which would provide both groups with an opportunity to serve the woman faced with an unwanted pregnancy."

Such efforts would bring both sides into closer alignment with the majority of Americans, most of whom regard the issue with profound ambivalence. Nonetheless, the battle over abortion no doubt will continue to rage for some time to come—in the media, on the sidewalks before abortion clinics, in state and national legislatures, in the courts, in the churches, and within the medical profession. For this reason, it is important for Americans, whether they are deeply involved in the conflict or simply are concerned observers, to understand what the battle is about. Though understanding may not bring agreement, it can bring compassion, empathy, and a willingness to talk; with these come the possibility of finding the common ground that does exist. As Faye Ginsburg (1989) discovered in her study of abortion activists in Fargo, North Dakota, "Whether pro-life or pro-choice, activists express their motivation for social action as a desire to alter the meaning and circumstances of procreation in order to make conditions better for the next generation. In other words, they are concerned, as female activists, with their role in reproducing the culture, but in terms different from the present" (p. 144).

It is possible that the struggle over abortion presents a greater opportunity than is at first apparent amidst the smoke from the fires of passionate debate. Perhaps it represents an opportunity that can only be discovered on the common ground where lies the hope for a better world, a world in which each child—each person—is loved, welcomed, and respected, in which all life is valued, and in which everyone has the opportunity for fulfillment and self-expression, however they define it. This book is dedicated to the search for that common ground.

About This Book

The purpose of this book is to provide access to the available information, as well as the full spectrum of thought, on abortion. It is not intended to promulgate any view, except the view that all voices should be heard and listened to. Historical and factual background information is presented, along with resources for further exploration into the social, psychological, legal, medical, political, and moral aspects of abortion. Because it pulls together a wide array of information not available in any other single source, this book may prove helpful to many different people— students, researchers, writers, journalists, historians, and activists, as well as individuals who are interested in clarifying their own thoughts and feelings about abortion. Be warned, however—the more you know, the less clear those thoughts and feelings may become. Such is the nature of this complex, troubling, and endlessly fascinating topic.

Organization

Like other titles in the Contemporary World Issues series, this book is meant to serve as both a "one-stop" resource and as a guide to further research. Chapter 1 sets the historical context with a chronology that includes significant legislation, court decisions, medical developments, trends, political events, religious proclamations, and other relevant occurrences. Chapter 2 contains biographical sketches of some of the key players in the debate, including activists, doctors, lawyers, and politicians. Chapter 3 contains statistical and factual information about abortion, including laws and policies, statistics, medical techniques, complications and risks, embryonic and fetal development, harassment of abortion providers, and public opinion about abortion. Chapter 4 is an annotated directory of organizations, including activist groups, research organizations, educational organizations, legal defense funds, political lobbying groups, and support services that include alternatives to abortion. Chapter 5 is an annotated bibliography of print resources, including bibliographies, anthologies, books and monographs, and periodicals. Chapter 6 is an annotated listing of nonprint resources, including a computer database search service, films, and videocassettes. A glossary of important terms and an index complete the volume.

About the Language Used in This Book

Language has become a major sub-issue in the abortion debate, with people on each side employing different terms to describe themselves and their opponents. It is difficult for a writer not to get caught up in the crossfire or to keep from being accused of taking sides based on her or his terminology. In an effort to be both balanced and descriptive I have adopted the following approach: when describing specific individuals or organizations I have tried to use the terms they would use themselves, most often "pro-life" or "pro-choice." In more general contexts, however, I have used terms that describe the participants in relationship to their specific stance on abortion; for example, "abortion rights supporters" or "advocates of legal abortion" on the one side and "anti-abortion groups" or "opponents of legal abortion" on the other. I hope most readers will find these terms acceptable.

References

Agee, Mary Cunningham, *Unique and Differentiating Characteristics of the Nurturing Network* (descriptive paper, undated).

Ginsburg, Faye D., *Contested Lives* (Berkeley: University of California Press, 1989).

Luker, Kristin, *Abortion and the Politics of Motherhood* (Berkeley: University of California Press, 1984).

Tribe, Laurence H., *Abortion: The Clash of Absolutes* (New York: W. W. Norton and Company, 1990).

Acknowledgments

I thank the many people who responded to my requests for information, in particular Dave Andrusko, Dr. Jane Hodgson, Dr. Joseph Stanton, and Wendy Wright, all of whom took time from busy schedules to aid my search and all of whom provided me with information, suggestions, and "leads" that have enriched the content and broadened the scope of this book.

Chronology

Roman Empire

Despite official pronatalist policies promoting at least three children per couple among the upper classes, abortion and contraception are frequent and widespread among those who can afford it (among the poor, infanticide and abandonment are common). According to Roman law, the "child in the belly of its mother" is not a person, and abortion, therefore, does not constitute murder. Such legal regulation of abortion as exists in the Roman Empire at this time is aimed at protecting the rights of fathers, not of fetuses. Wives who procure an abortion without their husband's consent are subject to exile, as are women who administer contraceptives or abortifacients. References are made to abortion in the writings of Ovid, Juvenal, Seneca, and Pliny, who lists abortifacient drugs.

Ancient Greece

In *The Republic,* Plato states that women who become pregnant after the age of 40 should be compelled to have abortions. Aristotle believes that the state should determine the number of children a married couple may have and that any woman becoming pregnant after reaching the allotted number should have an abortion. He proposes that the fetus first has a vegetable soul, which is succeeded by an animal soul, and finally, when the body is fully developed, by a human soul, so that early abortion is not the killing of a human being. Hippocrates, however, disapproves of abortion and includes a clause against it in his medical oath.

Beginning of Christian Era
(First through Seventh Centuries)

From the first century onward, Christian thought is divided as to whether early abortion is murder. An early church document, the *Didache,* condemns abortion, saying, "You shall not kill the fetus by abortion or destroy the infant already born" (Hurst, 1989, p. 6). Many early documents indicate that during this period abortion is considered a sin if it is used to conceal evidence of the sins of fornication or adultery. St. Augustine, while condemning birth control and abortion because they break the proscribed connection between the sexual act and procreation, does not hold abortion to be homicide if it occurs before hominization of the fetus. Hominization—also referred to as formation, animation, vivification, or ensoulment of an embryo—is thought to occur at 40 days for a male and 80 days for a female embryo; in questions of ambiguity the embryo is considered female.

Middle Christian Era
(Eighth through Sixteenth Centuries)

According to Hurst (1989), throughout this period abortion is treated as a serious sin of a sexual nature, but is not considered homicide. The *Irish Canons,* written around A.D. 675, specify one penalty for abortion before hominization and a different and more serious penalty after hominization. Writing around A.D. 1100, church scholar Ivo of Chartres, while condemning abortion, states that abortion of an "unformed embryo" is not homicide. This stance will be reiterated 40 years later by Gratian, whose writings on the subject would form the basis of canon law for the next 700 years.

In practice, particularly because of the uncertainty as to when pregnancy actually began, the concept of delayed hominization means that early abortions are not considered criminal acts; further, there is some debate as to whether even late abortions were actually prosecuted under common law.

In his writings on the subject, St. Thomas Aquinas puts forward the concept of hylomorphism, which says that human beings are a unity of two elements: primary matter, or the potentiality of the body, and substantial form, or the actualizing principle of the soul. Both elements are necessary for a human being to exist, which implies that the embryo must have a fully human body—one developed beyond the early stages of pregnancy—before it is capable of receiving the soul and becoming human. St. Thomas, however, believes both contraception and abortion to be vices against nature and sins against marriage; his views are adopted as the official doctrine of the Roman Catholic Church.

1588   Pope Sixtus V issues a papal bull declaring that abortion at any stage of pregnancy is a homicide, both a moral sin and a secular crime, and is punishable by excommunication.

1591   Pope Gregory XIV issues a papal pronouncement that reinstates the concept of delayed hominization and recommends that church penalties for abortion of an unanimated fetus be no stricter than civil penalties.

Seventeenth and Eighteenth Centuries

In colonial America and the early United States, abortions are not explicitly prohibited in any written law, nor are they prosecuted under common law. Abortion is generally regarded as both legal and moral if it occurs prior to quickening, the first perception of fetal movement by the mother. Prior to quickening, the embryo is believed to be inanimate.

1621   Paolo Zacchia, a Roman physician, publishes a treatise proposing that a rational soul is present in humans from the moment of conception, a concept that will gradually gain acceptance and influence.

Nineteenth Century

From 1800 to 1900, the fertility rate for white American women (the only statistics available) will drop from 7.04 to 3.56 children, largely due to increased use of abortion. During the first half of the century, abortion becomes increasingly visible in the United States, and by

1850, abortionists are advertising openly in newspapers, magazines, popular health manuals, and religious publications, which also carry ads for abortifacients and home remedies for "menstrual blockage." Most home medical manuals also contain abortifacient information in sections explaining how to release "obstructed menses," as well as lists of things to avoid during a suspected pregnancy because they are thought to bring on abortion.

Prior to 1840, most observers believe that the vast majority of American women seeking abortions are unmarried. As the century progresses, however, an increasing number of married women— primarily native-born, upper- and middle-class white Protestants— seek abortions to limit the size of their families and/or to space their children.

1803   As part of an omnibus crime bill known as Lord Ellenborough's law, the English Parliament passes a law making abortion by any method before quickening punishable by exile, whipping, or imprisonment, and abortion through the use of poisons after quickening becomes a capital offense. In the United States, however, the distinction between quick and unquick remains "virtually universal" through the early 1800s, and common law continues to treat pre-quickening abortions as legal.

1812   The Massachusetts Supreme Court dismisses charges levied against Isaiah Bangs for preparing and administering an abortifacient potion, on the grounds that the indictment against him did not state that the woman was "quick with child" at the time the potion was given. This ruling confirms the generally accepted belief that abortion early in pregnancy is beyond the scope of the law and therefore not a crime. *Commonwealth v. Bangs* will remain the ruling precedent for abortion cases through at least the first half of the nineteenth century.

1821   Connecticut passes a law prohibiting the inducement of abortion through "dangerous poisons"; the law, which seems primarily intended to protect women from dying as a result of taking potions meant to induce abortions, applies only to abortions after quickening. The maximum penalty is life imprisonment.

1825   Missouri passes an abortion statute; like Connecticut's, it is primarily an anti-poison measure.

1827   Illinois passes an abortion poison control measure on the model of Connecticut's 1821 statute.

1828   England's 1803 anti-abortion statute is revised to make instrumental abortion after quickening a capital offense and thus equal to abortion through the use of poisons.

New York passes a bill outlawing abortion by any means after quickening. The statute only includes successful abortions—either the woman or the fetus must die for an offense to have occurred. The maximum penalty for the person performing the abortion is one year in jail and/or a fine of $500. The bill sets an important legal precedent by explicitly permitting abortion to save the life of the mother. The bill will be signed into law in 1829 and take effect in 1830, but in reality it will have little impact on abortion practice, largely as a result of popular resistance to the regularization and regulation of medicine.

1830   Following the English lead, Connecticut revises its statute to outlaw instrumental abortion, as well as the use of poisons, after quickening. Under the new law, a person who attempts to perform an abortion can be punished by seven to ten years in prison.

1834   Ohio passes a law making attempted abortion a misdemeanor, without reference to quickening. The law also makes the death of either the mother or the fetus after quickening a felony.

1838   Great Britain modifies its abortion law to remove the concept of quickening and to eliminate the death penalty for abortion.

1840   By this time 10 of the 26 states have some statutory restrictions on abortion. Most of the laws apply only after quickening, but the Maine code makes attempted abortion of any pregnant woman by any method a crime, "whether such child be quick or not." The Maine law also includes an exception for therapeutic abortions in the event the mother's life is threatened.

In practice, most of the early anti-abortion laws are enforced laxly, if at all. All of them were passed, not on their own, but as parts of major revisions of criminal codes or as parts of omnibus crime bills. As Mohr (1978) says, "This was significant because it indicates that there was no substantial popular outcry for antiabortion activity; or, conversely, no evidence of public disapproval of the nation's traditional common law attitudes. . . . The first wave of abortion legislation in American history emerged from the struggles of both legislators and physicians to control medical practice rather than from public pressures to deal with abortion per se" (pp. 42, 43).

1840
cont.

Mohr also points out that a major loophole in all of the laws "was the necessity to prove intent, which was simply impossible to do, given the tolerant attitude of the American courts toward abortion when an irregular physician treated an unquickened woman for something he claimed he thought was not pregnancy" (p. 41). Further, the laws were designed to punish only the person who administered a potion or performed the surgery; none of them punished the woman involved.

1845
Massachusetts passes the first state law to deal separately and exclusively with abortion; it makes attempted abortion a misdemeanor punishable by one to seven years in jail and a $2,000 fine. If the abortion leads to the woman's death, the crime is elevated to a felony punishable by five to twenty years in the state prison. By midcentury, six other states—New York, Michigan, Vermont, Virginia, California, New Hampshire, New Jersey, and Wisconsin—will have enacted initial anti-abortion statutes, and Massachusetts will have strengthened its law by making it a crime to advertise abortion services or products.

1847
The American Medical Association (AMA) is founded. The impetus behind the birth of the AMA is a drive to professionalize the practice of medicine and to gain control of a market served not only by schooled physicians (called "regulars") but also by midwives, local healers, homeopaths, and abortionists. The campaign to criminalize abortion, carried on through the latter half of the nineteenth century, will be a key component in the physicians' successful struggle to gain a monopoly in the medical marketplace. The physicians do not seek to unconditionally outlaw abortions; instead they want laws giving them the exclusive power to determine a woman's need for a "therapeutic" abortion. Thus, the doctors will lobby against attempts by legislatures to define specific circumstances where abortion is or is not justified (Mohr, 1978).

1857
Dr. Horatio Storer, obstetrician and gynecologist, launches what will become a national drive to end legal abortion. The campaign has two primary goals: to turn public opinion against abortion and to persuade state legislatures to pass specific legislation making abortion a crime.

1859
Dr. Horatio Storer succeeds in persuading the AMA to pass a resolution condemning induced abortion, including those performed before quickening, and urging state legislatures to pass laws forbidding it. The AMA drive includes a large-scale media and lobbying campaign that focuses on the fetus's right to life. Another aspect of the campaign aims at awakening fears of "race suicide" among the

1859
cont.   Protestant middle and upper classes, based on declining birth rates among native-born whites (due in part to abortion) compared to high fertility among predominantly Catholic immigrants.

1861   England passes the Offenses against the Person Act, which states that anyone procuring an "unlawful abortion" (which was not defined), including the woman herself, is subject to life imprisonment, while a person aiding or abetting an abortion can be sentenced to three years in prison.

1864   The AMA establishes a prize to be awarded to the best anti-abortion book written for the lay public.

1865   The AMA anti-abortion prize committee, which is made up of prominent Boston physicians and chaired by D. Humphreys Storer, awards its first gold medal to Dr. Storer's son, Dr. Horatio R. Storer, for "The Criminality and Physical Evils of Forced Abortion." Expanded into book form, the paper is published by the AMA under the title *Why Not? A Book for Every Woman.*

1867   Dr. Edwin M. Hale, a homeopathic physician, publishes *The Great Crime of the Nineteenth Century,* in which he claims that "two-thirds of the number of conceptions occurring in the United States . . . are destroyed criminally"—undoubtedly a gross exaggeration (Mohr, 1978, p. 78). In two earlier volumes, *On the Homeopathic Treatment of Abortion* (1860) and *A Systematic Treatise on Abortion* (1866), Hale had defended abortion, which he believed to be common (he estimated the rate at one out of five pregnancies), often advisable (as in cases of seduction or threat to the health or life of the mother), and quite safe. Along with Hale, most homeopaths will soon join the regular physicians in condemning abortion.

1868   Doctors Horatio R. Storer and Franklin Fiske Heard publish *Criminal Abortion: Its Nature, Its Evidence, and Its Law,* a "careful large-scale and systematic attempt to calculate midcentury American abortion rates" (Mohr, 1978, p. 78). The book, which is intended to substantiate more general claims made by Storer and other anti-abortion physicians, is aimed primarily at lawyers and legal scholars rather than at the general public; it estimates the ratio of abortions to live births in New York State and elsewhere in the nation as being about one to four. Later estimates will put the number of abortions as high as one out of every three pregnancies.

1869   Pope Pius IX issues the papal enactment *Apostolicace sedis,* which abandons the previously existing limitation that excommunication was to be imposed only for abortions of "ensouled" fetuses. By

1869
cont.
implication, the enactment lays the groundwork for the Church's subsequent position that all abortion is murder.

1871
A report by the AMA Committee on Criminal Abortion describes women seeking abortions as "unmindful of the course marked out for [them] by Providence" and characterizes them as selfish and immoral, "[yielding] to the pleasures—but [shrinking] from the pains and responsibilities of maternity . . ." (cited in Tribe, 1990, p. 33). Mohr notes that along with the doctors' campaign against abortion, "most doctors were bitterly and stridently condemning what one of them called the '*non-infanto* mania' that afflicted the nation's women and desperately decrying the unwillingness of American wives to remain in their 'places' bearing and raising children" (Mohr, 1978, p. 168).

1873
Passage of the Comstock Laws, which prohibit sending "obscene" materials through the mails, including contraceptives and abortifacients as well as any information about them. Section 211 of the Federal Criminal Code provides a maximum of five years' imprisonment and a $5,000 fine for sending through the mail any "paper, writing, advertisement or representation that any article, instrument, substance, drug, medicine or thing may, or can be, used or applied, for preventing conception" or for abortion, or any "description calculated to induce or incite a person to so use or apply any such article, instrument, substance, drug, medicine, or thing" (Fryer, 1966, p. 117). A clause exempting physicians from the law is omitted when the bill is presented to Congress; it passes on the first vote with no debate. Anthony Comstock, the major force behind the law's passage, becomes a special agent of the Post Office Department empowered with enforcing the new law. From 1873 to 1880, he will be responsible for indicting more than 55 persons whom he identifies as abortionists, among them the infamous Madame Restell.

1878
April. Anthony Comstock arrests the notorious Madame Restell, New York's most successful, wealthy, and famous abortionist, after purchasing abortifacient preparations from her. Restell, whose real name is Anna Lohman, will make international headlines by committing suicide the day before her trial.

1879
Helgar dilators are invented. These are metal rods of progressively larger diameter, used to dilate the cervix so that instruments may be inserted to remove the embryo or fetus and placenta.

1880
By this time, 40 states have passed anti-abortion statutes, making induced abortion at any stage of pregnancy a criminal act. Most of the laws contain exceptions for therapeutic abortions, which are

1880
cont.
permitted when it is a physician's opinion that they are necessary to save the woman's life. Enforcement of the laws is sporadic—in Michigan, for example, there will be 156 indictments and only 40 convictions from 1893 to 1932; in Minnesota there will be 100 indictments and 31 convictions between 1911 and 1930. Although struck down by the *Roe v. Wade* ruling of 1973, versions of these nineteenth-century laws remained on the books in more than 30 states as of 1990. If *Roe v. Wade* is overturned, some of them could become enforceable without further action by current legislatures.

Also by this time, nearly all home health manuals specifically condemn abortion and avoid any discussion of procedures that might be used to induce abortion, in marked contrast to manuals published earlier in the century.

During the next decade, obstetrical textbooks begin to recommend use of antiseptic techniques for abortion (which most states still permit for therapeutic reasons) as well as for childbirth. This will reduce but not end deaths from puerperal fever, which will continue to be a major and often fatal complication of abortion well into the second half of the 1900s.

1892
Canada makes it a crime to possess "obscene" materials, including contraceptives and abortifacients.

1899
Abortion becomes a crime in Japan.

Twentieth Century

1920
The government of the Soviet Union issues its first abortion decree, calling abortion a necessary "evil" and suggesting its causes are rooted in social illnesses left over from the czarist regime. The purpose of the legalization is to protect public health and help keep women in the labor force, rather than to give women control over their reproductive abilities.

1929
England enacts the Infant Life (Preservation) Act, stating that termination of pregnancy, particularly with a viable fetus, is unlawful. Excepted are abortions done in "good faith" to protect the life of the woman. According to Tribe, the law "raised more questions than it answered, requiring women and doctors to negotiate the murky waters of good faith, viability, and necessity" (1990, p. 67).

1936   Frederick J. Taussig publishes a study in which he estimates, on the basis of vital statistics and medical questionnaires, that more than 500,000 illegal abortions are being performed annually in the United States.

In the U.S.S.R., Joseph Stalin outlaws abortion, declaring that motherhood is not a private matter but one of "great social importance" (Tribe, 1990, p. 57). The unavailability of contraceptives, a long-standing tradition of using abortion as birth control, and the problems of obtaining housing and other necessities ensure that illegal abortion will remain common, however, and two decades later the government again legalizes abortion for "public health reasons" (Tribe, 1990, p. 58).

1938   In England, obstetrician Aleck Bourne is tried under the 1861 statute for performing an abortion on a 14-year-old who had been raped by two soldiers. Bourne is acquitted, on the basis that in certain situations doctors may act to safeguard a woman's mental or physical health as well as to save her life; the judge further states that in some circumstances a doctor may have an "affirmative duty to terminate a woman's pregnancy" (Tribe, 1990, p. 67).

1941   In Germany, the Third Reich bans the production and distribution of contraceptives as part of a policy that includes forced impregnation of "suitable women" and regards abortion as a criminal offense. By 1943, the penalty for performing an abortion on a "genetically fit" woman is death, and allowing one's premises to be used for an abortion merits a prison sentence. By contrast, abortions are encouraged among Jewish and other "unfit" women, as a complement to a program of mandatory sterilization of "genetically inferior" persons begun in 1933.

1942   Switzerland becomes the first Western European nation to liberalize abortion laws, permitting abortion in cases of rape, incest, danger to the woman's health, or likelihood of fetal defect. Because of the relatively broad interpretation of "health," women from countries with more restrictive laws, including the United States, sometimes come to Switzerland seeking abortions.

1948   Japan passes the Eugenic Protection Laws, which permit abortions "to prevent the increase of the inferior descendants from the standpoint of eugenic protection and to protect the life and health of the mother" (Tribe, 1990, p. 60). A year later the act is amended to include economic hardship as a health consideration; effectively the act makes abortion available on demand.

1950s U.S. hospitals begin creating abortion committees to mediate requests for abortions, which are still illegal except to, in the judgment of the physician (and the committee), "save the life of the mother."

Alfred Kinsey releases his report on American sexuality. Among other findings, he reports that among the women he surveyed, 9 out of 10 premarital pregnancies had been ended by abortion. Among married women, 22 percent had had at least one abortion by the age of 45.

1958 The vacuum aspiration technique for early abortions is pioneered in Communist China.

1959 The American Law Institute (ALI) proposes legalizing therapeutic abortions in cases that would "gravely impair the physical or mental health of the mother"; where the child would be born "with grave physical or mental defects"; or where the pregnancy is the result of rape or incest. The ALI code will provide a model for the liberalized abortion laws passed in several states beginning in 1967.

1960 May 9. The Food and Drug Administration (FDA) approves commercial distribution of oral contraceptives ("the pill"). By 1966, an estimated six million women—one-fifth of those of child-bearing age—are using the pill.

1962– An outbreak of German measles (rubella) leads to births of 15,000
1965 congenitally abnormal babies; in some states, physicians who perform abortions on pregnant women who have the disease risk losing their licenses. The rubella outbreak adds impetus to the medical profession's growing shift toward favoring liberalized abortion laws.

1962 Abortion makes national headlines in the case of Sherry Finkbine, an Arizona mother of four who had decided to have an abortion after learning of the possible effects of thalidomide, which she had taken in early pregnancy. The day before her scheduled abortion, Mrs. Finkbine seeks publicity to warn other pregnant women of the dangers of thalidomide; as a result the abortion is cancelled by the hospital, which refuses to perform it (despite a judge's recommendation) out of fears of legal prosecution. Mrs. Finkbine eventually obtains an abortion in Sweden; the embryo is severely deformed.

The United Presbyterian Church becomes the first major religious organization to urge uniform laws for therapeutic abortions. It will be joined a year later by the American Lutheran Church Executive Committee and the Unitarian Universalist Association.

1962
cont.
In Grove, Oklahoma, Dr. W. J. Bryan Henrie is convicted of performing abortions and sentenced to jail, in a case that Lawrence Lader (1973) will call "the first time that a licensed doctor had become a *cause célèbre* after conviction for abortion" (p. 6). After serving his two-year sentence, Dr. Henrie begins a solo campaign to change the abortion laws, traveling by bus to speak at conferences, meetings, and legislative hearings around the country and publishing a magazine called *Destiny, Voice of the Silent Ones*. In one issue he writes, "I am ashamed of a law that must be broken to save the honor and respect of many women."

1963
The Eleventh All-Union Congress of Gynecologists includes a presentation on the use of vacuum aspiration for early abortion; the technique soon spreads worldwide, particularly to Eastern Europe and Japan.

March. Pope John XXIII institutes a commission to study the question of birth control.

1964
In response to pressure from Dr. James McNulty, a Catholic physician on the California State Medical Board, the board conducts an investigation of nine San Francisco physicians who performed abortions on pregnant women who had had rubella. The experiences of the "San Francisco Nine" will deter other California doctors from performing such abortions and will help bolster efforts to pass reform measures in that state.

1965
In *Griswold v. Connecticut* (381 U.S. 479, 485 [1965]), the Supreme Court strikes down a state law banning the use of contraceptives by married couples, overturning an individual's conviction for providing a married person with contraceptives and information regarding their use. The opinion, written by Justice William O. Douglas, cites the "zone of privacy created by several fundamental constitutional guarantees." The ruling will serve as a critical precedent to the 1973 *Roe v. Wade* decision.

The first National Right to Life Committee is formed; it is essentially an information clearinghouse. Local organizations in each state provide the group's political power.

In California, Patricia Maginnis founds the Society for Humane Abortion, calling for repeal of all laws restricting abortion.

1966
March 30. The Association for the Study of Abortion (ASA) is incorporated in New York. The ASA is primarily an educational organization that will refrain from direct political action to keep its

1966
cont.
tax-exempt status; however, according to Lader (1973), the board of prominent lawyers, doctors, and theologians "gave abortion the prestige and authority that was invaluable at the start" (p. 58).

July. In California, Patricia Maginnis announces a series of free, public classes to teach women self-abortion techniques which she had twice used on herself. The classes also cover contraception, abortion referrals overseas and in the United States, after-abortion care, and police tactics. The classes are a deliberate attempt to mount a public challenge to restrictive abortion laws and to dramatize the refusals by hospitals and doctors to assume responsibility for fighting the laws.

November. The National Conference of Catholic Bishops (NCCB) is formed to fight "coercive" use of birth control. Six months later, the NCCB will launch a nationwide anti-abortion education campaign directed at both Catholics and non-Catholics, with an initial budget of $50,000.

1967
Colorado becomes the first state to pass a liberalized abortion law, following the guidelines proposed by the American Law Institute (ALI) in 1959. By 1972, 13 other states (Arkansas, California, Delaware, Florida, Georgia, Kansas, Maryland, Mississippi, New Mexico, North Carolina, Oregon, South Carolina, and Virginia) will pass legislation to permit therapeutic abortions based on the ALI guidelines. In reality, the Colorado law does not make abortion much more available than it was previously, because the requirements are very strict and abortions cost at least $500. During the first 14 months the law is in effect, only 338 abortions are performed, 100 of them on women from outside Colorado.

In California, Dr. Leon Belous is arrested for providing a woman with the phone number of another doctor who had performed an abortion on her. Determined to test and overthrow the state's restrictive abortion laws, Dr. Belous insists on basing his defense on constitutional grounds (see 1969).

At the 1967 conference of the one-year-old National Organization for Women (NOW), the right of women to control their reproductive rights is included in the organization's Women's Bill of Rights, despite the reservations of mainstream professional women who fear that focusing on the abortion issue will take attention away from their economic goals.

The English Parliament passes the British Abortion Act, permitting abortion until viability as long as two doctors certify that the

1967
cont.

pregnancy poses a greater risk than abortion to the life or mental or physical health of a woman or to her existing children—in essence making early abortion available on request. Viability, as set by the Infant Life (Preservation) Act of 1929, is set at 28 weeks of gestational age. The act, which applies only to Great Britain and not to Ireland, serves as a model for legislation in a number of countries. In the years following the bill's passage, England maintains a fairly high rate of legal abortion, with a significant number of abortions performed on non-English women who come from countries with more restrictive laws, especially Ireland, where abortion is illegal, and Spain, until that country legalizes abortion in 1985. The law will survive numerous attempts by anti-abortion groups during the next two decades to pass new restrictions.

February 20. Patricia Maginnis and Rowena Gurner are arrested in Redwood City, California, for holding public classes on abortion techniques and referrals. At their trial, their defense claims abridgment of their constitutional rights of free speech and press; the judge finds in their favor.

April 6. At a lecture at Boston University, activist Bill Baird publicly challenges the constitutionality of the Massachusetts "crimes against chastity" statute, under which only married couples can receive birth control information or materials, and then only from physicians. Before an audience of 1,500, Baird offers to distribute packages of contraceptive foam and reads the names of Tokyo clinics specializing in abortion; when 12 single women step forward to take the foam, Baird is duly arrested. His case will eventually reach the Supreme Court (see 1970).

May. Reverend Howard Moody of the Judson Memorial Church in Greenwich Village organizes the Clergy Consultation Service for Abortion. On May 27, Moody and 21 Protestant ministers and Jewish rabbis announce that they will refer women to doctors who they know perform safe and legitimate abortions; the announcement is reported on page 1 of the *New York Times*. At its peak, the service will include some 1,200 clergy members in more than 20 states, including Protestant ministers, Jewish rabbis, and even some Catholic priests. The members refer women to doctors in Puerto Rico, Great Britain, and even the United States.

July. The vacuum aspiration method for early abortions reaches the United States, with the publication of two articles in *Obstetrics and Gynecology.*

1968   President Lyndon Johnson's Presidential Advisory Council on the Status of Women, chaired by former senator Maurine Neuberger (D-OR), releases its report, calling for repeal of all abortion laws.

May 1. In Washington, D.C., Dr. Milan Vuitch is arrested for performing an abortion on "Mrs. Donald R.," a secretary at the Navy Munitions Building whose husband had deserted her and impregnated two other women before impregnating her during a temporary reconciliation. When she refused to live with him or bear his child, Mr. R. went to the police and offered to cooperate in the arrest of Dr. Vuitch. The Serbian-born Dr. Vuitch had performed hundreds of low-cost abortions since 1966, mounting what was in effect an open challenge to restrictive laws. In his trial, Dr. Vuitch challenges the constitutionality of the abortion laws, asserting that, as Mrs. R.'s doctor, only he had the right to decide whether her health was threatened by her pregnancy and whether an abortion was necessary (see 1969).

July 29. Pope Paul VI issues the *Humanae Vitae* encyclical, which reaffirms the doctrine that Catholics may not use any form of birth control other than the rhythm method or abstinence.

1969   The American Civil Liberties Union (ACLU) and the Planned Parenthood Federation of America voice support for abortion rights, reversing Planned Parenthood's long-standing position against abortion.

In Chicago, members of the Chicago Women's Liberation Union begin the illegal feminist abortion collective known as "Jane," which grows out of an abortion referral and counseling service on the University of Chicago campus. Originally the collective steers women to safe and relatively inexpensive illegal abortions. Gradually, however, members learn how to perform the abortions themselves. Over its four years of operation, Jane will provide more than 11,000 abortions, most of them done in members' own homes. Although the nominal charge is $100, the average payment is $40, and no women are turned away because of inability to pay. The collective's safety record compares favorably with legal abortion clinics in New York and California—its single death is a woman already suffering a severe infection, probably from an attempt at self-induced abortion, when she arrives at Jane. The collective places special emphasis on intensive and caring counseling as "the heart of the procedure," in the belief that the medical and counseling components of abortion should not be separated and in the attempt both to provide sisterly support and to demystify the abortion experience.

1969
cont.

Of the dozens of activists involved in Jane, only seven members are arrested during its existence; the charges against them will be dropped in 1973.

Canada adopts a law allowing abortions in hospitals that have an appointed committee of three or more physicians when the committee has determined that continuing a pregnancy would threaten the life or health of the pregnant woman.

In Ashland, Pennsylvania, Dr. Robert Spenser dies at the age of 80. According to Lader (1973), for more than 40 years Dr. Spenser "had handled more abortions than anyone on the East Coast," charging between $10 and $50 until the 1960s, when he raised his price to $100 (p. 4). Dr. Spenser, who often let women from out of town stay free at his clinic, performed some 30,000 abortions with only 1 death—of a woman who was bleeding when she arrived at his clinic—for which a jury exonerated him. Considered a leading citizen of his community, Dr. Spenser counted the mayor, the police chief, and most county officials among his close friends. "He became a legend," Lader writes, "not by challenging the law, but by ignoring it. The community protected him. He treated unwanted pregnancies as well as pneumonia for over forty years because the community wanted it that way" (p. 5).

Senator Robert Packwood (R-OR) introduces legislation to legalize abortions in the District of Columbia and the entire United States; he will reintroduce the legislation in the 1971–1972 session of Congress, but no action will be taken on either bill.

By the end of this decade, estimates of illegal abortions in the United States range from 200,000 to 1.2 million annually.

February. The First National Conference on Abortion Laws, held in Chicago, establishes the National Association for the Repeal of Abortion Laws (NARAL), which will become the National Abortion Rights Action League in 1973. NARAL's sponsors include feminists, radical clergy, liberal lawyers and politicians, health professionals, population control and welfare rights advocates, and more conservative groups such as Church Women United, the Young Women's Christian Association, and the Commission on Uniform State Laws.

March. The Redstockings, a radical women's liberation group, holds an "Abortion Speak Out" at the Washington Square Methodist Church in New York City. Hundreds of women attend the meeting, where individual women stand to describe publicly their experiences with illegal abortion.

1969
cont.
June 12. Reverend Robert Hare of Cleveland is indicted in Massa-chusetts for violation of anti-abortion statutes, for referring a woman to a Massachusetts physician, Dr. Pierre Brunelle, as part of his work for a clergy counseling service. The indictment is dismissed, but the prosecutor appeals, and the case is still dragging through the courts as of January 1973, when the *Roe v. Wade* decision strikes down all state anti-abortion laws. Reverend Hare is the only American clergy-man to be indicted on an abortion charge. Dr. Brunelle is convicted and sent to prison.

September 5. In the case of Dr. Leon Belous, the California Supreme Court, by a vote of four to three, declares the state law restricting abortion unconstitutional and exonerates the doctor, saying that "The fundamental right of a woman to choose whether to bear children follows from the Supreme Court's and this court's repeated acknowledgment of a 'right of privacy' or 'liberty' in matters related to marriage, family and sex." The decision, which is the first state supreme court decision to declare any anti-abortion statute uncon-stitutional, sets a precedent for numerous forthcoming challenges to state laws (Lader, 1973, pp. 109–110).

November 10. Citing the recent Belous decision in California, Judge Arnold Gesell of the U.S. District Court of the District of Columbia reaches a verdict in the case of Dr. Milan Vuitch that exonerates the doctor and declares the D.C. law unconstitutional. It is the first time a federal court has overthrown an abortion law. The case is imme-diately appealed to the Supreme Court, which agrees to hear it (see 1971). Dr. Vuitch reopens his clinic a few blocks from the White House; he is soon taking 100 abortion cases per week.

December. In Dallas, Texas, attorneys Linda Coffee and Sarah Weddington meet with Norma McCorvey, a pregnant woman who has been trying unsuccessfully to get an abortion, to ask her to be the plaintiff for what they hope will be a landmark case challenging the constitutionality of Texas's restrictive abortion laws. Coffee and Weddington, both recent graduates of the University of Texas Law School (where they were two of the five women in their class), have been seeking a plaintiff for their suit for several months; McCorvey agrees to participate even though they tell her that the time involved will make it virtually impossible for her to get the abortion she seeks. For 10 years, until she herself comes forward, McCorvey will be known to everyone but Coffee and Weddington as "Jane Roe."

1970
In *Baird v. Eisenstadt* (405 U.S. 438, 453 [1972]), the Supreme Court rules that the Massachusetts "crimes against chastity" law is uncon-stitutional, thus legalizing access to birth control for single persons.

1970
cont.

The *Baird* decision will provide a strong precedent for the *Roe v. Wade* decision three years later.

The Family Planning Services and Population Research Act, passed by Congress to fund family planning services abroad, includes a provision that states, "None of the funds appropriated under this title shall be used in programs where abortion is a method of family planning."

In response to pressure from a growing abortion rights coalition, Hawaii becomes the first state in the Union to repeal its abortion law, legalizing abortions performed in the first 20 weeks of pregnancy. The bill, which does contain a residency requirement, is signed into law by the Catholic governor.

New York repeals its abortion law with a bill permitting abortion on demand up to the twenty-fourth week of pregnancy. The bill is passed with a dramatic last-minute vote change by Assemblyman George Michaels, who was convinced by his wife and his son, an intern who had seen firsthand the effects of illegal abortion, to vote against the wishes of his conservative, mostly Catholic constituents. The vote will cost Michaels his political career. During the first 6 months after the bill is signed into law by Governor Nelson Rockefeller, 69,000 legal abortions are performed in New York City, half on women from out-of-state. Within 9 months, the number of legal abortions passes 100,000.

Following Hawaii's and New York's lead, Alaska and Washington repeal their abortion laws, the latter as a result of a popular referendum. Efforts to pass liberalized laws fail, however, in 31 other states.

Dr. Jane Hodgson, a Minnesota physician, becomes the first doctor in U.S. history to be convicted of performing an abortion in a hospital, on a 23-year-old woman who had contracted rubella. Hodgson had performed the abortion in a deliberate attempt to challenge Minnesota's restrictive abortion laws, but the Supreme Court will refuse to hear her case. Her conviction will be reversed by the Minnesota Supreme Court after the 1973 *Roe v. Wade* decision.

1971

The Supreme Court agrees to hear 2 of the more than 70 criminal and civil abortion cases pending in 20 states. One of these, *Roe v. Wade*, is a Texas case challenging a typical nineteenth-century anti-abortion statute. The other, *Doe v. Bolton*, questions the constitutionality of a Georgia law that allows therapeutic exceptions based on the ALI code.

1971
cont.
The March of Dimes, as part of a comprehensive birth defects program, begins making grants for genetic services programs, including amniocentesis, a move that will be strongly opposed by anti-abortion groups and the Catholic Church.

Dr. Jack Willke, a Cincinnati physician, and his wife, Barbara, publish *Handbook on Abortion*. The book, which will later be called the "bible of the pro-life movement," is the first to show color pictures of aborted fetuses.

India passes the Medical Termination of Pregnancy Act, permitting abortions in the likelihood of birth defects or if the birth threatens a woman's physical or mental health. Broad latitude in interpreting the law means that legal abortions are generally readily available, despite opposition to abortion from a number of Hindu and Muslim religious groups. Over the next two decades, a disturbing trend in use of abortion for sex selection and a decline in the proportion of women to men leads several Indian state governments to restrict access to amniocentesis and other sex determination tests and adds fuel to the ongoing abortion debate.

April 21. In *United States v. Vuitch* (402 U.S. 62 [1971]), the Supreme Court upholds the constitutionality of the Washington, D.C., law by a vote of five to two, with two justices not voting. The decision actually strengthens abortion rights in the District of Columbia, however, by broadening two existing rights. The law permitted abortion to save a woman's "health"; the Court expanded the definition of health to include "psychological as well as physical well-being." Further, the Court placed the burden of proof as to whether an abortion was necessary on the prosecution rather than on the physician, stating, "We are unable to believe that Congress intended that a physician be required to prove his innocence." Following the decision, Washington's abortion facilities—which include the Preterm Clinic, owned by a nonprofit coalition of prominent citizens; an outpatient clinic at Washington Hospital Center; and a number of private physicians performing in-office abortions—soon are among the country's busiest. The Preterm Clinic uses suction machines and a simplified procedure that bypasses the need for a sterile operating room and prepping, shaving, and scrubbing patients. Its carefully kept records on more than 20,000 patients, with no deaths and few complications, demonstrate the safety of free-standing clinics.

1972
The Centers for Disease Control (CDC) begins its Abortion Surveillance Division, which publishes annual statistical reports on abortions and the characteristics of women obtaining them.

1972
cont.
In response to pressure from right-to-life and Catholic groups, the March of Dimes agrees to adopt a policy forbidding the use of any of its funds for abortion.

Michigan voters turn down a referendum to legalize abortion in the first 20 weeks of pregnancy. The campaign against the referendum includes distribution to over 2 million households of a glossy color brochure, *Life and Death,* which contrasts a photograph of a child alleged to have been born at 22 weeks of pregnancy with one of a saline-aborted fetus. The referendum is defeated 62 percent to 38 percent, despite pre-election polls showing 59 percent support for the measure. A similar campaign in North Dakota also helps defeat a referendum in that state.

Connecticut passes a law allowing abortion only to save the life of the pregnant woman and imposing a maximum five-year prison term for abortionists. An amendment to allow abortions in the case of rape or incest is voted down during the debate. Although the law is declared unconstitutional, it is allowed to remain in effect pending the decision in the *Roe v. Wade* case currently before the Supreme Court. During the latter part of 1972, about 100 women travel from Connecticut to New York each week in search of legal abortions.

President Richard Nixon's Commission on Population Growth and the American Future issues its report, calling on the federal government to ensure the availability of birth control counseling, birth control devices, and oral contraceptives to all Americans, especially teenagers and the poor. The commission report also recommends that the nation follow New York State's lead in making abortion available on demand. The report is immediately attacked by the National Conference of Catholic Bishops and others. Nixon rejects the section of the report dealing with abortion and later writes a letter to Cardinal Terence Cooke of New York expressing his support for the repeal of the New York law.

1973
January 22. The Supreme Court rules on *Roe v. Wade* (410 U.S. 113 [1973]) and *Doe v. Bolton* (410 U.S. 179 [1973]). In the *Roe* case, a Texas woman ("Jane Roe," a pseudonym used by Norma McCorvey) challenged that state's 1857 law making abortion illegal except to save the life of the mother. The Court ruling declares unconstitutional Article 1196 of the Texas statute, on the grounds that it makes no distinction between abortions performed earlier or later in pregnancy and that it does not permit legal abortions for any reason other than to save the life of the mother. Because ruling that single article unconstitutional would leave Texas with a law prohibiting all abortions for any reason, the whole statute is overturned.

1973
cont.

In making its decision on *Roe,* the Court applies the concepts of trimesters and viability, saying in essence that:

> The state does not have any compelling interest in regulating abortions during the first trimester (12 weeks) of pregnancy, except to require that an abortion be performed by a licensed physician in a medical setting.

> The state's only interest in regulating abortions during the second trimester (12 through 24 weeks) is to protect maternal health.

> When the fetus becomes viable (capable of independent survival outside the womb, with or without artificial life support) the state may choose to limit abortions to women for whom continued pregnancy would be life-threatening. The determination as to viability, however, is a medical and not a legal or judicial matter.

In *Doe v. Bolton,* the companion case to *Roe v. Wade,* the Court strikes down a Georgia statute requiring that:

> Abortions be performed in hospitals accredited by JCAH (Joint Commission on Accreditation of Hospitals)

> Abortions be approved by a majority vote of a three-doctor hospital committee, as well as by two physicians in addition to the woman's personal physician

> A woman receiving an abortion must be a Georgia resident

The rulings are largely based on the precedent of a constitutional right to privacy established in the *Griswold v. Connecticut* contraception ruling of 1965. The Court interprets the First, Fifth, Ninth, and Fourteenth Amendments to the Constitution to support a woman's right to an abortion, particularly the liberty clause in the Fourteenth Amendment, which reads, "No State shall . . . deprive any person of life, liberty, or property, without due process of law." The Court holds that the right to an abortion does not have to be spelled out to be included in the rights bestowed by the Constitution: "The right to privacy, whether it be founded in the Fourteenth Amendment's concept of personal liberty and restrictions upon state action or in the Ninth Amendment's reservation of the rights to the people, is broad enough to encompass a woman's decision whether or not to terminate her pregnancy" (*Roe v. Wade,* p. 177).

As Chief Justice Warren Burger notes explicitly in his concurring opinion on *Doe v. Bolton,* the decision does not give women a constitutional right to "abortion on demand." Instead, the decisions

1973
cont.

uphold the *physician's* right to make a medical decision (and, correspondingly, a woman's right to choose her own physician), with no provisions or guarantees for making abortions available. As Petchesky (1984) points out, "the decision did not so much [secure] the privacy of a woman's right to choose abortion as [define] the scope and limits of the state's authority to intervene" (p. 290). The justices specifically refrain from dealing with the question of "when life begins." Further, the decision states that although the Constitution never defines what the word *person* includes, *person* as used in the Fourteenth Amendment does not include the unborn. These distinctions will become important in later rulings regarding various state and federal restrictions on abortions and public funding for abortions.

Voting with the majority on both cases are Chief Justice Warren Burger and Justices Harry Blackmun, William Brennan, Lewis Powell, Potter Stewart, Thurgood Marshall, and William O. Douglas. Dissenting are Justices William Rehnquist and Byron White. (For detailed descriptions of these and other abortion-related Supreme Court decisions through 1989, see Drucker, 1990.)

A major effect of the two decisions, unforeseen by the abortion rights advocates who hail them as the beginning of the end of their fight, will be to galvanize the anti-abortion, or right-to-life, movement into action. During the next decade, the latter movement will mount a broad-based campaign to prevent women from exercising the Court-declared right to an abortion. Fought mostly at the state level, the campaign seeks to enact restrictions in the "gray zone of constitutionality" (Tribe, 1990, p. 144). Examples of such restrictions include 24-hour waiting periods, stringent record-keeping requirements, and spousal and parental consent laws. The anti-abortion activists also campaign intensively around the country to elect politicians who are opposed to legal abortion and to vote supporters of legal abortion out of office.

February. The National Conference of Catholic Bishops (NCCB) announces that any Catholic involved in any phase of abortion will be subject to immediate excommunication.

April. Representative Angelo Roncallo (R-NY) introduces a measure to ban fetal research. The measure passes in the House but does not become law. Instead, a Senate compromise places a temporary moratorium on fetal research and forms the National Commission for the Protection of Human Subjects to study the issue. The commission-appointed study group will report that past fetal research has provided great benefits and that the need for future research is even greater. However, fetal research restrictions modeled on the Roncallo proposals pass in 15 states.

1973
cont.

June. The current National Right to Life Committee (NRLC) is founded in Detroit. The organization has two board members from each stage. These directors are elected from boards at the state level; representatives to the state board are elected by committees of leaders from local affiliates. The NRLC receives initial support from the United States Catholic Conference Family Life Division, but soon cuts its ties to allow the church to maintain its tax-exempt status.

June. Senator James Buckley (R-NY) and six other senators introduce a bill for a constitutional amendment that would overturn *Roe v. Wade* and outlaw abortion except where the mother's life is threatened, by extending the legal category of "person" to all "human beings, including their unborn offspring at every stage of their biological development, irrespective of age, health, function or condition of dependency." By September, no fewer than 18 proposed constitutional amendments will have been introduced in Congress in response to *Roe v. Wade*. Some of these, like Buckley's, seek to extend the legal definition of "person"; others, such as one sponsored by Representative Lawrence Hogan (R-MD), seek to ensure that due process and equal protection under the Fourteenth Amendment be extended to all individuals "from the moment of conception"; and still others are "states' rights" amendments, which seek to restore the regulation of abortion to the individual states. A number of bills are also introduced that attempt to accomplish the same ends through a simple statute as opposed to a constitutional amendment.

Summer. Planned Parenthood and NARAL hold nationwide seminars on how to set up clinics to offer safe and low-cost abortions, modeled on New York City clinics set up after that state's repeal of its restrictive abortion law in 1970. The groups soon develop a national network of clinics to complement hospital-based services. The free-standing clinics generally can provide abortions at a much lower cost than hospitals (an average first trimester abortion costs $200–$300). Many clinics also provide other reproductive health services such as contraception, pap smears, and sterilization. The clinics set an important precedent—by the end of the 1980s, outpatient services for a wide variety of surgical procedures will be commonplace. Nonetheless, many women, particularly those in rural areas or in areas with mostly Catholic hospitals, will have difficulty obtaining legal abortions.

August. In response to intense lobbying spearheaded by the United States Catholic Conference, 38 CBS affiliates decide not to air reruns of two episodes of the television comedy *Maude* in which Maude decides to have an abortion. The campaign serves to demonstrate the considerable political clout of anti-abortion activists.

1973
cont.
November 13. The NCCB issues a resolution calling on Catholics to "embark on a political crusade" at the grass-roots level, with the goal of passing a constitutional amendment outlawing abortion.

1974
Congress passes legislation prohibiting use of U.S. funds for direct support of abortion services overseas; private family planning services may still receive U.S. aid if they use a separate, non–U.S. funded account for abortion services.

Congress passes a "conscience clause" bill permitting any individual or hospital opposed to abortion to refuse to perform the procedure; the application of the bill to hospitals poses a serious threat to abortion availability in places where a single hospital serves a large geographic area. Partly as a result of the conscience clause, as of 1975 only 17 percent of public hospitals and 28 percent of private, non-Catholic hospitals will perform abortions.

Congress passes an amendment to the Legal Services Corporation Act, which provides free legal aid to low-income individuals, prohibiting legal services lawyers from providing representation on some abortion-related matters. The restriction will later be tightened to prohibit any representation by legal services attorneys in abortion-related cases.

The National Science Foundation Authorization Act passed by Congress includes a provision prohibiting the use of federal funds for fetal research. Also, the National Research Service Award Act of 1974 reauthorizes the National Commission for the Protection of Human Subjects of Biomedical and Behavioral Research and places a moratorium on fetal research.

The Missouri legislature passes an anti-abortion bill that includes a spousal consent requirement for married women and a parental consent requirement for women under 18 and that outlaws saline abortions after the twelfth week of pregnancy—provisions that will be declared unconstitutional by the Supreme Court in 1976. The legislature also becomes the first to call for a Constitutional Convention to draft a human life amendment.

During this first year of legal abortion, 763,476 abortions are reported to the Centers for Disease Control. In the initial period of legality, women who qualify for assistance under the Medicaid program receive federal and/or state funding to pay for their abortions, a situation that outrages abortion opponents.

1974
cont.
January 22. About 6,000 demonstrators come to the Washington, D.C., March for Life in commemoration of the anniversary of the *Roe v. Wade* decision. The march will become an annual event.

November. Pope Paul VI approves a document specifying that abortion cannot be justified by any extenuating circumstances, not even a threat to the pregnant woman's life.

1975
In Congress, both the Senate and the House defeat amendments to the 1976 HEW-Labor appropriations bill that would bar the use of Medicaid funds for abortions.

Justice William O. Douglas retires from the Supreme Court; President Gerald Ford nominates John Paul Stevens, age 55, to take Douglas's place. Over the next 15 years, Justice Stevens, a moderate Republican, will consistently vote in favor of legal abortion.

In France, a law is passed guaranteeing "the respect of every human being from the commencement of life," except "in cases of necessity and under conditions laid down by this law" (Tribe, 1990, p. 73). The law prohibits abortion as a means of birth control, but permits abortion up to the tenth week for a woman who believes that being pregnant "place[s] [her] in a situation of distress" (Tribe, p. 73). The abortion must be preceded by counseling that encourages the woman to keep the child; if she still decides on abortion, social security will cover 70 percent of its cost.

January. In Massachusetts, Dr. Kenneth Edelin goes on trial for manslaughter in a case that garners national attention and generates public controversy. He is accused of not attempting to preserve the life of a fetus he had removed from a teenager during a hysterotomy (a technique used for late abortions in which the uterus is cut open and the fetus removed). Witnesses for the prosecution include several prominent anti-abortion physicians, including Fred Mecklenberg and Mildred Jefferson. The mostly Catholic jury convicts Edelin and he receives a one-year suspended sentence. In December of 1976, the state supreme court will overturn the conviction on appeal.

January 22. The second March for Life draws an estimated 25,000 people to Washington, D.C. Featured speakers include Senator James Buckley (R-NY), author of the original human life amendment.

March. Senator Birch Bayh's (D-IN) Senate Judiciary Subcommittee on Constitutional Amendments holds extensive hearings on proposed constitutional amendments to reverse the 1973 court decisions

1975
cont.   on abortion. The hearings include an unprecedented appearance by four Catholic cardinals who testify in favor of the amendment, which would convey legal personhood to the unborn child from conception onward and allow no exception to the ban on abortion. Testimony is also heard from numerous pro-life and pro-choice leaders, as well as from religious groups, doctors, and constitutional law experts. Six months later, the subcommittee votes not to report a number of the proposed constitutional amendments to the full Judiciary Committee.

April. The U.S. Commission on Civil Rights issues a 101-page report on the constitutional aspects of the right to limit child-bearing. The report opposes efforts to enact a constitutional amendment outlawing abortion and opposes any ban on the use of federal funds to pay for abortions for the poor. It states that such an amendment would violate the separation of church and state, in that it would establish one view of when a fetus becomes a person and thereby inhibit the free exercise of religion by others. In response, abortion opponents in Congress threaten to cut off the commission's appropriations.

August. The Department of Health, Education, and Welfare (HEW), following recommendations of the National Commission for the Protection of Human Subjects (see 1973), lifts most restrictions on funding for fetal studies. The regulations also give women the right to consent to the use of their aborted fetal material for research, along with establishing safeguards to prevent research on potentially viable fetuses.

October. A National Institutes of Health report finds amniocentesis to be a safe and effective procedure for detecting fetal defects such as chromosomal abnormalities, metabolic disorders, and structural malformations of the brain and spinal cord.

November. The Family Life Division of the National Conference of Catholic Bishops (NCCB) outlines the "Pastoral Plan for Pro-Life Activity," a plan to gain support for a constitutional amendment that would recriminalize abortion. The plan spells out specific roles for the bishops in Washington, D.C., Catholic regional and diocesan officials, parish priests, and Catholic laypeople. The NCCB gives unanimous approval to the plan.

1976   Right-to-life activist Ellen McCormack, a housewife from Merrick, Long Island, succeeds in entering or being listed as a Democratic candidate in presidential primaries in 19 states, as well as qualifying for federal matching funds and Secret Service protection. By September, she will win more than 267,000 votes and gain significant

1976
cont.

percentages in Massachusetts, Pennsylvania, Indiana, California, Wisconsin, New Jersey, and Florida. The McCormack candidacy sparks the beginning of the drive for a constitutional convention that would enact an amendment barring abortion. It also leads to anti-abortion planks being considered at both the Democratic and Republican conventions. The Democrats reject the move, but the Republicans adopt a plank favoring "the continuance of the public dialogue on abortion and supporting the efforts of those who seek enactment of a constitutional amendment to restore protection of the rights of the unborn child."

June 24. Freshman Representative Henry Hyde (R-IL) proposes an amendment to the HEW-Labor appropriations bill banning federal funds "to pay for abortion or to promote or encourage abortion." The amendment is adopted in the House and defeated in the Senate, but in September an agreement is reached on language that bans HEW funds for abortion "except where the life of the mother would be clearly endangered if the fetus were carried to term." Some observers suggest that Senate willingness to go along with the amendment reflects a belief that the Supreme Court will find it unconstitutional—a belief that later will seem to have been well founded when U.S. District Court Judge John F. Dooling issues a restraining order and a preliminary injunction blocking implementation of the amendment (see 1977).

July 1. The Supreme Court rules on *Planned Parenthood of Central Missouri v. Danforth* (428 U.S. 52 [1976]). The class action suit had been filed on behalf of physicians performing or desiring to perform abortions and pregnant women wishing to terminate their pregnancies, seeking relief from a Missouri abortion law enacted in 1974. The Court ruling strikes down provisions requiring all minors to obtain parental permission and married women to obtain spousal permission for an abortion, as well as a prohibition of saline infusion abortions after the first trimester and a requirement that physicians "exercise professional care to preserve the fetus' life and health" under penalty of a manslaughter charge. The Court upholds Missouri's statutory definition of viability, provisions requiring a woman's consent for abortion, and requirements for abortion reporting and record keeping with reasonable confidentiality requirements. Agreeing with the majority are Justices Blackmun, Brennan, Stewart, Marshall, Stevens, and Powell; dissenting are Chief Justice Burger and Justices White and Rehnquist.

July 1. The Supreme Court also rules on *Bellotti v. Baird* (428 U.S. 132 [1976]), a case challenging the parental consent clause in a set of anti-abortion laws passed by Massachusetts in 1974. The clause

1976
cont.
required minors to have the consent of both parents before obtaining an abortion, but allowed the parents' veto to be overridden by a judge. The law included provisions that the parents be notified and allowed to present their side of the dispute in court. The Supreme Court remands the case to federal district court for certification to the Supreme Judicial Court of Massachusetts, citing unresolved questions about the state legislature's intent and the meaning of several provisions; the case will reach the high court again in 1979.

1977
During this year, the federal government pays $90 million for approximately 300,000 abortions under Medicaid.

The March of Dimes announces that it will phase out its genetic services program, which was largely responsible for the development of amniocentesis techniques. Anti-abortion forces claim credit for the decision, due to years-long pressure that included calls to Catholics to boycott the organization's fund drives.

Father Charles Fiore founds the National Pro-Life Political Action Committee (NPL-PAC). At about the same time, Paul Brown forms another PAC, the Life Amendment Political Action Committee (LAPAC). Both PACs favor a no-exceptions human life amendment, in contrast to the version favored by the NRLC, which would allow abortions to save the life of the mother. Both groups also have strong affiliations with the New Right and the "pro-family" movement. Over the next few years, these PACs will target senators and representatives who disagree with their stance and will succeed in driving several out of office.

January 15. Ruling in a class action suit brought on behalf of women needing Medicaid abortions, Judge John Dooling of the U.S. District Court states that the Hyde Amendment, in excluding most medically necessary abortions from covered services, violates the First Amendment guarantees of the free exercise of religion or conscience and the Fifth Amendment rights of privacy, due process, and equal protection of the laws for poor women eligible under the program. The right of a poor woman to obtain a medically necessary abortion paid for by Medicaid, the judge writes, is "nearly allied to her right to be" (Jaffe et al., 1981, p. 194). The federal government appeals the case of *Harris v. McRae* to the Supreme Court, which will refuse to stay Judge Dooling's order. Pending a final decision, HEW resumes Medicaid payments for medically necessary abortions and notifies states that they are required to pay their share.

Representative Hyde again introduces an amendment to the 1978 HEW-Labor appropriations bill, calling for a total ban on abortion

1977
cont.

funding to prevent "the slaughter of innocent, inconvenient unborn children." The amendment, which is supported by President Jimmy Carter, passes in the House, but becomes the focus of a six-month debate in the Senate and heavy lobbying by Catholic and other anti-abortion groups. A compromise amendment passes on December 7, barring federal funds for abortions except in cases of promptly reported rape or incest, where the life of the mother is endangered, or where "severe and long-lasting physical damage to the mother would result if the pregnancy were carried to term when so determined by two physicians." Judge Dooling subsequently lifts his temporary injunction blocking implementation of the amendment.

June 20. The Supreme Court rules, in *Beal v. Doe* (432 U.S. 438 [1977]) and *Maher v. Roe* (432 U.S. 464 [1977]), that states can deny Medicaid funding for "nontherapeutic" (i.e., "elective") abortions for indigents, saying that "the Constitution does not provide judicial remedies for every social and economic ill." Voting with the majority are Chief Justice Burger and Justices Powell, Stewart, White, Rehnquist, and Stevens; dissenting are Justices Brennan and Blackmun. Prior to this, between 1973 and 1975, 13 states had adopted laws or administrative policies limiting Medicaid funding for abortions, but most of the laws had been thrown out by federal courts. Following these rulings and the passage of the 1977 Hyde Amendment, most states move to restrict abortion funding. By the end of 1979, amidst a storm of lobbying by both anti-abortion and abortion rights forces, 40 states have restricted Medicaid funding for abortions either by legislation or by executive or administrative decree. At the federal level, funds are restricted not only for Medicaid recipients but also for Peace Corps volunteers, military dependents, and working women who depend on employment-related pregnancy disability benefits.

1978

Abortion opponents in Congress succeed in barring the U.S. Commission on Civil Rights from conducting further abortion studies (see 1975). Congress also passes legislation denying health insurance coverage for abortions to Peace Corps employees.

Partially in response to pressure from the National Conference of Catholic Bishops, the House and Senate pass an anti-abortion amendment to a broadly supported bill designed to mandate inclusion of pregnancy-related conditions in employee fringe-benefit plans such as health insurance, sick leave, and temporary disability plans. The compromise amendment gives employers discretion in covering abortions under health insurance plans (except where the woman's health is endangered), but requires them to pay medical

1978
cont.
payments and earned sick leave or disability benefits for the treatment of abortion complications. Dissatisfied with the compromise, the NCCB files a class action suit to halt implementation of the bill's abortion provisions, but the suit is dismissed on technical grounds.

1979
January 9. In *Colautti v. Franklin* (439 U.S. 379 [1979]), the Supreme Court overturns a Pennsylvania law requiring a doctor to make efforts to sustain the life of an aborted fetus if, in his professional judgment, the fetus is viable or might be viable, as long as such efforts did not adversely affect the mother. Grounds for overturning the law are that it is "impermissibly vague." Voting with the majority are Justices Blackmun, Brennan, Stewart, Marshall, Powell, and Stevens; dissenting are Chief Justice Burger and Justices White and Rehnquist.

January 22. An estimated 60,000 people participate in the annual March for Life in Washington, D.C. At the same time, abortion rights activists announce the establishment of a fund to aid low-income women who are unable to get Medicaid funding for abortions because of the Hyde Amendment. The fund is named in honor of Rosie Jimenez, a 27-year-old Texas mother who died from an illegal abortion after failing to get government funding for a legal abortion. "Rosie" will become a symbol of the abortion rights movement's fight to restore government funding for abortions.

July 2. In *Bellotti v. Baird* (II) (443 U.S. 623 [1979]), the Supreme Court rules on the Massachusetts law that requires minors seeking abortions to get the consent of both parents, finding that the provision is constitutionally defective in that:

> It permits courts to deny an abortion to a "mature and fully competent minor"

> It requires parental notification and consultation regardless of the minor's maturity, without giving her the opportunity to obtain an "independent judicial remedy"

Voting with the majority are Justices Burger, Stewart, Rehnquist, Stevens, Marshall, Brennan, and Blackmun, with Justice White dissenting.

1980
The Republican Party platform includes strong support for a human life amendment and advocates appointing federal judges on the basis of their demonstrated opposition to abortion. The party nominates Ronald Reagan for president. Reagan is an avowed anti-abortionist who, as governor of California, had reluctantly signed that state's liberalized abortion law in 1967.

1980
cont.

January 19. Senator Jesse Helms (R-NC) introduces the Human Life Bill (S. 158), which would define *person* to include an embryo from the moment of conception, thus, it is argued, having the same effect as a constitutional amendment extending constitutional protection to fetuses. On the same day, Representative Henry Hyde (R-IL) introduces a similar bill in the House.

About the same time, Senator Orrin Hatch (R-UT) introduces the Hatch Human Life Federalism Amendment, which would override *Roe v. Wade* by a constitutional amendment that would let the states or Congress decide whether to outlaw abortion. The two approaches spark conflict among pro-life forces, with the Catholic Church and mainstream groups like the NRLC supporting the Hatch Amendment, while the New Right and its supporters back the Helms-Hyde Bill.

January 20. An estimated 50 people representing a dozen organizations meet in Washington, D.C., for the first annual Respect Life Leadership Conference to discuss common issues and concerns, prominent among them the passage of a human life amendment. That same week, abortion rights activists in 35 states launch a lobbying and political action campaign aimed at countering the political efforts against abortion.

June 30. In *Harris v. McRae* (448 U.S. 297 [1980]), the Supreme Court, by a one-vote majority, affirms the constitutionality of the Hyde Amendment in its most restrictive version, rejecting Judge Dooling's opinion that the amendment violates Fifth Amendment rights of poor women. The ruling effectively shuts off any further litigation of the amendment and eliminates virtually all federal funding for abortion. The justices also rule that the Medicaid law does not require participating states to fund medically necessary abortions if there were no federal reimbursement and extends the earlier *Maher v. Roe* ruling to include "the right of a state or the federal government to subsidize childbirth while refusing to pay for abortion, even if the abortion is deemed medically necessary and its denial could endanger the health of the mother or the health (or even survival) of the baby that is finally born" (Jaffe et al., 1981, p. 201). In a minority opinion, Justices Brennan, Marshall, and Blackmun charge that the Hyde Amendment unconstitutionally coerces poor women to have babies that they do not want. In a separate minority opinion, Justice Stevens charges the majority with placing protection of the potential life of the fetus before protection of the pregnant woman's health, thus "shirking a duty imposed on it by *Roe v. Wade*" (Jaffe et al., p. 201).

1980 June 30. In a companion decision, *Williams v. Zbaraz* (448 U.S. 358
cont. [1980]), the Supreme Court holds that Illinois is not required under
Title XIX of the Social Security Act to pay for abortions for which
federal funds are unavailable under the Hyde Amendment and that
Illinois funding restrictions do not violate the Equal Protection
Clause.

1981 In the Senate, the Hatch Amendment and the Helms Human Life
Bill are debated in Judiciary Committee subcommittees. Anti-
abortion groups are split on their support for the two bills; this
fragmentation contributes to the inability of the bill's sponsors to
move either legislation to the Senate floor.

Congress moves to make the Hyde Amendment more restrictive by
removing funding of abortions for victims of rape or incest.

Congress decides that public health service clinics receiving federal
funds must notify parents of minors for whom contraceptives have
been prescribed.

Justice Potter Stewart, one of the *Roe v. Wade* majority, retires, and
President Ronald Reagan appoints Sandra Day O'Connor, age 51,
to take his place. In the first abortion ruling in which she takes part,
City of Akron v. Akron Center for Reproductive Health (1983), Justice
O'Connor will side with the minority.

January 22. An estimated 50,000 people come to Washington, D.C.,
for the annual March for Life.

March 23. In *H. L. v. Matheson* (450 U.S. 398 [1981]), the Supreme
Court upholds a Utah statute requiring physicians to notify the
parents of unemancipated minors living with and dependent on their
parents prior to performing abortions, on the grounds that since the
law does not give parents "veto power" over the abortion, it is not
unconstitutional. Parental notification, the majority declares, is
needed to "protect adolescents" by giving parents the opportunity
"to supply essential medical and other information to a physician"—
information needed because of the "potentially traumatic and permanent consequences" of abortion for teenagers. (Drucker, 1990,
pp. 80–81). Agreeing with the majority are Chief Justice Burger and
Justices Stewart, White, Powell, Rehnquist, and Stevens; dissenting
are Justices Marshall, Brennan, and Blackmun.

1982 January 22. The annual March for Life in Washington, D.C., draws
an estimated 25,000 demonstrators.

1982
cont.
March. Senator Jesse Helms (R-NC) introduces an expanded version of the Human Life Bill (S. 2148), which includes a provision that would permanently prohibit virtually all federal funding for abortions except when a woman's life is threatened. The bill would also restrict abortion coverage under federal employees' health insurance policies, referrals for abortion, and training in abortion techniques.

August 15. Hector and Rosalie Zevallos, the owner/operators of an ob-gyn clinic in Granite City, Illinois, disappear. Two days later a man identifying himself as a member of the "army of God" calls the FBI office in nearby St. Louis, saying that he is holding the Zevalloses and demanding that President Reagan publicly denounce abortion and call for an end to it. He threatens to kill the couple if the demand is not met within three days. Reagan declines comment and an FBI search is unsuccessful, but a few days later the Zevalloses are released unharmed. The Zevallos incident is one in an increasing number of violent acts against abortion clinics since the mid-1970s, including arson, bombings, vandalism, and threats to clinic personnel and directors and their families.

August 16. Senator Jesse Helms (R-NC) introduces an anti-abortion amendment to the resolution to extend the debt ceiling, but Senator Robert Packwood (R-OR) and 12 colleagues defeat the amendment by conducting a filibuster that lasts nearly a month.

1983
By a two-thirds vote in a popular referendum, the 1861 English law banning abortion is incorporated into the Irish Constitution. Thereafter, about 4,000 Irish women annually travel to Great Britain to obtain legal abortions.

January 22. An estimated 26,000 demonstrators rally in Washington, D.C., in the annual March for Life. At the same time abortion rights activists hold rallies, fund-raisers, and news conferences to mark the end of a decade of legal abortion.

June 15. In a mixed decision on *Planned Parenthood of Kansas City, Missouri v. Ashcroft* (462 U.S. 476 [1983]), the Supreme Court rules as unconstitutional Missouri's requirement that abortions after 12 weeks of pregnancy be performed in a hospital. The Court upholds state requirements for pathology reports for each abortion performed, the presence of a second physician during post-viability abortions, and parental or judicial consent for unemancipated or unmarried minors seeking abortions.

June 15. In *City of Akron v. Akron Center for Reproductive Health* (462 U.S. 416 [1983]), the Supreme Court rules that the government

1983
cont.

cannot impose a fixed waiting period on any woman seeking an abortion. The ruling also strikes down a parental consent requirement for minors under 15, a requirement that second trimester abortions be performed in hospitals, specific requirements for disposal of fetal tissue, and a requirement that a woman seeking an abortion must receive detailed descriptions of fetal development as well as information on particular physical and psychological risks associated with abortion and must be reminded that assistance is available from the father or social services should she choose to have the baby. Voting with the majority are Chief Justice Burger and Justices Powell, Brennan, Marshall, Blackmun, and Stevens; dissenting are Justices O'Connor, White, and Rehnquist.

June 15. In *Simonopoulos v. Virginia* (462 U.S. 506 [1983]), the Supreme Court upholds a Virginia requirement that second trimester abortions be performed in a licensed hospital because the statute defines *hospital* to include outpatient clinics.

June 28. After two days of debate, by a 49 to 50 vote, the Senate defeats a revised version of the Hatch Amendment, which states simply, "A right to abortion is not secured by this Constitution."

November. Congress passes a continuing resolution prohibiting federal employee health insurance programs from paying for abortions.

1984

For the first time, abortion becomes a key issue in the presidential election.

January 23. A crowd of 30,000 to 50,000 people rally against abortion in Washington, D.C., joined by thousands in other cities around the country. Abortion rights activists hold smaller rallies of their own.

August. At the Mexico City International Conference on Population, the United States declares that it will deny funds to any private organization that performs or promotes (as through counseling) abortion as a method of family planning. Further, countries where abortion is legal can only receive U.S. population assistance through segregated accounts. The "Mexico City Policy" also threatens the United Nations Fund for Population Activities (UNFPA) with a cut-off of funds if it supports abortion or coercive family planning programs in any member nations.

October. A full-page ad in the *New York Times* contains a declaration of support for Democratic vice-presidential candidate Geraldine Ferraro, who has been condemned by the Catholic Church for her support of legal abortion. The declaration, signed by 24 nuns and

1984
cont.
more than 70 religious leaders, testifies to the diversity of opinion regarding abortion among Catholics. Church leaders warn the participating nuns that they must recant or be dismissed. A year later, a second ad will appear, declaring support for the original signatories and attesting to the right of Catholics to disagree with church teachings.

1985
Despite the legality of abortion, services are still not available in many areas, particularly rural areas and small towns. According to the Alan Guttmacher Institute, the number of abortion providers has actually declined since 1982, from 2,908 to 2,680. During the same period, the number of hospitals providing abortion services has decreased 15 percent, from 1,570 to 1,405, and 20 percent of public hospitals have stopped providing abortions. This year, only 2 percent of abortions will be performed in rural communities or small towns. Free-standing clinics, the vast majority of them in metropolitan areas, provide over 87 percent of all abortions. Further, more than half of all abortion providers now refuse to perform abortions after the first trimester.

January 22. President Ronald Reagan addresses the annual March for Life. Although he has met with leaders of earlier marches, this is his first address to the group as a whole. More than 70,000 people cheer as the president expresses his solidarity with their struggle. The same day, movement leaders preview *The Silent Scream,* a film produced by former abortionist Dr. Bernard Nathanson, which will generate a storm of criticism and controversy among abortion rights supporters while galvanizing opposition to abortion.

1986
Supreme Court Chief Justice Warren Burger retires. President Reagan appoints William Rehnquist, the most conservative sitting justice, as chief justice and appoints Antonin Scalia, age 50, to fill the vacancy.

In *Diamond v. Charles* (106 S. Ct. 1697 [1986]), the Supreme Court rules that, in the absence of an appeal by the state, a physician's status as a pediatrician, parent, or "protector of the unborn" does not give him or her standing to challenge an Illinois abortion law.

January 22. An estimated 36,000 people hear President Reagan address the annual March for Life for the second time.

April. More than 100,000 people answer a call from the National Organization for Women to join in a March for Women's Lives in Washington, D.C.; another 20,000 march in Los Angeles in support of abortion rights.

1986
cont.
June 11. In a hotly debated decision on *Thornburgh v. American College of Obstetricians and Gynecologists* (106 S. Ct. 2169 [1986]), the Supreme Court strikes down "extreme" reporting requirements that would make detailed information about the woman, the doctor, or the circumstances of an abortion available to the public. The ruling also declares as unconstitutional a Pennsylvania requirement for giving prospective abortion patients, under "informed consent," detailed information about gestational age and risks of abortion and childbirth, as well as information on medical assistance available for prenatal and neonatal care and childbirth and the legal obligations of the father. The Court also holds that a physician is not required to try to preserve the life of a "viable" fetus if doing so poses any additional risk to the health of the pregnant woman. Justices Blackmun, Brennan, Marshall, Powell, and Stevens side with the majority; Chief Justice Burger and Justices White, O'Connor, and Rehnquist dissent. Justice White and Justice O'Connor each file dissenting opinions, in which Justice Rehnquist concurs, harshly criticizing the "opposition" and the Court itself, not only for this ruling but also for nearly all its abortion rulings since *Roe v. Wade.*

1987
Supreme Court Justice Lewis F. Powell retires. President Reagan nominates Judge Robert Bork to replace him, but the nomination goes down to defeat in the Senate after a heated and often bitter debate. The president then nominates Judge Douglas Ginsberg but is forced to withdraw the nomination after it is revealed that Ginsberg smoked marijuana in college. The president's final nominee is Anthony Kennedy, a California law school professor with no expressed opinion on abortion. Of the sitting justices, only four remain who have previously expressed a commitment to abortion rights.

President Reagan directs Surgeon General C. Everett Koop to prepare a comprehensive report on the health effects of abortion on women.

January 25. Five thousand demonstrators gather in a driving snowstorm for the fourteenth annual March for Life, the smallest gathering since the march's inception.

December 14. In *Hartigan v. Zbaraz,* the Supreme Court splits four to four, thus invalidating an Illinois law that would have required parental notification and a 24-hour waiting period before teenagers could have abortions.

1988
The Reagan administration changes the rules for distribution of family planning funds under Title X. About $200 million per year is currently distributed under the program, which began in 1970 and

1988
cont.
which serves nearly 5 million low-income women annually. Under the "gag rule," physicians and counselors at clinics receiving Title X funds are prohibited from providing any information about abortion to patients. Women who ask about abortion are to be told that "this project does not consider abortion an appropriate method of family planning." The regulation further stipulates that all pregnant women are to be given a list of providers of prenatal care "that promotes the welfare of mother and unborn child." To provide abortion counseling, clinics must maintain physically separate facilities with separate personnel, accounting, and record keeping and must fund those facilities privately.

A growing number of state courts hear "father's rights" cases in which men seek to block their wives or partners from having abortions. Some of these cases will be appealed to the Supreme Court, which as of mid-1991 has refused to hear any of them.

In the case of Dr. Henry Morgentaler, a Quebec physician who provided easy access to abortions in violation of the 1969 Canadian statute, the Canadian Supreme Court invokes *Roe v. Wade* and holds that the 1969 law imposed an impermissible restriction on a woman's right to have an abortion; in effect the ruling makes abortion available on request in Canada. Over the next two years abortion will continue to be a major issue in Canadian politics, as anti-abortion groups attempt to gain passage of laws restricting abortion.

January 22. An estimated 50,000 demonstrators gather for the annual March for Life in Washington, D.C.

July. Operation Rescue, a group based in Binghamton, New York, receives national media attention when it mounts a blockade of Atlanta abortion clinics during the Democratic National Convention. During the next two years, thousands of people will participate in "rescues" in New York, Illinois, Pennsylvania, California, Connecticut, Colorado, and other states. Thousands of the demonstrators will be arrested; many of them will elect to serve jail sentences rather than pay their fines.

September 16. In Indiana, 17-year-old Becky Bell dies in a Marion County hospital. The cause of death is listed as "septic abortion with pneumonia." Becky soon becomes a *cause célèbre* of the abortion rights movement, which claims that she died because of Indiana's parental consent laws. Because she was unwilling to disappoint her parents by telling them she was pregnant, Becky had an illegal abortion and died from its complications. Following their daughter's death, Becky's parents become national spokespersons

1988
cont.
arguing against parental consent laws; they also participate in the filming of a video that they hope will lead to appeal of parental consent legislation. The facts of the case are disputed by some anti-abortion groups, which claim that Becky actually had a spontaneous abortion (miscarriage) and that, had her parents known of her pregnancy, they would have been able to seek medical help in time.

September 23. The French government approves the marketing of an "abortion pill" developed by a French biochemist, Dr. Etienne-Emile Baulieu. When taken orally during the earliest stage of pregnancy, RU 486 blocks the fertilized egg from implanting in the uterus. In later stages (up to about seven weeks since the last menstrual period, or LMP), RU 486 can be combined with prostaglandin to induce abortion.

October 26. Roussel-UCLAF, the pharmaceutical company that makes RU 486, announces cancellation of plans to distribute the drug in France, citing pressure from French and American anti-abortion groups. Two days later, French Health Minister Claude Evin orders the company to resume distribution of the drug, saying, "From the moment governmental approval for the drug was granted, RU 486 became the moral property of women, not just the property of the drug company" (Klitsch, 1989, p. 1). Roussel-UCLAF complies with the order, and by mid-1990 RU 486 will have been used in more than 50,000 abortions.

1989
During this year, Operation Rescue protests and civil disobedience tactics at abortion clinics will lead to more than 20,000 arrests.

January. Surgeon General C. Everett Koop decides not to release a report commissioned by President Reagan in 1987 on the health effects of abortion. In his letter to the president, Dr. Koop writes that "in spite of a diligent review on the part of many in the Public Health Service and in the private sector, the scientific studies do not provide conclusive data about the health effects of abortion on women."

January 22. An estimated 67,000 people rally in Washington, D.C., in the annual March for Life. The event takes on special significance because of anticipation surrounding the pending Supreme Court decision in the *Webster* case (see below).

February. The Reproductive Health Equity Act (RHEA; H.R. 857) is introduced in the House. The bill would restore full federal funding for abortion in all federal programs, including Medicaid, Indian Health Service, federal and military employees' health benefit programs, the Peace Corps, and federal penal institutions.

1989
cont.

April 9. Abortion rights activists gather to march in Washington, D.C., in one of the largest demonstrations ever held in the capital. Organizers of the demonstration hope to influence the pending Supreme Court decision in the *Webster* case (see below). Police estimate the crowd at 300,000, though some organizers claim the demonstrators number twice that.

April 28. In response to the earlier abortion rights march and also in an attempt to influence the pending *Webster* decision, the NRLC holds a national Rally for Life in Washington, D.C. Organizers estimate the crowd at 350,000; police and media estimates, however, are smaller.

July 3. In *Webster v. Reproductive Health Services*, in a fragmented, no-majority decision, the Supreme Court upholds a Missouri statute that:

Prohibits the use of public facilities (including private facilities built on land leased from the state) or public employees to perform abortions

Requires physicians to test for fetal viability

Bans the use of state funding for "encouraging and counseling women on the abortion procedure"

In their opinions, four justices indicate their desire to overturn the fundamental privacy right to choose abortion established in *Roe v. Wade*. In ruling on the provision for testing fetal viability, the justices explicitly reject the trimester framework established in *Roe v. Wade* and speak of the "State's 'compelling interest' in protecting potential human life throughout pregnancy." By a five to four majority, the Court declines to rule on the constitutionality of the preamble to the Missouri statute, which states that "It is the intention of the general assembly of the state of Missouri to grant the right to life to all humans, born and unborn," on the basis that the preamble merely expresses the state's value judgment favoring childbirth over abortion and is not used to restrict individuals' actions.

During the months before the announcement, both sides view the *Webster* case as a potential challenge to *Roe v. Wade*, prompting numerous groups to file amicus curiae briefs and thousands of individuals to send letters to the justices. While not explicitly overturning *Roe v. Wade*, the decision continues to erode that earlier ruling and sets the stage for legislative activity at the state level. Both sides interpret the decision as a victory for the anti-abortion movement, setting off a wave of abortion rights activity. In the following months, bills restricting abortion will be introduced in several state legislatures.

1989
cont.

August. The House of Representatives defeats an amendment preventing the District of Columbia from using local tax revenues to provide funding for abortions—the first time since September 1980 that an abortion spending restriction has been defeated in the House. The Senate also passes an appropriations bill permitting the district to fund abortions with its own tax money, without a separate vote on the issue. The bill and a slightly modified later version are both vetoed by President George Bush.

October. For the second year in a row, the Senate approves a Labor and Health and Human Services (the successor agency to HEW) appropriations bill containing a provision requiring Medicaid funding for abortions for rape or incest victims. The House follows suit, voting after intense debate to approve the funding amendment 216–206. President Bush vetoes the measure, and an override attempt fails in the House by a vote of 231–191.

November. By narrow majorities, Congress restores U.S. funding to the United Nations Fund for Population Activities (UNFPA), but is forced to remove the provision when President Bush vetoes the entire Foreign Assistance Appropriation because of it.

November. Representatives Don Edwards (D-CA), Patricia Schroeder (D-CO), and Bill Green (R-NY) and Senators Alan Cranston (D-CA), Robert Packwood (R-OR), and Howard Metzenbaum (D-OH) introduce the Freedom of Choice Act (FCA) (H.R. 3700, S. 1912). The purpose of the FCA is to codify the *Roe v. Wade* decision into federal law as a means of protecting legalized abortion nationwide. It would prohibit states from restricting the right of a woman to choose abortion "before fetal viability or at any time, if such termination is necessary to protect the life or health of the woman" and would allow states only to "impose requirements necessary to protect the life or health of women." In addition to the 50 states, the bill would apply to the District of Columbia, Puerto Rico, and any other U.S. possessions or territories, including Guam. As of early May 1990, the bill will have 121 co-sponsors in the House and 25 co-sponsors in the Senate, where it will be assigned to the Human Resources Committee.

November. The Reproductive Health Equity Act (RHEA) is introduced in the Senate (S. 1946). (See February 1989.) Because the bill involves a number of federal programs, it is sent to several committees in the House and the Senate, including Post Office and Civil Service and Government Affairs, Armed Services and Foreign Affairs, and Judiciary.

1989
cont.

November 12. In their second major demonstration this year, hundreds of thousands of abortion rights supporters gather in Washington, D.C., to protest the *Webster* decision and show support for keeping abortion legal.

1990

Violence and civil disobedience actions against abortion clinics continue. Since 1977, extremists have bombed or set fire to 129 clinics and threatened 250 others, have invaded 266 clinics, and have vandalized 269 clinics. In a number of communities, members of Operation Rescue, the most visible of the radical anti-abortion groups, receive heavy fines and jail sentences after convictions on various charges, including racketeering. For their part, abortion rights groups work to counter demonstrations and "sidewalk counseling" actions by providing escorts for women seeking to enter abortion clinics and mobilizing supporters to defend and keep open clinics targeted for blockades.

A survey by the Alan Guttmacher Institute shows that between 1985 and 1988, the number of abortion providers decreased by 19 percent. The vast majority of providers are located in metropolitan areas— among rural counties, more than 90 percent do not have any facility that performs abortions.

The California Medical Association (CMA) passes a resolution demanding the availability of the French "abortion pill," RU 486, for use in "extensive clinical investigation and, if indicated, clinical practice." (Under a 1939 statute, California may approve drugs separately from the federal Food and Drug Administration.) Also in California, the legislature votes to restore funding for abortions under the state's MediCal program.

In England, the House of Commons passes a bill that would restrict availability of abortions to the first 18 weeks.

Belgium becomes one of the last Western European countries to pass a liberalized abortion law, which permits abortion in the first 12 weeks of pregnancy for women "in a state of distress." King Baudoin refuses to sign the bill into law and is temporarily suspended by the government; the law is ratified by the prime minister.

The European Commission on Human Rights agrees to hear a case presented by the Dublin Well Women Centre, which has been enjoined by the Irish Supreme Court from providing women with information on how and where to obtain legal abortions in Britain.

1990
cont.

January 22. A crowd estimated by police at 75,000 turns out for the annual March for Life in Washington, D.C.

March. The territory of Guam passes the most restrictive abortion law in the United States, outlawing abortion except to save the life of the mother; under the law, abortion providers would receive third-degree felony prison terms, and persons who obtain or "solicit" abortions would be punished with up to one year in jail. The law is signed by the governor but is immediately challenged by Janet Benshoof of the American Civil Liberties Union's Reproductive Freedom Project. In the resulting court hearings the law is enjoined by U.S. District Judge Alex Munson. Attorneys for the ACLU subsequently ask for the law to be permanently enjoined and still are awaiting a ruling as of mid-1991. Also during March, the Idaho state legislature passes a bill that prohibits abortions except in the case of rape, incest, severe fetal deformity, or danger to the pregnant woman's life or health; under threats of a potato boycott by abortion rights supporters, the bill is vetoed by Governor Cecil Andrus.

March. In Rumania, thousands of women seek abortions and contraceptives, newly legalized after the downfall of Nicolae Ceausescu's repressive government. Under the Communist regime, women were required to bear four children apiece—reportedly, women were even subjected to monthly pregnancy tests to ensure that they had not had illegal abortions. Some of the children born under this policy were sold by Ceaucescu, many developed AIDS, and hundreds of thousands are growing up in government orphanages.

April. In a widely publicized and controversial decision, the National Conference of Catholic Bishops (NCCB) awards a $5 million, five-year contract to the public relations firm of Hill & Knowlton and the Wirthlin Group, a Republican polling organization, to develop a campaign to end public support for legal abortion. Several weeks later, the Catholic fraternal group Knights of Columbus announces that it will provide $3 million for the campaign.

April 30. Doctors at the University of Colorado (CU) Health Sciences Center announce that a transplant of brain tissue from an aborted fetus produced "substantial improvement" in a patient with Parkinson's disease. Because of the federal ban on funding for fetal tissue research, the CU project is funded completely from private sources. Despite the lack of federal money, privately funded research also continues on the use of fetal tissue transplants to treat diabetes, immunodeficiency disorders, and several metabolic diseases. Other conditions that may someday be treated with fetal tissue transplants include leukemia, Huntington's disease, and Alzheimer's disease.

1990
cont.

June. The Louisiana state legislature passes a bill that would prohibit abortion in all cases and impose a sentence of 10 years' hard labor on any doctor convicted of performing an abortion; after it is vetoed a second bill is hastily passed with provisions for rape and incest, but it too is vetoed by Governor Buddy Roemer.

June 5. New York Cardinal John O'Connor issues a public warning to Roman Catholic politicians that they risk excommunication if they persist in supporting legal abortion. A few weeks later Rachel Vargas, administrator of the Reproductive Services Clinic in Corpus Christi, Texas, becomes the first U.S. Catholic to be formally excommunicated because of her activism on reproductive rights issues, in an action that garners national publicity.

June 25. In *Hodgson v. Minnesota*, the Supreme Court upholds a 1981 Minnesota statute requiring that both parents of a minor be notified 48 hours prior to performance of an abortion. The statute includes a judicial bypass option as well as contingencies in the event that: (1) one parent "cannot be located through diligent effort"; (2) emergency treatment is "necessary to prevent the woman's death"; or (3) the minor is a victim of sexual abuse or physical abuse that has been reported to the proper authorities. Five justices (Rehnquist, White, O'Connor, Scalia, and Kennedy) vote to uphold the two-parent notification requirement. Six (the above plus Stevens) uphold the 48-hour waiting period. By a five to four vote, with Justice O'Connor voting with the majority, the court strikes down an alternative portion of the statute that would have eliminated the judicial bypass option and required "absolute notice" of both parents except in the contingencies cited above.

June 25. In a companion decision, *Ohio v. Akron Center for Reproductive Health*, the Supreme Court upholds by a six to three vote a 1985 Ohio statute requiring an abortion provider to notify one parent 24 hours before performing an abortion on a minor; the statute includes a judicial bypass option. In writing their opinions for these cases, the majority of the court holds that a woman's interest in obtaining an abortion is a "liberty interest." This is a significant departure from the "fundamental right" wording of earlier decisions and means that, to regulate abortion, states need show only a "rational basis" for their restrictions, as opposed to a "compelling interest," which is much more difficult to prove. Accordingly, the two decisions are hailed as victories by the anti-abortion movement and decried by abortion rights supporters. At the time of the rulings, 38 states have parental notification or consent laws on the books, but the laws are being enforced in only 14 states.

1990
cont.
July. Supreme Court Justice William Brennan, considered the court's most liberal member, retires, leaving only two of the original *Roe v. Wade* majority, both of whom are over 80, still sitting on the Court, along with John Paul Stevens, who has consistently voted in favor of abortion rights since his 1975 appointment. President George Bush nominates David Souter to take Brennan's place, asserting that no "litmus test" for abortion was applied in the nomination. Despite protests from abortion rights groups, Judge Souter wins easy confirmation in the Senate and takes his place on the Court a week after the opening of the 1990 session.

August. A federal judge strikes down portions of Pennsylvania's restrictive abortion law, ruling that requirements for spousal notification, a 24-hour waiting period, and parental consent or a court order for a minor are unconstitutional. The ruling is quickly appealed in a case abortion opponents hope will reach the Supreme Court.

October. Minnesota passes a law requiring hospitals and clinics to arrange for the burial or cremation of aborted fetuses. Also in October, the House of Representatives defeats a bill that would have permitted taxpayer financing of abortions in the District of Columbia, and the Senate passes an amendment requiring organizations receiving federal funds to notify the parents of minors seeking abortions before performing the procedure.

November. Abortion becomes an increasingly visible issue in gubernatorial elections and in legislative races at both the state and national levels.

1991
January. Utah passes the nation's most restrictive abortion law, sparking national attention when legal researchers say that the law could potentially cause women or doctors to be prosecuted for murder. The bill is later amended to remove abortions from the state's criminal homicide act, to permit abortions in case of rape or incest (which may be reported by a third party), and to cover only "intentional" abortions (so that women are allowed, for example, to use IUDs). In anticipation of court challenges, legislators also create a fund allowing the state to receive private donations that will be used to defend the laws. The law's passage prompts abortion rights supporters to call for a boycott of Utah tourism.

February 25. The Supreme Court agrees to decide whether anti-abortion demonstrators may be prohibited from blocking entrances to abortion clinics under an 1871 civil rights law. The Restoration-era law, known as the Ku Klux Klan Act, provides the right of

1991
cont.
damages and injunctive relief against people who conspire to deprive any person or class of persons of their civil rights. Virginia abortion clinics, the National Organization for Women, and Planned Parenthood of Metropolitan Washington invoked the law in the fall of 1989 in order to obtain an injunction against Operation Rescue, after the anti-abortion group vowed to shut down several Washington area clinics. The injunction was upheld by the Fourth Circuit U.S. Court of Appeals. Operation Rescue appealed to the high court, which will hear the case sometime in the fall of 1991.

May. The defense-spending passage approved by the House of Representatives includes a provision restoring abortion services in overseas military hospitals, although women would have to pay for the abortions themselves.

May 30. In a five-to-four decision on *Rust v. Sullivan,* the Supreme Court upholds the "gag rule" on clinics receiving federal funds under Title X. Imposed by the Reagan administration and continued under President Bush, the regulations prohibit the more than 3,900 clinics that receive federal family planning funds under Title X from giving patients any information about abortion (see 1988). Planned Parenthood of New York City and the New York City and New York state governments had challenged the regulations on the grounds that they violated both Title X and the guarantee of freedom of speech under the First Amendment, and several lower courts had issued injunctions prohibiting the regulations from taking effect, though with conflicting conclusions on their constitutionality. The Bush administration defended the regulations but asked the Court to resolve the issue in light of the conflicting rulings. In his first abortion-related case while on the Court, Justice David Souter provides the crucial swing vote for the majority, although during hearings on the case he had voiced concern about the regulations' impact on doctors' professional speech and ability to counsel patients. Analysts hesitate to speculate on what, if anything, Souter's vote indicates about his stance on future abortion cases. Justice Sandra Day O'Connor votes with the minority.

The Court's decision has far-ranging implications not only for the future of legal abortion but for issues involving freedom of speech and separation of powers. It reignites the abortion controversy, provoking celebration among abortion opponents and outrage among abortion rights supporters, who express concern about its impact not only on abortion services, but on other family planning services that the affected clinics provide to millions of poor and low-income women. In the wake of the decision, some clinics vow to continue providing abortion referrals and services and do without Title X funding, while others say that they will have to close down.

1991
cont.
The ruling also promises to stir up additional action in Congress, where earlier in the year Representatives Ron Wyden (D-OR) and John Porter (R-IL) had introduced legislation that would strike down the administration's regulations.

June 26. The House votes overwhelmingly (353–74) to approve the Labor and Health and Human Services Appropriations Bill, which includes an amendment, sponsored by Representative John Porter (R-IL), forbidding the Secretary of Health and Human Services to use the appropriations funds to enforce the "gag rule." The amendment would provide federally funded clinics with a one-year reprieve from enforcement of the administration's regulation. It wins the support of a number of representatives who, while opposed to abortion, also oppose the counseling ban because, in Porter's words, it "stifles free speech, interferes with the doctor-patient relationship, and denies women complete access to information on reproductive matters" (ACLU, June 28, 1991, p. 2). The appropriations bill goes to the Senate, which will act on it in late July or early August.

June 28. Justice Thurgood Marshall, one of the two remaining justices from the *Roe v. Wade* majority, announces his resignation from the Supreme Court, citing health reasons. Four days later, President Bush announces his nominee to succeed Marshall: Judge Clarence Thomas, a 43-year-old black conservative who was appointed to the U.S. Court of Appeals for the District of Columbia in 1990. Thomas previously served as chair of the Equal Employment Opportunity Commission under President Reagan; in that role he was frequently criticized for failing to enforce antidiscrimination laws and for not acting on thousands of complaints of age discrimination. Although Thomas has not ruled on any abortion-related cases during his time on the appellate court, abortion rights groups vow to oppose his nomination. They base their opposition on interviews, articles, and speeches, which they believe indicate that Thomas is opposed to abortion, citing his support for a "natural law" that supersedes human laws.

July 17. On a voice vote, the Senate passes a bill introduced by John Chaffee (R-RI) that would overturn the "gag rule." As originally written, the bill required that pregnant women being seen at federally funded family planning clinics must be advised of all their options, including abortion; before passage it is rewritten to say that women may be provided with the information but that such provision is not required. The bill passes only after the addition of two parental notification amendments. One, introduced by George Mitchell (D-MN) and passed 54–45, would allow a doctor, member of the clergy, or judge to give permission for an abortion in cases

1991 where a minor aged 17 or younger was unable to obtain parental
cont. consent. The other, introduced by Dan Coats (R-IN) and passed
52–47, would require doctors at federally funded clinics to notify one
parent or guardian 48 hours before performing an abortion on a
minor, allowing exceptions only in cases of incest or in cases where
a girl's life is in imminent danger.

Also in 1991. Abortion-related activity continues at a furious pace
in state legislatures and courts. Numerous state legislatures are
considering bills restricting abortion. The restrictions range from
parental consent or notification bills introduced in the wake of the
Hodgson decision (see 1990) to near-complete bans which include
criminal penalties for doctors performing abortions. The most restrictive bills are intended to provoke challenges that abortion opponents hope will eventually lead to the Supreme Court and the
overturning of *Roe v. Wade.* Other states are considering legislation
that will preserve the right to legal abortion should *Roe v. Wade* be
struck down. In some states, as well as in the United States Congress,
bills restricting abortion are competing for passage with bills codifying the right to abortion.

Demonstrations and violence against abortion clinics continue.
At the same time, the number of doctors willing to perform abortions
continues to decline, as does the number of facilities that perform
abortions. In many, if not most, states, abortions are now virtually
unobtainable outside of major urban areas.

References

American Civil Liberties Union/Reproductive Freedom Project, *Reproductive Rights Update,* Vol. III, Nos. 1–9, inclusive. January 4–July 26, inclusive.

Benshoof, Janet, *Benshoof in Guam* (Washington, DC: ACLU Reproductive Freedom Project, 1990).

Committee on Government Operations, 101st Congress, *The Federal Role in Determining the Medical and Psychological Impact of Abortion on Women* (Washington, DC: U.S. Government Printing Office, 1989).

Drucker, Dan, *Abortion Decisions of the Supreme Court, 1973–1989* (Jefferson, NC: McFarland and Company, Inc., 1990).

Faux, Marian, *Roe v. Wade: The Untold Story of the Landmark Supreme Court Decision That Made Abortion Legal* (New York: Macmillan, 1988).

———, *Crusaders: Voices from the Abortion Front* (New York: Birch Lane Press, published by Carol Publishing Group, 1990).

Francome, Colin, *Abortion Freedom: A Worldwide Movement* (London: George Allen & Unwin, 1984).

Fryer, Peter, *The Birth Controllers* (New York: Stein and Day, 1966).

Glendon, Mary Ann, *Abortion and Divorce in Western Law* (Cambridge, MA: Harvard University Press, 1987).

Hodgson, Jane, ed., *Abortion and Sterilization: Medical and Social Aspects* (London: Academic Press, 1981).

Hurst, Jane, *The History of Abortion in the Catholic Church: The Untold Story* (Washington, DC: Catholics for a Free Choice, 1989).

Jaffe, Frederick S., Barbara L. Lindheim, and Philip R. Lee, *Abortion Politics: Private Morality and Public Policy* (New York: McGraw-Hill, 1981).

Keller, Allan, *Scandalous Lady: The Life and Times of Madame Restell, New York's Most Notorious Abortionist* (New York: Atheneum, 1981).

Kennedy, David, *Birth Control in America: The Career of Margaret Sanger* (New Haven: Yale University Press, 1970).

Klitsch, Michael, *RU 486: The Science and the Politics* (New York: Alan Guttmacher Institute, 1989).

Lader, Lawrence, *Abortion II: Making the Revolution* (Boston: Beacon Press, 1973).

Luker, Kristin, *Abortion and the Politics of Motherhood* (Berkeley: University of California Press, 1984).

Merton, Andrew, *Enemies of Choice: The Right-to-Life Movement and Its Threat to Abortion* (Boston: Beacon Press, 1981).

Mohr, James, *Abortion in America: The Origins and Evolution of National Policy* (New York: Oxford University Press, 1978).

Nathanson, Bernard, *Aborting America* (New York: Doubleday, 1979).

National Abortion Federation, "Antiabortion Violence, 1977–1990" (Washington, DC: National Abortion Federation, 1991).

Olasky, Marvin, *The Press and Abortion: 1838–1988* (Hillsdale, NJ: Lawrence Erlbaum Associates, 1988).

Packwood, Bob, "The Rise and Fall of the Right-to-Life Movement in Congress," in Butler, J. Douglas, et al., eds., *Abortion, Medicine and the Law*, 3d ed. (New York: Facts on File, 1986).

Paige, Connie, *The Right-to-Lifers: Who They Are, How They Operate, Where They Get Their Money* (New York: Summit Books, 1983).

Petchesky, Rosalind, *Abortion and Woman's Choice: The State, Sexuality, and Reproductive Freedom* (Boston: Northeastern University Press, 1984, 1990).

Roe v. Wade (410 U.S. 113 [1973]).

Smolowe, Jill, "Gagging the Clinics," *Time*, Vol. 37, No. 22 (June 3, 1991): 16–17.

Tietze, Christopher, and Stanley K. Henshaw, *Induced Abortion: A World Review, 1986* (New York: Alan Guttmacher Institute, 1986).

Tribe, Laurence H., *Abortion: The Clash of Absolutes* (New York: W. W. Norton and Company, 1990).

2

Biographical Sketches

TO LIST ALL OF THE PEOPLE WHO HAVE FIGURED SIGNIFICANTLY in the abortion debate would require a volume in itself, so selecting individuals to appear in a list such as this is indeed a daunting task. Following are brief portraits of some of the movers and shakers on either side of the controversy. By no means comprehensive, the list is a representative sampling of those who have made and/or are making significant contributions to their respective movements.

Luz Alvarez-Martinez (1943?–)

Luz Alvarez-Martinez is a co-founder and the director of the Oakland-based National Latina Health Organization/Organización Nacional de La Salud de La Mujer Latina (NLHO), which is dedicated to achieving bilingual access to quality health care and the self-empowerment of Latinas through educational programs, outreach, and research. Reproductive choice has been a major focus of the NLHO since its inception, and Alvarez-Martinez is an outspoken advocate of reproductive rights, particularly for women of color. The seventh of 11 children and a first-generation Mexican-American, Alvarez-Martinez grew up in the then mostly white city of San Leandro, near Oakland, California. The mother of 4 sons, she devoted most of her time to her family until 1977, when she returned to school with the intention of becoming a nurse-midwife. She became involved in school politics, the Women's Center, and the Berkeley Women's Health Collective (BWHC) and was part of a group that founded a satellite clinic of the BWHC, operated for and by women of color. In 1981, newly divorced and a single parent, Alvarez-Martinez enrolled in a baccalaureate nursing program at Hayward State University but was forced to quit in 1983 due to financial and emotional stress.

A Roman Catholic by upbringing, Alvarez-Martinez left the Church in 1964 when she was told she could not practice birth control and be within the laws of the Church. In 1983, hospitalized for a tubal ligation, she found out by accident that women making decisions about birth control were shown two different films: the English-language version stressed alternative types of birth control, while the Spanish version emphasized sterilization. This and other experiences, as well as stories told to her by other Latinas, contributed to her growing awareness of reproductive abuses and inequities against Latinas and to her determination to fight those abuses. In 1983 she attended the First National Conference of the National Black Women's Health Project (NBWHP), where "for the first time I saw how powerful a group of women of color could be." She stayed involved with the NBWHP, traveling to Kenya for the United Nations International Conference Ending the Decade of Women and participating in a number of local, national, and international conferences focusing on women's health issues.

On International Women's Day, 1986, Alvarez-Martinez and three other Latinas founded the NLHO, with which she has been involved ever since. In April 1989, she became a national board member of the National Abortion Rights Action League (NARAL), with the express intent of working toward expanding the abortion issue to one of full reproductive freedom and of involving more Latinas and women of color at the national level. In February 1990, Alvarez-Martinez joined with other Latinas in creating Latinas for Reproductive Choice, a special project of the NLHO. She continues to speak frequently at both the local and national levels and has written several articles on Latinas and reproductive choice.

Byllye Avery (1936–)

Byllye Avery, founder and executive director of the National Black Women's Health Project (NBWHP), is one of a growing number of women of color who have become key participants in the reproductive rights movement, which until recently was peopled mostly by white middle- and upper-class women. A longtime health care activist, Avery has become a chief spokesperson for the new arm of the movement, which has been largely responsible for expanding the agenda beyond abortion rights to a demand for full reproductive freedom. This includes the right to have, as well as not to have, children and calls for access to such services as prenatal care and affordable, quality day care as well as safe, effective contraceptives and legal, affordable abortion.

In the early 1970s, while living in Gainesville, Florida, Avery found herself identified as one of three "women who could help other women get abortions." She referred the women—most of whom were white and middle class—to a phone number in New York, where abortion was legal. She grew increasingly frustrated, however, at her inability to help black women, who generally didn't have the money to make the trip, much less pay for an abortion. When abortion became legal in 1973, Avery co-founded the Gainesville Women's Health Center, which provided abortion services as well as a well-woman gynecology clinic where "the educational work went on about getting in control of your body." Many of the clinic's clients were poor black women whose abortions were paid for by Medicaid until the Hyde Amendment cut off Medicaid funding in 1977. Around that time Avery also became involved in the birthing movement, opening an alternative birthing center in Gainesville. She found that poor women faced the same kinds of barriers and the same lack of choice when it came to giving birth as they did in seeking abortions—"We have a medical system in which care is given in terms of money, so that poor women don't have options."

Avery has devoted her career to expanding those options. In 1979, she moved to Atlanta and opened the National Black Women's Health Project, a self-help and advocacy organization that seeks to empower black women to achieve and maintain physical, mental, and emotional health. While the NBWHP is involved in all aspects of black women's health, a recently opened Washington, D.C., office is focusing primarily on reproductive health and rights issues. Avery is a frequent and welcome speaker at reproductive rights events and conferences. A recent recipient of the coveted MacArthur Foundation Fellowship for social contribution, she also received the 1989 Essence Award for community service. She currently serves on the boards of the New World Foundation, the International Women's Health Coalition, the Committee for Responsive Philanthropy, and the Advisory Committee for the Kellogg International Fellowship Program.

Bill Baird (1932–)

Bill Baird has been called the bête noire of the reproductive rights movement. His confrontational stance and insistence on publicly airing controversial opinions have brought him into conflict with the pro-choice "establishment"—groups such as Planned Parenthood, NOW, and NARAL—which he accuses of being "bureaucratic wastelands" more concerned with maintaining their organizations than with fighting for women's rights. Although others in the movement find him to be overly radical, even embarrassing, there is no denying that Baird has made significant contributions to the cause at great personal cost. His public challenges to restrictive birth control and abortion laws have led to eight jailings in five states, several felony convictions, frequent bouts with poverty, and, he is convinced, the loss of his family.

Baird first became involved in reproductive rights after financial difficulties forced him to quit medical school and he went to work for Emko Foam, distributing contraceptives from tables set up in stores and other public places. To teach women about birth control, he drove his mobile "plan van" into the poorest areas of New York, using a mannequin and colloquial and slang terms to explain the facts of reproduction. These activities led to his first arrest on May 14, 1965, for indecent exposure of obscene objects. In 1967, he publicly challenged the Massachusetts "crimes against chastity" laws, in a case that went to the Supreme Court (*Baird v. Eisenstadt*) and that would be favorably cited six times in the 1973 *Roe v. Wade* decision legalizing abortion. That same year, he testified in hearings for the Colorado abortion reform act, arguing against the rape, incest, and mental instability provisions on the basis that most women have abortions for economic and social reasons—a fact that, even now, some in the abortion rights movement seem reluctant to acknowledge.

Throughout his unusual career, Baird has seemed to delight in confronting not only the state, but also his pro-life opponents, picketing their conventions and attending their meetings in order to challenge speakers. He believes men have an important role to play in achieving reproductive freedom but feels that he and other men have been pushed aside, largely because of their gender. Whether because he is a man or because he is simply too radical for the movement's mainstream, it is true that Baird, once a popular speaker and media darling, no longer occupies center stage. He continues to be active in abortion-related issues, most recently in the case of Nancy Klein, the New York woman who was in a coma and whose husband sought an abortion in hopes of saving her life. For the most part, however, except for the occasional speaking engagement or interview, Baird has been relegated to the sidelines, feeling betrayed by the movement to which he has dedicated his life and to which, as Lawrence Lader wrote in *Abortion II*, "he added a wild, unorthodox zest that was essential to the campaign." Baird hopes to write a book about his experiences and contributions.

Janet Benshoof (1947–)

Janet Benshoof is the director of the American Civil Liberties Union's Reproductive Freedom Project (RFP), a post she has held since 1977. Benshoof, who is a nationally recognized expert on reproductive rights and privacy law, directs federal litigation and public education in the areas of abortion rights, contraception, and sterilization. A native of Minnesota, Benshoof graduated summa cum laude from the University of Minnesota and received her law degree from Harvard Law School. Since her admission to the New York Bar in 1972, Benshoof has devoted her career to litigating in the field of health and women's rights. She has argued a number of prominent cases before the Supreme Court, including *City of Akron v. Akron Center for Reproductive Health, Harris v. McRae,* and *Hodgson v. Minnesota* (see Chapter 1 for case descriptions), as well as a case challenging the constitutionality of the Adolescent Family Life Act.

Benshoof speaks extensively on reproductive rights issues around the country, participating in media interviews, panel discussions, and conferences and lecturing at such law schools as Yale, Rutgers, and Columbia. In March 1990, she flew to Guam to attempt to persuade the governor not to sign the territory's recently passed abortion law, the most restrictive in the nation. When the governor refused to see her and signed the bill, Benshoof mounted a deliberate challenge by giving a speech about the law, freedom of speech, freedom of religion, privacy rights, and the failure of the Constitution in Guam. She also told women where they could go in Honolulu (a five-hour flight from Guam) to have abortions. As expected, she was arrested for soliciting abortions, thus creating a test case that the ACLU used to win a judicial injunction against enforcement of the new law. Her action also ignited public discussion of abortion and stimulated a surge of abortion rights activity in Guam. As of this writing, Benshoof and the RFP are engaged in preparing for federal action on the Guam statute, which may provide the Supreme Court with the opportunity to review *Roe v. Wade.*

In addition to her work with the project and her speaking activities, Benshoof has contributed articles on reproductive rights issues to such journals as the *Harvard Law Review* and New York University's *Journal of International Law and Politics.* She has also contributed chapters to several books on topics related to abortion and constitutional law. She has received several awards, including the *Ms.* Foundation for Women's Gloria Steinem Award (1989), the National Abortion Foundation's Humanitarian Award (1988), and the Margaret Sanger Award for the Advancement of Family Planning (1986), and was named by *Esquire* magazine in 1984 as one of the "Men and Women under 40 Changing America."

Judie Brown (1944–)

Judie Brown is widely recognized as one of the foremost leaders of the pro-life movement. Indeed, Brown's role is such that author Connie Paige wrote in her 1983 book *The Right-to-Lifers,* "If any single person is responsible for the growth of the right-to-life movement, that person is Judie Brown." Since the mid-1970s, Judie and her husband, Paul, who have strong ties to such New Right leaders as Paul Weyrich and Richard Viguerie, have been major players in bringing abortion to the forefront as a political issue in the United States.

Brown first became involved in the abortion issue in Seattle in 1969, when she and her husband passed out literature on street corners as part of an unsuccessful campaign to defeat a referendum to liberalize Washington's abortion law. Paul's job required frequent transfers, and the couple moved next to Atlanta, where Judie became involved with Birthright, then to North Carolina, and then to Ohio. With each move Judie's involvement in the movement deepened. In 1976 she was one of those chosen to represent Ohio Right to Life in the annual March for Life. She returned from the rally eager to move to Washington, D.C.; serendipitously, Paul was offered a transfer to the capital soon after. In Washington, Judie volunteered for the National Right to Life Committee and was soon offered a paid position as public relations director and right-hand woman to then president Mildred Jefferson. During her tenure at NRLC, Judie showed a tremendous flair for public relations. She began sending mailings to independent groups as well as to NRLC state affiliates and developed several different kinds of mailings, including educational material, legislative updates, medical developments, and media alerts. She made it a point to send people something every three months, keeping the committee in the front of everyone's minds. During the three years she was there, Judie helped to substantially increase not only NRLC's membership but also its influence, both with its own affiliates and in the public arena.

In 1977, Paul quit his job to work full-time combatting abortion and other "anti-life" issues, forming a political action committee to campaign for a human life amendment. Having worked her way almost to the top of the nation's largest pro-life organization, Judie became disillusioned with NRLC's "cumbersome structure" and internal squabbling. She was particularly unhappy with what she perceived as the movement's too narrow educational and legislative initiatives, which she felt were not "addressing the root cause of the abortion holocaust: the ascension of the anti-life ethic in America." Accordingly, in 1979 Judie left the NRLC and founded her own organization, the American Life League, to "attack the anti-life ethic at its roots rather than battle its symptoms." Within two years ALL claimed 68,000 newsletter subscribers; current membership numbers around 250,000. Through ALL, the devoutly Catholic Browns have worked to expand the abortion debate to include abortifacient contraceptives such as the IUD, as well as classroom sex education, euthanasia, and religious questions. Judie Brown has also played a key role in the debate over medical care for handicapped infants. She appears frequently in the print and electronic media and has contributed editorial pieces to major newspapers and magazines.

Carolyn Gerster (1931?–)

Carolyn Gerster has been a prominent voice against abortion since the 1970s. She is also a respected physician and community leader whose many activities include speaking to students on the hazards of smoking, conducting seminars for older adults on hypertension and coronary artery disease, and serving as a board member of Aid to Adoption of Special Kids. The only child of Protestant parents, Gerster was a superior student who graduated from the University of Oregon Medical School at the age of 21, having worked her way through college and medical school as a press operator, long-distance telephone operator, and carhop. She interned in Hawaii, then joined the army, becoming in 1957 the only woman among 250 military physicians at Fort Sam Houston in Texas. She was later stationed in Paris and Frankfurt, where she met her husband Josef, who is also a doctor. In 1959, the couple moved to Scottsdale, Arizona, where they have been in private practice together since 1962.

The mother of five grown sons, Gerster had a sixth son who died in infancy, another child who was stillborn, and two miscarriages. It was one of the miscarriages that aroused her interest in abortion. About 13 weeks into her third pregnancy, Gerster began cramping and ran into the bathroom in time to catch the flow of blood in a basin. Later she ran water over the bloody tissue and recovered the 3½-inch long fetus. "I just stood there and it hit me: My God, I've had a baby." About the same time, Gerster became concerned about "the erosion of the Judeo-Christian ethic concerning the intrinsic value and dignity of each human life." In 1971 she became a co-founder and president of the Arizona Right to Life Committee. As director from Arizona to the National Right to Life Committee, she served on the executive committee that drew up the NRLC bylaws in 1973. She served as NRLC vice-president from 1973 to 1975, was chairman of the board of directors from 1975 to 1978, and served as president from 1978 to 1980. Since 1980 she has been the NRLC's vice-president in charge of international affairs.

A powerful speaker, Gerster has talked about abortion, infanticide, and euthanasia to audiences in local high schools, universities, medical and law schools, and organizations around the United States and abroad. She was a 1984 delegate to the United Nations International

Conference on Population in Mexico City and a 1985 delegate to the U.N. Focus on Women Conference in Nairobi. She has appeared on national television and testified before U.S. Senate committees and state legislatures, as well as contributing articles to professional and religious journals. An active Episcopalian, she is a member of that church's Standing Commission for Human Affairs and Health. She also is serving a term on the Arizona Board of Medical Examiners. Dr. Gerster is the recipient of numerous awards, among them the Arizona Mother of the Year for 1987.

Nellie Gray (1924–)

Nellie Gray is best known as the guiding force behind the March for Life, the march and rally held each year in Washington, D.C., on January 22, the anniversary of the 1973 *Roe v. Wade* decision legalizing abortion. The first demonstration she organized in 1974 drew about 6,000 people; the March for Life has since grown to an annual event attended by tens of thousands. Born in Big Spring, Texas, Gray served in the army from 1944 through 1946, working as a secretary and attaining the rank of corporal. After leaving the service, she attended college on the G.I. bill, earning a B.S. in business administration and an M.A. in economics. In 1950, Gray became an economic research assistant for the State Department. She moved to the Department of Labor 2 years later and spent 17 years as a manpower legislation expert, attending Georgetown University Law Center at night to earn her law degree.

A devout Catholic, Gray was horrified by the 1973 *Roe v. Wade* decision, and in June of that year quit her job to devote her life to making abortion illegal in all circumstances. Following the first March for Life in 1974, Gray registered as a full-time lobbyist and has since spent her time lobbying and organizing the annual march. Her goal is to obtain the passage of the Paramount Human Life Amendment, which would guarantee the right to life for every human being from the moment of fertilization, with "no exceptions or compromises." Gray believes that a pregnant woman's life has "equal value" with that of the fetus, but that, given modern medicine and technology, there is no such thing as a conflict between preserving the life of the woman and that of her unborn child.

David Allen Grimes (1947–)

David Grimes is a physician and researcher who has spent much of his career developing better and safer abortion techniques. Most recently, he has become the United States' best-known researcher of RU 486, the French "abortion pill." Grimes first became interested in the abortion issue while still in medical school and during his residency in Chapel Hill, North Carolina, where he became involved in research on the use of prostaglandins for late term abortions, following up on an interest in population biology that dated to his undergraduate days at Harvard. He spent his junior year in medical school working for the newly formed Abortion Surveillance Division at the Centers for Disease Control (CDC). After serving two years as a resident at Chapel Hill, he interrupted his residency to join the military and served two years as a surgeon at CDC, where he returned again when his residency was complete.

Grimes served as assistant chief of the Abortion Surveillance Branch from 1979 through 1982 and as chief of the branch from 1982 to 1983. At CDC, Grimes and colleague Willard Cates produced numerous studies on abortion and did pioneer work in the field, until they were both transferred to the Sexually Transmitted Diseases division in 1984. In 1986, citing political heat and censorship of his writing, Grimes left the CDC and moved to California, where he joined the faculty of the University of Southern California School of Medicine and began doing research at the Los Angeles County–University of Southern California Medical Center's Women's Hospital, the only institution in the nation involved in RU 486 research. He spent several years doing clinical trials of the drug, in studies involving almost 400 women.

In February 1990, Roussel-UCLAF, the drug's manufacturer, stopped supplying it, citing anti-abortion opinion in the United States. While waiting for supplies to be resumed, and despite threats from anti-abortion activists, Grimes spends much of his time lecturing internationally and in the United States on RU 486 and the worldwide tragedy of illegal abortion. He also continues both to teach abortion techniques and to provide abortions—he is one of the few doctors who will perform abortions on AIDS patients—as well as continuing to work on other research projects. He is optimistic that RU 486 will eventually be marketed in this country—"It's safe, effective, and popular"—and even predicts that the drug's inventor, Dr. Etienne-Emile Baulieu, will win the Nobel Prize.

A member of the boards of directors of the Planned Parenthood Federation of America and the Association of Reproductive Health Professionals, Grimes has received numerous honors and awards, including the Christopher Tietze Humanitarian Award from the National Abortion Federation. He has authored or co-authored numerous articles for professional journals and book chapters on abortion and other reproductive health–related topics.

Jane Hodgson (1915–)

Jane Hodgson holds the distinction of being the first doctor convicted for performing an abortion in a hospital—a conviction that arose from her deliberate attempt to challenge Minnesota's restrictive abortion law. She is also one of the pioneers of and chief contributors to the abortion rights movement. A practicing obstetrician since 1947, a founding Fellow of the American College of Obstetrics and Gynecology, and a past president of the Minnesota Society of Obstetricians and Gynecologists, Hodgson had devoted most of her career to improving fertility and helping women deliver healthy babies; but during the 1960s she gradually realized that denying abortion to women who sought it was "lousy medicine." She became convinced that the only solution was total legality, although she doubted it would happen in her lifetime.

Gradually Hodgson became determined to challenge the law and started looking for a test case. She found it in April 1970, in Nancy Widmyer, a mother of three who had contracted rubella and wanted an abortion. Backed by a lawyer provided by the Clergy Counseling Service (CCS), Hodgson began the legal motions to challenge the law in federal court. When the court refused to hear the case, she performed the abortion and was duly arrested, indicted, and convicted: "I really wanted to come to court—I thought that was the only way to educate the legislature. I expected the legislature would promptly pass a new law! But it didn't work out that way." Concerned about losing her license while her case was appealed, Hodgson continued to refer women through the CCS but did not perform abortions again until 1972, when she went to Washington, D.C., to become the director of the recently opened Preterm clinic, which became a model for the outpatient abortion clinics that sprang up around the country in the wake of *Roe v. Wade*.

Jubilant over the *Roe v. Wade* decision and the overturning of her Minnesota conviction, Hodgson returned to Minnesota, where, in addition to her private practice and teaching duties, she opened a fertility control clinic and worked on the development of safer techniques for second trimester abortions. She spent much of her time training younger doctors in abortion techniques and still considers such training a major focus of her work. She also worked to raise funds to help pay for abortions for low-income women, who were denied funding under Minnesota law, and testified as an expert witness in numerous abortion cases.

In 1981, Hodgson became the major plaintiff in a challenge to Minnesota's parental notification law. As the medical director of three clinics, she saw many teenage patients, some of whom had hitchhiked in the winter from rural areas to seek abortions. *Hodgson v. Minnesota* eventually reached the Supreme Court, which handed down a decision upholding the law in June of 1990. Despite the setback, Hodgson continues to work and speak out in favor of abortion rights, including an appearance in a recent video produced by the Fund for the Feminist Majority. She has received numerous awards, including one named in her honor, the Jane Hodgson Reproductive Freedom Award, and has published many articles on abortion and related topics. She also edited a book, *Abortion and Sterilization: Medical and Social Aspects* (London: Academic Press, 1981), which has been widely used in arguing court cases and as a medical textbook. Hodgson was featured in a book by Peter Irons, *The Courage of Their Convictions: Sixteen Americans Who Fought Their Way to the Supreme Court* (New York: Free Press, 1988).

Dennis J. Horan (1932–1988)

For many years, until his sudden death at the age of 56, Dennis J. Horan was the star attorney and one of the most beloved and respected figures of the pro-life movement. A founder and past president of the Illinois Right to Life Committee and a former chairman of the National Right to Life Legal Advisory Committee, Horan also served as pro-life legal counsel for the United States Catholic Conference and as chairman of the National Conference of Catholic Bishops' Committee on Law and Public Policy. In 1979, he helped to found Americans United for Life, the nation's only public law firm dedicated to fighting abortion and euthanasia, serving as its chairman until his death. A graduate of Loyola University School of Law, which awarded him its Medal of Excellence in 1984, Horan also had a successful legal career. From 1970 to 1979 he was a lecturer at the University of Chicago Law School, from 1979 to 1982 he lectured on medical law at the University of Chicago, and from 1982 until his death he headed a major Chicago law firm, which under his direction tripled in size, to over 300 attorneys with 15 offices in four states.

A Roman Catholic, Horan believed that abortion was, in the words of his brother-in-law, physician and fellow activist Bart Hefferman, "a violent tragedy for women and unborn children [and] an ominous threat to the value of human life itself." Accordingly, he devoted himself to the struggle to reverse *Roe v. Wade* and recriminalize abortion, contributing thousands of hours of his time to abortion-related cases. In 1980 he appeared before the Supreme Court, arguing successfully in defense of the Hyde Amendment in *Harris v. McRae*, a case he took on a pro bono basis.

A published poet, Horan wrote numerous articles on the legal rights of the unborn and the handicapped as well as editing and contributing to several books, including *Abortion and Social Justice* (Thaxton, VA: Sun Life, 1972), *New Perspectives on Human Abortion* (Frederick, MD: University Publications of America, 1981), and *Abortion and the Constitution* (Washington, DC: Georgetown University Press, 1987). A past chairman of the American Bar Association Medicine and Law Committee and the Right to Live/Right to Die Subcommittee, in 1987 Horan was named to the newly created congressional Biomedical Ethics Committee. Horan's legal expertise and dedication are much missed by others in the movement, who called him the "dean of pro-life lawyers."

Henry Hyde (1924–)

Henry Hyde was first elected to the United States Congress in 1974. The Republican representative from Illinois is probably best known for the Hyde Amendments that restrict federal funding for abortions for poor women. Born in Chicago, Hyde attended Catholic schools before winning admission to Georgetown University on a basketball scholarship. He interrupted his education to serve in the navy from 1944 to 1946, then graduated from Georgetown and attended Loyola University Law School, receiving his law degree in 1949 and being admitted to the Illinois Bar in 1950. Like his parents, Hyde was a Democrat until 1952, when he supported Dwight Eisenhower against Adlai Stevenson. Increasingly concerned by what he saw as the leftward drift of the Democratic Party, Hyde changed his affiliation to Republican in 1958. In 1966 he ran for the state legislature, serving four terms before he was elected to Congress in 1974.

A staunch conservative, throughout his legislative career Hyde has supported the death penalty and more stringent antidrug legislation and opposed the Equal Rights Amendment. In his first term in Congress, he was elected chairman of the 17-member freshman Republican class and won seats on the influential Judiciary and Banking and Currency Committees. It was as Congress' leading crusader against abortion, however, that he rose to fame. In 1976, Hyde and co-sponsor Robert Bauman of Maryland introduced a hastily written amendment to the fiscal 1977 appropriations bill for the Departments of Labor and Health, Education, and Welfare, prohibiting the use of federal funding for elective abortions under Medicaid. To Hyde's surprise, the amendment passed, and versions of it have passed every year since. The amendment permits abortions only to save the life of the pregnant woman, with the result that since 1977 federal funding for abortions has been virtually nonexistent. (In 1989, in the first serious challenge to the amendment, Congress passed legislation allowing funding in cases of rape or incest, but President Bush vetoed the measure.) In 1981, along with Senator Jesse Helms (R-NC), Hyde introduced the Helms-Hyde bill in an attempt to codify the belief that life begins at conception. The bill, however, was criticized not only by pro-choice activists but also by pro-life groups who preferred a constitutional amendment to legislation that would be subject to judicial challenges. The bill eventually died in committee.

In recent years, Hyde has confounded liberal forces by joining them in advocating legislation that would promote better health care for women and reduce infant mortality. In 1989 he joined reproductive rights advocate Barbara Boxer, a Democratic representative from California, in sponsoring a bill that would criminalize the practice of surrogate child-bearing. He has also worked to encourage federal funding of adoptive services and other alternatives to abortion and has called for an end to the welfare system, which he says encourages illegitimate births. In a move that surprised both friends and foes, Hyde also voted in favor of the 1990 Family Leave Act, which was later vetoed by President Bush.

Hyde's success in championing their cause in Congress and his willingness to travel around the country speaking in defense of the unborn have endeared him to the pro-life community. A witty, dynamic speaker and skilled debater, he once introduced himself to a National Right to Life convention as a "626-month fetus." Although he denies that his opposition to abortion grows out of his Roman Catholic faith, he rejects the idea that religious values should not be part of political debate and has challenged other Catholic politicians to join him in saving the unborn and in building a consensus against abortion.

Mildred Faye Jefferson (1927–)

Mildred Jefferson has been a moving force in the pro-life movement for more than 20 years. As a black, divorced, childless woman and a Protestant who has disassociated herself from organized religion, she symbolizes diversity in a movement whose image is one of domination by white Catholic men. Born in Carthage, Texas, Jefferson was an only child. Her mother was a teacher and both her father and grandfather were Methodist preachers. A brilliant student, she graduated from Texas College in Tyler, Texas, at the age of 18, then attended Tufts University and Harvard Medical School, receiving her M.D. in 1951. She did postgraduate work at Tufts and interned at Boston City Hospital, later going into practice as a general surgeon.

Jefferson's interest in abortion dates back to 1970, when she was asked to sign a petition protesting an American Medical Association resolution declaring that it was not unethical for doctors to perform legal abortions. When the resolution passed anyway, Jefferson and several other physicians founded the Value of Life Committee to disseminate information about abortion and fetal development. By June 1975, she had risen far enough in the movement to be elected president of the National Right to Life Committee. As NRLC's president, she formed alliances with other conservative groups, expanded the membership, and brought the organization to national prominence. In 1978, however, she lost the presidency in a move that foreshadowed the factionalism that has continued to dog the pro-life movement. Since 1978, Jefferson has continued to campaign vigorously not only against abortion but also against a national health care system, which she sees as a socialistic move to "erect a monolithic health care system" that would enslave doctors and lead to a rationing of health care. Like many in the movement, she believes legal abortion could lead to mandatory abortion, especially for poor and minority women, since "once you do something voluntarily, you have no grounds to object if it is required." A firm believer in the sanctity of life ethic, she also sees herself as an accommodator reaching out to a wide range of people who share her opposition to abortion, regardless of political or religious orientation.

In 1990, Jefferson made a bid for the U.S. Senate seat in Massachusetts, but failed to get on the ballot for the Republican primary. She attributes her loss to racism and sexism within the Republican Party, whose nomination process she is challenging in court. A powerful, eloquent speaker, she is in high demand throughout the country and speaks to "every organization that asks me." She is president of the Right to Life Crusade, an outreach group; contributes columns to the *National Right to Life News;* and is currently working on three books.

Frances Kissling (1943–)

As president of Catholics for a Free Choice (CFFC), Frances Kissling is one of the most controversial voices in the Catholic Church, which would probably just as soon pretend she and her organization didn't exist. Kissling, who at one time planned to become a nun, has been involved in reproductive rights for 20 years. She first became involved in social activism during the 1960s, protesting the war in Vietnam and joining the feminist movement. In 1970, she took a job running an abortion clinic in New York, which at that time was one of two states where abortion was legal. During 1974–1975, she worked as a consultant helping to establish abortion clinics in Italy, Austria, and Mexico. In 1976, she founded the National Abortion Federation, serving as its director until 1980. She became president of Catholics for a Free Choice in 1982, and under her leadership CFFC has steadily gained in both notoriety and influence.

When Kissling returned to the Catholic Church, it was with the intent to act as a "social change agent" to transform it into a church that is "more sensitive to all powerless people," including women. Accordingly, she talks to Catholics all over the world, promoting her message that the real issue in the struggle over abortion is not reproductive rights or the preservation of fetal life but control over women. If the church is really concerned about abortion, she asserts, they would be better off spending money to prevent unwanted pregnancy—a strategy that would conflict with the church's position on birth control. She sees the church's understanding of sexuality as "misconceived," a position that "leaves no room for such values as love and companionship." The bishops are concerned over the fact that Catholic women have abortions at the same rate as other women, she says, because it indicates that they have not been able to control women through the church— and therefore they are attempting to use the state to enforce control over not just Catholics, but all women. Kissling, however, is determined to get the church to recognize women as free moral agents and to trust them to make good decisions.

With views such as these, it is not surprising that Kissling has many detractors, some of whom accuse her of not being a real Catholic. She insists, however, that the church can accommodate a pro-choice viewpoint and continues to call on everyone, not just Catholics, to focus on values, not just rights. "It is time," she said during a 1988 address in Albuquerque, "for us to talk about the survival of this planet and about the kind of people we want to be—not the things we want to be allowed to do."

In addition to her work with CFFC, Kissling is a founder and treasurer of the Global Fund for Women, serves on the standing Committee on Women's Rights of the American Public Health Association, and is active in Women-Church Convergence, a coalition of Catholic organizations committed to promoting women's rights within the Roman Catholic Church. Named by *Ms.* magazine as one of "80 Women to Watch in the '80s," Kissling is a frequent public speaker both in the United States and abroad, has appeared on network television, and is frequently interviewed by national media. She coauthored *Rosie: The Investigation of a Wrongful Death* with Ellen Frankfort (New York: Dial Press, 1978) and is a frequent contributor of articles and op-ed pieces to newspapers and religious magazines.

Kate Michelman (1940–)

Kate Michelman has headed the National Abortion Rights Action League (NARAL) since 1985. Under her tenure, NARAL has grown to more than 400,000 members and established its position as the political arm of the abortion rights movement. Michelman's involvement with abortion rights grows out of both personal and professional experience. In 1970, she was a 30-year-old college student with three children, and pregnant with a fourth, when her husband left her for another woman. With no money, no car, and no credit, she was faced with deciding whether to "push my family into an unmanageable crisis or terminate the pregnancy and carry on with getting a job and nurturing my family back to health and stability." She went before a hospital review board, which required her to have her husband's written consent before she could obtain an abortion. She told them they would have to find him to get it. They did, and Michelman had the abortion and went on to finish her degree and begin work as a developmental psychologist. Much of her early career was spent working with abused children and their families, and "it was very clear to me that many of the problems originated because women didn't have many choices about reproduction." In 1978, Michelman developed and implemented a multidisciplinary diagnostic therapeutic treatment program for developmentally disabled preschool children and their families, a program that has been replicated by early childhood specialists in other parts of the country.

In 1980, Michelman became the director of Planned Parenthood in Harrisburg, Pennsylvania, holding that position until 1985, when she became the executive director of NARAL. As head of NARAL, she led the successful 1987 campaign to block U.S. Senate confirmation of Supreme Court nominee Robert Bork and rallied 1,000 delegates to represent the abortion rights vote at the Democratic National Convention. More recently, Michelman was largely responsible for the slogan, "Who Decides?," which has become a unifying theme for the abortion rights movement and has served to focus the debate around the issue of individual liberty—an issue that has hit home for many people previously unconcerned with the abortion controversy. Named by *Washington* magazine as one of the 100 most powerful women in Washington, Michelman is an articulate and thoughtful speaker who spends much of her time traveling throughout the country to promulgate NARAL's message that the right to choose abortion is a fundamental one and that the government should not intrude into such private, personal decisions as whether or not to bear a child.

Bernard Nathanson (1926–)

Bernard Nathanson is perhaps the only person to have played a major role on both sides of the abortion debate. An alumnus of Cornell University and the McGill University Medical College, Nathanson has practiced obstetrics and gynecology since 1957, following in his father's footsteps. In New York in the late 1960s, he was a staunch and vocal advocate for abortion rights. In 1969, he helped to found the National Association to Repeal Abortion Laws (later the National Abortion Rights Action League), and from February 1971 through September 1972 he directed the Center for Reproductive and Sexual Health in New York City, the largest abortion clinic in the world. He continued to play an important part in NARAL until 1975, when he resigned from his position on the board of directors and focused his attention on the growing science of fetology, which was causing him to have serious second thoughts about abortion.

In 1979, Nathanson published *Aborting America* (New York: Doubleday), the story of his gradual realization that abortion is not the simple, humane procedure he had thought it to be. "There are 75,000 abortions in my past medical career," he wrote, "those performed under my administration or that I supervised in a teaching capacity, and the 1,500 that I have performed myself. The vast majority of these fell short of my present standard that only a mother's life, interpreted with appropriate medical sophistication, can justify destroying the life of this being in inner space which is becoming better known to us with each passing year. I now regret this loss of life" (p. 248).

Nathanson is perhaps best known for his role in producing and narrating *The Silent Scream*, the most famous and controversial abortion film ever made. In 1983 he wrote *The Abortion Papers* (New York: Frederick Fell Publishers), a scathing indictment of the "abortion people" and what he and many others in the movement see as the pro-abortion bias of the media. In 1987 he produced another video, *Eclipse of Reason* (two more videos are in the works as of this writing). In his speeches, videos, and writing, Nathanson places heavy emphasis on the profits made by the abortion industry, a "billion dollar a year industry" that he claims "invites skimming" and corruption. An avowed atheist who bases his opposition to abortion on nonreligious moral grounds, Nathanson is not opposed to contraception and in fact advocates better contraception as a way to prevent abortions. Though severely criticized by the abortion rights activists who were once his friends and colleagues, he is highly respected in the pro-life movement, for which he is a prominent and authoritative spokesperson. With his wife, Adelle, he currently publishes a free bimonthly newsletter, *Bernadell Technical Bulletin*, which contains abstracts of medical literature on topics related to "life issues" and accompanying commentary by Nathanson, as well as other educational materials on bioethical issues.

Joseph Scheidler (1927–)

In the fight against abortion, Joseph Scheidler is a top commander and one of the leading strategists—columnist Patrick Buchanan once called him the "Green Beret of the pro-life movement." A self-described "traditional Catholic" who once studied for the priesthood, Scheidler decided against ordination because he "didn't like the way the Church was going" in the years prior to Vatican II. As a seminary student, Scheidler studied abortion and delved into the concepts of ensoulment and hominization, concluding that abortion was not only homicide, but also an "especially grievous sin [that] always caused one to lose membership in the Church." He recalls that he has always felt protective of children, a feeling he dates to his reaction to the Lindbergh kidnapping when he was quite young: "It frightened me to think that adults would use a child as a convenience to make money."

Scheidler's feelings did not translate into activism until 1973, when the *Roe v. Wade* Supreme Court decision so appalled him that he quit his job in public relations and founded the Chicago Office for Pro-life Publicity, believing that if "Americans knew about the humanity of the unborn child and the dangers of abortion, they would resist this new ruling." Scheidler now heads the Pro-Life Action League, an activist organization that undertakes activities based on the methodology outlined in Scheidler's 1985 book *Closed: 99 Ways To Stop Abortion* (Westchester, IL: Good News Publishers). He believes that the movement has not yet done enough to educate the public about the realities of abortion, a gap he attempts to bridge as he travels throughout the United States and abroad promoting his view that abortion is never moral or permissible, because "when you come down to the issue of human life, you can't compromise." His recent trips include a journey to France as part of the fight against the "abortion pill," RU 486.

In addition to speaking engagements, Scheidler appears frequently on television and radio and participates in "sidewalk counseling" and "rescues" at abortion clinics around the country, where he and his ever-present bullhorn are familiar figures. He also states that he has salvaged as many as 5,000 unborn children from clinic trash receptacles and given them proper funerals. An artist at generating publicity, Scheidler once hired private detectives to track down the address of an 11-year-old girl scheduled for an abortion and later attempted to remove her from her mother's custody. Scheidler was one of the main "stars" of *Holy Terror*, a video on the pro-life movement; he has also produced his own video, *The Abortion Providers*, featuring former abortion clinic operators and doctors who have since come out against abortion. As of this writing, Scheidler was working on two new books and two new videos; he is also a regular guest columnist in *USA Today* and has published articles in several national publications.

Eleanor Smeal (1939–)

Eleanor Smeal has been active and visible in women's rights issues for many years; her interest in abortion rights grew out of her wider concerns with women's rights in general. As president of the National Organization for Women (NOW) from 1977 through 1982 and again from 1985 through 1987, she helped build that organization from 35,000 to over 220,000 members. During her second term, she led the National March for Women's Lives in 1986, in addition to organizing seven other marches around the nation, working to defeat anti-abortion referenda in four states, and developing an aggressive legal strategy against violence and harassment aimed at abortion clinics. She continues to serve NOW as the national advisory chair and has gone on to form her own organization, the Feminist Majority, of which she is president. Reproductive rights issues are a major focus for the Feminist Majority, which has produced two videos on abortion, *Abortion: For Survival* and *Abortion Denied: Shattering Young Women's Lives*. Smeal is also on the National Abortion Rights Coalition Steering Committee. In addition to being a frequent speaker at abortion rights rallies and events, she has appeared on many national television shows.

A Phi Beta Kappa graduate of Duke University, Smeal holds an M.A. from the University of Florida. She has won a number of honors, including being named by *The World Almanac* for 1983 as the fourth most influential woman in the United States and being named by *Time* magazine as one of the "50 Faces for America's Future" in its August 6, 1979, cover story. She was also featured as one of the six most influential Washington lobbyists in a story by *U.S. News and World Report*. President Jimmy Carter appointed her to presidential commissions concerned with International Women's Year and the White House Conference on the Family. She also served on the Executive Committee of the Leadership Conference on Civil Rights; was a member of the Council of Presidents, an organization of major women's rights groups; and serves on the boards of many other civil rights and women's rights organizations.

Joseph Stanton (1920–)

Joseph Stanton could be called the patriarch of the pro-life movement. He is also its chief archivist and historian, as well as an activist who speaks and writes unceasingly about abortion, euthanasia, and related issues and who has served time in jail for his protest activities. He has addressed committees of the United States Congress, contributed writings to the *Congressional Record,* argued before state legislatures, and met with three presidents, and he gives lectures throughout the United States and in Canada and Australia. He is credited with bringing many people into the pro-life movement, particularly liberal Protestant academics, and with helping to give the movement professional credentials.

As a teenager, Stanton was stricken with either rheumatoid arthritis or rheumatic fever, which left him bedridden for more than six months. This was followed by an attack of polio that nearly killed him. He recovered, though with disabilities that have increased over the years. His bout with polio left Stanton with a special sensitivity for the ill and disabled: "When I hear people talking about 'vegetables' and 'I wouldn't want to live like that' as reasons for aborting a defective child or as justification for euthanasia, I think back on that child in an iron lung. What if someone had said then, 'He isn't likely to survive, and even if he does, he may never completely recover' and had decided to remove me from the iron lung before I was able to breathe again on my own?"

After graduating from Boston College in 1942, Stanton attended Yale Medical School, hoping to follow in his father's footsteps by becoming a surgeon. The polio, however, had left him unable to oppose his thumb, and he surrendered the dream of surgery to pursue a career in research and internal medicine. A devout Catholic, Stanton opposes contraception and sterilization as well as abortion—he nearly passed up a residency at Yale–New Haven Hospital because he did not want to participate in performing tubal ligations. Throughout his career he has advocated the rights of the unborn, the disabled, the ill, and the elderly. Shocked by the legalization of abortion in New York in 1970, he became actively involved in the fledgling pro-life movement and helped to found both Massachusetts Citizens for Life and the Value of Life Committee (VOLCOM).

Since his retirement from active medical practice in 1985, Stanton has devoted himself to the battle against such "ethic of death" practices as abortion, euthanasia, and in vitro fertilization. Throughout his long involvement, he has been aided by his wife, Mary, and their 11 children, who harbor memories of stuffing envelopes for VOLCOM mailings. He especially credits his wife with providing the support that has made his work possible, particularly as he has become increasingly disabled. A scholar by nature, Stanton has collected volumes of press clippings, books, and other materials dealing with abortion and related topics, and VOLCOM holds what is perhaps the most complete archival library on the subject. Though slowed in recent years by his continuing struggle with the after-effects of polio, Stanton continues to write and speak and to participate in "rescue" activities. A book is currently being written about Stanton's life and contributions.

Randall Terry (1959–)

In the late 1980s, Randall Terry skyrocketed to national fame as the founder and leader of Operation Rescue, the New York–based organization that has staged hundreds of demonstrations and clinic blockades around the country, leading to thousands of arrests. Terry himself has been arrested at least 35 times in nine cities and has spent more than seven months in jail. The intense, charismatic Terry, who makes no secret of his political ambitions, sees his battle against abortion as nothing less than a crusade to save the nation from God's judgment, which he believes will bring down immense suffering on Americans as punishment for their continued tolerance of abortion.

A New York native, Terry graduated from the Elim Bible Institute in Lima, New York, in 1981. While at Elim he learned about the work of Francis Schaeffer, an evangelical author who advocated political action to attack the moral decay of Western culture—a decay that he attributed in large part to abortion. On January 22, 1984, Terry rode a bus to Washington, D.C., to participate in the annual March for Life. His preaching ability was already becoming known around Binghamton, and it was during that trip to Washington that Terry says he first envisioned Operation Rescue. Later that year he and his wife, Cindy, began Project Life, standing outside abortion clinics in Binghamton— she full-time, he during lunch hours and days off—trying to persuade women not to enter. The two were soon joined by other members of their church. In October 1984, the Terrys opened a Crisis Pregnancy Center, followed three years later by a home for unwed mothers.

During this time Terry began appearing on television and radio shows and giving newspaper interviews. In January 1986, he and six others carried out their first "rescue mission," locking themselves in one of the inner rooms of an abortion clinic before the clinic personnel were due to arrive. The protesters were arrested, convicted, and fined $60 each. Terry refused to pay and was sentenced to jail for the first time. Nearly two years later, on November 28, 1987, he mounted his first large-scale "rescue." Three hundred people blocked the Cherry Hill Women's Clinic in Cherry Hill, New Jersey. Since Cherry Hill, Operation Rescue has conducted more than 500 "rescue" operations, generating huge amounts of publicity and incurring the wrath of abortion rights groups.

Terry has appeared on national television and has been the subject of several news documentaries. He is the star of a video about his organization, *Operation Rescue,* and the author of two books, *Operation Rescue* (Binghamton, NY: Operation Rescue, 1988) and *Accessory to Murder* (Brentwood, TN: Wolgemuth and Hyatt, 1990). A singer and songwriter who plays saxophone and piano, Terry has also recorded two record albums, including a collection of anti-abortion songs called *When the Battle Raged.* Though both he and his organization have suffered numerous financial and legal setbacks, including lawsuits by abortion rights groups and convictions under the federal racketeering law (RICO), and media coverage of his activities has begun to diminish, Terry continues apparently undaunted, speaking frequently around the United States and rallying his troops in the ongoing fight against abortion, infanticide, and euthanasia.

Faye Wattleton (1943–)

Since Faye Wattleton became president of the Planned Parenthood Federation of America (PPFA) in 1978, PPFA has become the largest and most prominent institution in the fight for reproductive rights, and Wattleton, the movement's most visible and articulate spokesperson. Although Planned Parenthood's 172 affiliates provide a wide range of medical and educational services (only 5 percent of Planned Parenthood clients received abortions in 1988), the organization has come to symbolize the fight for access to safe, legal, affordable abortion. Much of this is due both to Wattleton's organizational leadership and to her nearly constant presence in the media. On taking the helm of PPFA— the first black and the first woman to do so—she imposed a corporate structure on the organization, hired media consultants and pollsters, opened a Washington lobbying office, and increased fundraising efforts. By 1989, the organization boasted 600,000 members and an operating budget of $323 million.

The daughter of a factory worker and a seamstress who was also a missionary for the Church of God, Wattleton entered Ohio State University at the age of 16 to study nursing, having skipped both kindergarten and first grade. She received her degree in 1964 and taught nursing for two years in Dayton before receiving a full scholarship to Columbia University, where she earned a master's degree in maternal and infant health care, specializing in midwifery. While in New York, she worked at Harlem Hospital, where many of the patients were women suffering from the effects of botched abortions—an experience that left her with lasting impressions and a firm commitment to reproductive rights.

Returning to Dayton in 1967, Wattleton became assistant director of the Montgomery County Combined Health District. She joined the local board of Planned Parenthood and a year and a half later became the affiliate's executive director. In 1975, literally while in labor with her daughter, she was elected chairman of PPFA's National Executive Director's Council, which acts as a liaison between PPFA affiliates and the national office. In 1978 Wattleton was appointed to her current position, where her combination of thoughtful intelligence, missionary zeal, and consummate professionalism have made both her and her organization powers to be reckoned with—such that conservative Senator Orrin Hatch of Utah was once overheard telling her, "I wish you were on our side."

Among Wattleton's numerous honors and awards are the American Public Health Association's 1989 Award of Excellence, the Better World Society's 1989 Population Medal, the 1989 Congressional Black Caucus Foundation Humanitarian Award, the World Institute of Black Communicator's 1986 Excellence in Black Communications Award, the 1986 Women's Honors in Public Service from the American Nurses Association, and the 1986 American Humanist Award, as well as several honorary doctorates. She is featured in a national photography exhibit, "I DREAM A WORLD: Portraits of Black Women Who Changed America." A frequent guest on radio and television, Wattleton has also been featured in or interviewed for numerous national magazines. She lectures frequently on college campuses and speaks before professional and lay organizations concerned with women's rights, civil rights, health care, social service, politics, and religion, as well as consulting to American business and political leaders and with heads of state, ambassadors, and cabinet ministers of other countries on family planning issues.

Sarah Weddington (1945–)

In 1967, as a young attorney fresh out of the University of Texas School of Law, Sarah Weddington was looking to make her mark on the world. By 1973 she had done so, as the lawyer who argued for the winning side in one of the most famous (or infamous) cases ever to be decided by the Supreme Court, *Roe v. Wade*. Born in Abilene, Texas, Weddington grew up in small, rural Texas towns, the daughter of a Methodist preacher and a college business teacher. After graduating from law school, she found the opportunities for women attorneys in Texas rather limited. For the next two years she worked as assistant reporter for the American Bar Foundation Special Committee on the Reevaluation of Ethical Standards. In 1969, Weddington met with a group of women who wanted to know if they would be breaking the law by referring women to places where they could get safe abortions in Mexico. In the process of researching their question, Weddington decided to challenge the constitutionality of Texas's restrictive abortion laws. She enlisted the help of Linda Coffee, who had been in her law school class, and by December of that year the two women had succeeded in locating a plaintiff for their case—Norma McCorvey, who would be known to the world as "Jane Roe." As they had hoped, the case eventually ended up in the Supreme Court, where Weddington became, as far as is known, the youngest woman ever to win a case.

In the meantime, Weddington had gone into private practice in Austin as a family law specialist and had become the first woman from Austin to be elected to the Texas House of Representatives. She served three terms before going to Washington, D.C., as general counsel for the U.S. Department of Agriculture. From 1978 to 1981 she served as assistant to President Jimmy Carter on women's issues and appointments. After a year spent as a law professor at the University of New Mexico, she returned to Washington and became the top lobbyist for the state of Texas as Director of the Office of State-Federal Relations.

Although currently in practice in Austin, Weddington spends a great deal of her time traveling and lecturing on the *Roe v. Wade* decision and other law topics related to abortion and reproductive rights. She is in constant demand as a speaker, giving as many as three speeches a week at campuses, state bar conventions, law schools, and attorneys' organizations and appearing on radio and national television. She also teaches part-time at the University of Texas at Austin in the departments of government and American studies and serves on the boards of several nonprofit foundations. She has written columns and articles for national magazines and is "in the initial stages" of writing a book. Weddington has received numerous honors and awards, including being named an "Outstanding Young Leader" by *Time* magazine, receiving the *Ladies Home Journal* "Woman of the Future Award," being named one of the 10 "Outstanding Women in America" in 1979, and being named an "American under 40 Making Things Happen" by *Esquire* magazine in 1984. She has received several honorary doctorates and was named by the National Association for Campus Activities as 1990 Lecturer of the Year.

John C. Willke (1925–)

John C. Willke is one of the most powerful and best known leaders in the pro-life movement. He is president of the International Right to Life Federation and a founding board member and past president of the National Right to Life Committee, the country's largest pro-life organization, with 50 state and nearly 3,000 local chapters. He also hosts a daily radio program, "Pro-life Perspective," which is broadcast on more than 300 stations, and serves as a principal pro-life contact for members of Congress and the presidential administration.

A native of Ohio, Willke attended Catholic schools before graduating from Oberlin College and the University of Cincinnati Medical School. He went into private practice as a physician in Cincinnati in the early 1950s, not long after marrying Barbara, a nurse. Devout Catholics, the Willkes have been fighting abortion since 1970, when they began incorporating abortion into their sex education lectures. They had begun giving talks on sex in 1953, first to Bible study classes and then in churches and at church-related functions. Soon they were doing pre-marriage counseling and talking to parents about how to teach their children about sex. In 1964, the Willkes published *How To Teach Children the Wonders of Sex,* the first of 10 books the couple has written in the fields of abortion and sexuality. The popular book was recently revised, after 16 printings in 20 years.

Soon after they began talking about abortion, the Willkes began collecting pictures of aborted fetuses to use in their presentations. In 1971, they incorporated the pictures into the *Handbook on Abortion,* which has been called the "bible of the pro-life movement." It has since been supplanted by *Abortion: Questions and Answers,* a pocket-size book of over 1,000 questions and answers that is meant to be carried in a purse or wallet. In addition to their own books, the Willkes have contributed to 4 other books, have published articles in more than 70 publications, and have had their works translated into 19 languages; they have also appeared in 5 educational movies and numerous videos. Through their own publishing company, Hayes Publishing, the Willkes produce and market a wide array of materials on abortion and related issues, including books, slide presentations, videos, posters, flyers, and brochures. A frequent guest on radio and national television, John Willke has also been featured in *People* magazine. He travels widely both in the United States and abroad to participate in debates, conferences, and other events.

Molly Yard (1915?–)

As president of the National Organization for Women (NOW), Molly Yard is at the forefront of the struggle for reproductive rights. Although NOW has always had a commitment to reproductive rights, the 1989 *Webster* decision propelled the organization into the front lines of the battle over abortion. Yard has thrown herself into this battle, as she has into numerous feminist and social causes throughout her long and full career. Born in China as the third daughter of Methodist missionaries, Yard was aware from an early age of the unequal treatment of women. She still can recall hearing young girls cry out in pain at night as their feet were bound and unbound. When she returned to the United States at age 13, however, Yard soon found that girls were not exactly on an equal standing with boys here, either. Thanks to a mother determined to give her daughters the opportunities she had been denied, Yard attended Swarthmore College in Swarthmore, Pennsylvania, majoring in political science. There she had her first experience as a political activist, campaigning successfully for the abolition of the school's sororities and fraternities after a Jewish friend was refused admittance to that tradition-bound system.

Yard comes by her activism honestly—her father lost two jobs as a result of his determination to speak out on behalf of the powerless and the oppressed. Through the years she has played key roles in the trade union movement, the civil rights movement, and the Democratic Party, in addition to the women's movement. She counted Eleanor Roosevelt among her close friends, a relationship dating from the days when Yard served first as secretary and then as chairperson of the American Student Union. Yard has been active in NOW since 1974, having joined the organization's national staff in 1978 during the ratification drive for the Equal Rights Amendment. She was elected president of NOW in 1987—becoming the first grandmother to serve in that role—and is currently in her second term.

Under Yard's leadership NOW's membership has nearly doubled, from 140,000 to 250,000. A key speaker during the April and November 1989 reproductive rights rallies in Washington, D.C., Yard spent much of 1990 touring the country with the Freedom Caravan for Women's Lives, speaking on campuses and at rallies in an effort to galvanize support for abortion rights candidates. She is also devoting considerable effort to bringing the French "abortion pill," RU 486, to the United States. In February 1990, Yard was honored in Paris by the Alliance des Femmes pour la Democratisation as an international leader on reproductive rights.

3

Facts and Statistics

THIS CHAPTER PROVIDES GENERAL FACTS AND STATISTICS relating to abortion in several areas, so that readers may construct a basis for evaluating what they read, see, and hear about abortion in other books, in the media, and from individuals and organizations. The information given is as factual as possible; of course, interpretations of the meaning or significance of a given fact or statistic will vary greatly with respect to individual positions and feelings on the issues involved. Of necessity, the information is relatively brief. Therefore, suggestions for further reading are included where appropriate.

The chapter includes seven sections:

Abortion Laws and Policies Worldwide. An overview of abortion laws and policies in the United States and throughout the world.

Abortion Statistics. An overview of abortion statistics, with particular emphasis on abortions in the United States. Included are statistics on the number, rate, and frequency of abortions; characteristics of women having abortions; weeks of gestation; types of techniques used; why women have abortions; reasons for having late abortions; abortion-related deaths; and abortion providers in the United States.

Abortion Techniques. Brief descriptions of abortion techniques, including instrumental techniques such as vacuum aspiration, medical techniques such as intraamniotic instillation, surgical techniques, and folk methods. Also included in this section is a discussion of RU 486, the so-called French abortion pill.

Abortion Complications and Long-term Impact. An overview of the possible medical complications and long-term risks of abortion, including a discussion of the difficulties of determining the long-term impact of abortion. Also included is a brief discussion of the psychological effects of abortion.

Overview of Embryonic and Fetal Development. A descriptive overview of the stages of human development from fertilization through birth.

Harassment of Abortion Providers. A statistical overview of violence and illegal or harassing acts directed at abortion providers since the legalizing of abortion in 1973.

Public Opinion and Abortion. A brief discussion of the issues involved in measuring public opinion about abortion, with references for further research.

Abortion Laws and Policies Worldwide

Worldwide, the laws and policies governing induced abortion range from complete prohibition to abortion on request, at least in the early stages of pregnancy. According to Henshaw (1990), as of January 1, 1990:

> Approximately 53 countries (including dependent territories) with populations of 1 million or more prohibit abortions except to save the life of the pregnant woman; these countries together constitute 25 percent of the world's population.
>
> Forty-two countries, constituting 12 percent of the world's population, permit abortion on broad medical grounds, including threats to the woman's general health. In some countries, the woman's physical health must be threatened; others explicitly or by interpretation allow for threats to mental health as well. Some of these countries also permit abortion for genetic or juridical indications, as in the case of rape.
>
> Fourteen countries, constituting 23 percent of the world's population, allow abortions for social or social-medical indications, including "adverse social conditions." Practically speaking, abortion is available virtually on request in many of these countries, including Australia, Finland, Great Britain, Japan, and Taiwan.

Twenty-three countries, constituting about 40 percent of the world's population, permit abortion on the request of the pregnant woman. These include China, the Soviet Union, the United States, and about half of Europe. Sweden and Yugoslavia are among several countries that explicitly define abortion as the right of a pregnant woman.

Table 1 shows a detailed breakdown of countries in each category. According to Hartmann (1987):

In Japan, the U.S.S.R., and Western Europe, abortion is used as a primary means of population control

Half of abortions worldwide (30 million to 50 million per year) are estimated to be illegal

United States

In the United States, since the 1973 *Roe v. Wade* Supreme Court decision, abortion is essentially legal on request throughout the country. In recent years, however, legislation at the state level has put a number of restrictions on access to abortions; increasingly these restrictions are being upheld by the Supreme Court, which has grown progressively more conservative as justices have retired and been replaced by judges appointed by presidents Reagan and Bush.

The *Roe v. Wade* decision established the trimester system of regulating abortion. Under this system, the Supreme Court ruled that:

The state does not have any compelling interest in regulating abortions during the first trimester (12 weeks) of pregnancy, except to require that an abortion be performed by a licensed physician in a medical setting.

The state's only interest in regulating abortions during the second trimester (12 through 24 weeks) is to protect maternal health.

When the fetus becomes viable (capable of independent survival outside the womb, with or without artificial life support), the state may choose to limit abortions to women for whom continued pregnancy would be life-threatening. The determination as to viability, however, is a medical and not a legal or judicial matter. (Although they technically may be considered legal under *Roe v. Wade*, abortions are virtually unavailable in the

TABLE 1   Countries, by restrictiveness of abortion law,
              according to region, January 1, 1990

Law	Africa	Asia & Oceania	Europe	North America	South America
To save a woman's life	Angola Benin Botswana Burkina Faso Central Afr. Rep. Chad Côte d'Ivoire Gabon Libya Madagascar Malawi Mali Mauritania Mauritius Mozambique Niger Nigeria Senegal Somalia Sudan Zaire	Afghanistan Bangladesh Burma Indonesia Iran Iraq Laos Lebanon Oman Pakistan Philippines Sri Lanka Syria United Arab Emirates Yemen Arab Rep. Yemen, Peoples' Democratic Rep.	Belgium Ireland	Dominican Rep. El Salvador*,† Guatemala Haiti Honduras Mexico* Nicaragua Panama	Brazil* Chile Colombia Ecuador* Paraguay Venezuela
Other maternal health reasons	Algeria Cameroon* Congo Egypt† Ethiopia Ghana*,† Guinea Kenya Lesotho Liberia*,† Morocco Namibia*,† Rwanda Sierra Leone South Africa*,† Tanzania Uganda Zimbabwe*,†	Hong Kong*,† Israel*,† Jordan* Korea, Rep. of *,† Kuwait† Malaysia*,† Mongolia Nepal New Zealand*,† Papua New Guinea Saudi Arabia Thailand*	Albania Northern Ireland Portugal*,† Spain*,† Switzerland	Costa Rica Jamaica Trinidad & Tobago	Argentina* Bolivia* Guyana Peru
Social and social-medical reasons	Burundi Zambia†	Australia† India**,†† Japan*,†,§§ Korea, Dem. Rep.*,† Taiwan*,†	Bulgaria*,†,‡ Finland*,†,‡,‡‡ German Fed Rep.*,†,‡‡,*† Great Britain† Hungary*,†,‡,‡‡ Poland*,§§,‡‡		Uruguay*,§
On request	Togo Tunisia‡‡	China Singapore Turkey§§ Vietnam	Austria‡‡,*† Czechoslovakia‡‡ Denmark‡‡ France§§ German Dem. Rep.‡‡ Greece‡‡ Italy‡‡ Netherlands Norway‡‡ Romania‡‡ Soviet Union‡‡ Sweden*‡ Yugoslavia††	Canada Cuba†† Puerto Rico United States	

United States past the twenty-fourth week. Further, in recent years, the number of facilities offering second trimester abortions has declined markedly.)

Current Abortion Restrictions

Several recent Supreme Court decisions have upheld state-imposed restrictions on abortion. These include parental consent and notification laws, which were upheld in *Hodgson v. Minnesota* and *Ohio v. Akron Center for Reproductive Health*. As of late 1990, 38 states had parental consent and/or notification laws on the books. The laws were being enforced in 17 states; they had been enjoined or stayed in 14 states and were not being enforced in the remaining 7 states.

In April 1989, the Supreme Court announced its ruling in *Webster v. Reproductive Health Services*. The controversial decision upheld a number of Missouri restrictions on abortion, including:

A prohibition against using public facilities (including private facilities built on land leased from the state) or public employees to perform abortions

A requirement that physicians test for fetal viability before performing a late abortion

A ban on the use of state funding for "encouraging and counseling women on the abortion procedure"

In May 1991, the Supreme Court also upheld the "gag rule" which prohibits any mention of abortion by doctors or counselors at family planning clinics receiving federal funds under Title X. The regulation, which was imposed by the Reagan administration in 1988 and

---

TABLE 1   NOTES

*Includes juridical grounds, such as rape and incest.   †Includes abortion for genetic defects.

‡Approval is automatic for women who meet certain age, marital and/or parity requirements.

§Not permitted for health reasons but may be permitted for serious economic difficulty.

**During the first 20 weeks.   ††During the first 10 weeks.

‡‡During the first three months or 12 weeks.

§§No formal authorization is required, and abortion is permitted in doctor's office; thus, abortion is de facto available on request.

*†Gestational limit is for interval since implantation.   *‡During the first 18 weeks.

Notes: Table does not include countries with fewer than one million inhabitants or those for which information on the legal status of abortion could not be located (e.g., Bhutan and Kampuchea). All abortions are permitted only prior to fetal viability unless otherwise indicated in footnotes.

SOURCE: Stanley K. Henshaw, "Induced Abortion: A World Review, 1990," *Family Planning Perspectives*, Vol. 22, No. 2 (March/April 1990): 77. © 1990 The Alan Guttmacher Institute.

continued under President Bush, does not directly affect the legality of abortion. The Court's upholding of the regulation, however, means that the 3,900 clinics that receive Title X funds, and that serve some four million poor and low-income women, must either stop providing abortion referrals, information, and services or lose their federal funding (see Chapter 1, 1988 and 1991).

As of this writing, several other laws, including statutes passed in Pennsylvania and in the territory of Guam, are being challenged in cases that may reach the Supreme Court. Laws restricting abortion are also pending or are expected to be introduced in a number of state legislatures during their 1991–1992 sessions. Also pending or expected to be introduced are a number of bills codifying women's right to an abortion, including a bill in Congress, the Freedom of Choice Act, which may reach the House and/or Senate floors during the 1991–1992 session.

Sources of further information or discussion on abortion laws and policies include (starred items are described in Chapter 5):

*Butler, J. Douglas, and David F. Walbert, eds., *Abortion, Medicine and the Law*, 3d ed. (New York: Facts on File, 1986).

*Glendon, Mary Ann, *Abortion and Divorce in Western Law* (Cambridge, MA: Harvard University Press, 1987).

Henshaw, Stanley K., "Induced Abortion: A World Review, 1990," *Family Planning Perspectives*, Vol. 22, No. 2 (March/April 1990): 76–89.

*Noonan, John T., Jr., *A Private Choice: Abortion in America in the Seventies* (New York: Free Press/Macmillan Publishing Co., 1979).

*Tietze, Christopher, and Stanley K. Henshaw, *Induced Abortion: A World Review, 1986* (New York: Alan Guttmacher Institute, 1986).

Several organizations listed in Chapter 4 have legislative hotlines and/or publish periodic updates and/or analyses of current and pending legislation and court decisions, including:

American Civil Liberties Union Reproductive Freedom Project

Americans United for Life

National Abortion Rights Action League (NARAL)

National Council of Jewish Women—NCJW Choice Campaign

National Organization for Women (NOW)

National Right to Life Committee

National Women's Law Center

Religious Coalition for Abortion Rights

See also Chapter 1, "Chronology," for descriptions of individual court decisions and legislation affecting abortion.

Abortion Statistics

Number and Frequency of Abortions

The frequency of abortion is measured in three ways:

Absolute numbers of abortions

Abortion ratio—the number of abortions per 1,000 live births

Abortion rate—the number of abortions for every 1,000 females of child-bearing age

Abortions in the United States

Prior to the legalization of abortion beginning in 1970, abortion rates could only be estimated, other than the relatively low number of legal, "therapeutic" abortions performed each year. Estimates of abortion rates have, however, remained remarkably consistent since the middle of the nineteenth century, when the ratio of abortions to live births was estimated at anywhere from one-fifth to one-third. Estimates of illegal abortions in the years prior to 1973 range from 500,000 to 1 million or more annually, though some anti-abortion groups dispute these figures.

In 1969, the Centers for Disease Control (CDC), a division of the U.S. Department of Health and Human Services, began an annual abortion surveillance to "document the number and characteristics of women obtaining abortions and to assist efforts to eliminate preventable causes of morbidity and mortality associated with abortion." In June 1990, the CDC stated that the reported number of abortions in the United States had increased every year from 1970 to 1982, with the largest percentage increase occurring during the period from 1970 to 1972. The annual increase declined from 1976 to 1982, reaching a low of 0.2 percent for the period 1981–1983. Since 1983, the numbers, rates, and ratios of abortion have remained relatively stable, with year-to-year fluctuations averaging less than 3 percent (Figures 1–3).

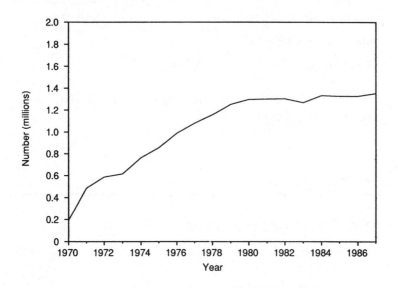

FIGURE 1   Legal abortions, by year, United States, 1970–1987. *Source:* Centers for Disease Control, *Morbidity and Mortality Weekly Report: CDC Surveillance Summaries,* Vol. 39, No. SS-2 (June 1990): 55.

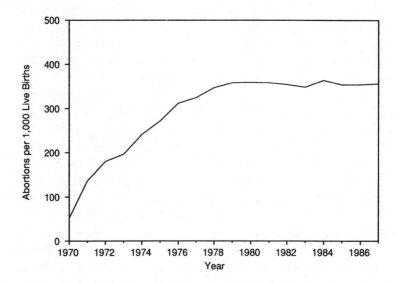

FIGURE 2   Abortion ratios, by year, United States, 1970–1987. *Source:* Centers for Disease Control, *Morbidity and Mortality Weekly Report: CDC Surveillance Summaries,* Vol. 39, No. SS-2 (June 1990): 55.

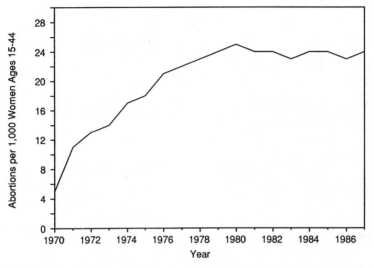

FIGURE 3   Abortion rates, by year, United States, 1970–1987. *Source:* Centers for Disease Control, *Morbidity and Mortality Weekly Report: CDC Surveillance Summaries,* Vol. 39, No. SS-2 (June 1990): 56.

While these figures provide a fairly reliable general picture of abortion in the United States, the number of abortions actually performed is certainly greater than the number reported to the CDC, which receives its information on abortions from central health agencies with widely varying requirements for reporting. Therefore, a frequently used source of abortion statistics is the Alan Guttmacher Institute (AGI), a private, nonprofit research organization that conducts periodic surveys of all identified providers of abortion services, including hospitals, free-standing clinics, and private physicians.

AGI attempts to locate all facilities that provide abortion services through a variety of sources, including Planned Parenthood affiliates, National Abortion Rights Action League state coordinators, state health departments, metropolitan area Yellow Pages directories, a newspaper clipping service, and mailing lists from companies and other organizations. Information is then obtained from the providers through a combination of mailed questionnaires, health department reports, and telephone interviews. Through this methodology AGI obtains a more complete picture of abortion statistics. In 1987, for example, the CDC reported approximately 13 percent fewer total abortions than AGI.

AGI surveys were conducted annually from 1974 to 1979, with each survey collecting data for the previous year. Thereafter, surveys were conducted biannually for the years 1979–1980, 1981–1982, 1984–1985, and 1986–1987. No data was collected for 1983. For the 1986

TABLE 2   Number and percentage distribution of legal abortions, abortion rate per 1,000 women, and percentage of pregnancies terminated by abortion, by age, United States, 1973–1983

Measure	1973	1974	1975	1976	1977	1978	1979	1980	1981	1982	1983
Number of abortions											
Total	744,610	898,570	1,034,170	1,179,300	1,316,700	1,409,600	1,497,670	1,553,890	1,577,340	1,573,920	1,575,000
<15	11,630	13,420	15,260	15,820	15,650	15,110	16,220	15,340	15,240	14,590	16,350
15–19	232,440	278,280	324,930	362,680	396,630	418,790	444,600	444,780	433,330	418,740	411,330
15–17	n.a.	n.a.	n.a.	(152,700)	(165,610)	(169,270)	(178,570)	(183,350)	(175,932)	(168,410)	(166,440)
18–19	n.a.	n.a.	n.a.	(209,980)	(231,020)	(249,520)	(266,030)	(261,430)	(257,398)	(250,330)	(244,890)
20–24	240,610	286,600	331,640	392,280	449,660	489,410	525,710	549,410	554,940	551,680	548,130
25–29	129,600	162,690	188,900	220,500	246,680	265,990	284,200	303,820	316,260	326,380	328,280
30–34	72,550	89,810	100,170	110,050	124,380	134,280	141,970	153,060	167,240	168,020	171,560
35–39	40,960	48,770	52,740	56,720	61,700	65,350	65,070	66,580	69,510	73,250	78,090
≥40	16,820	19,000	20,530	21,250	22,000	20,670	19,900	20,900	20,820	21,260	21,260
Percentage distribution of abortions											
Total	100.0	100.0	100.0	100.0	100.0	100.0	100.0	100.0	100.0	100.0	100.0
<15	1.6	1.5	1.5	1.3	1.2	1.1	1.1	1.0	1.0	0.9	1.0
15–19	31.2	31.0	31.4	30.8	30.1	29.7	29.7	28.6	27.5	26.6	26.1
15–17	n.a.	n.a.	n.a.	(13.0)	(12.6)	(12.0)	(11.9)	(11.8)	(11.2)	(10.7)	(10.6)
18–19	n.a.	n.a.	n.a.	(17.8)	(17.5)	(17.7)	(17.8)	(16.8)	(16.3)	(15.9)	(15.5)
20–24	32.3	31.9	32.1	33.3	34.2	34.7	35.1	35.4	35.2	35.0	34.8
25–29	17.4	18.1	18.2	18.7	18.7	18.9	19.0	19.6	20.0	20.7	20.8
30–34	9.7	10.0	9.7	9.3	9.4	9.5	9.5	9.8	10.6	10.7	10.9
35–39	5.5	5.4	5.1	4.1	4.7	4.6	4.3	4.3	4.4	4.7	5.0
≥40	2.3	2.1	2.0	1.8	1.7	1.5	1.3	1.3	1.3	1.4	1.4
Abortion rate*											
Total	16.3	19.3	21.7	24.2	26.4	27.7	28.8	29.3	29.3	28.8	28.5

TABLE 2   *continued*

Measure	1973	1974	1975	1976	1977	1978	1979	1980	1981	1982	1983
<15	5.6	6.4	7.2	7.6	7.6	7.5	8.3	8.4	8.6	8.3	9.2
15-19	22.8	26.9	31.0	34.3	37.5	39.7	42.4	42.9	43.3	42.9	43.5
15-17	n.a.	n.a.	n.a.	(24.2)	(26.2)	(26.9)	(28.8)	(30.2)	(30.1)	(30.1)	(30.8)
18-19	n.a.	n.a.	n.a.	(49.3)	(54.1)	(58.4)	(61.9)	(61.0)	(61.8)	(60.0)	(60.4)
20-24	26.2	30.4	34.3	39.6	44.3	47.2	49.9	51.4	51.1	51.2	51.1
25-29	16.4	19.6	21.8	24.1	26.9	28.4	29.6	30.8	31.4	31.5	31.1
30-34	10.9	13.0	14.0	15.0	15.7	16.4	16.5	17.1	17.7	17.7	17.8
35-39	7.1	8.4	8.9	9.3	9.8	9.8	9.4	9.3	9.5	9.3	9.6
≥40**	2.9	3.3	3.6	3.7	3.9	3.6	3.4	3.5	3.4	3.3	3.1
Percentage of pregnancies terminated by abortion++											
Total	19.3	22.0	24.9	26.5	28.6	29.2	29.6	30.0	30.1	30.0	30.4
<15	25.6	29.0	33.4	35.8	41.1	40.9	43.0	42.7	43.7	42.9	46.0
15-19	n.a.	n.a.	n.a.	n.a.	38.3	39.5	40.6	41.1	41.2	41.2	42.2
15-17	n.a.	n.a.	n.a.	n.a.	(38.7)	(39.7)	(41.3)	(42.4)	(42.2)	(42.0)	(43.2)
18-19	n.a.	n.a.	n.a.	n.a.	(37.9)	(39.3)	(40.1)	(40.1)	(40.3)	(40.5)	(41.4)
20-24	17.6	20.0	22.8	25.0	27.6	28.7	29.4	30.1	30.4	30.6	31.4
25-29	13.2	15.4	17.2	18.6	20.2	20.8	21.1	21.8	22.0	22.3	22.5
30-34	18.7	21.7	23.5	23.1	23.7	23.5	23.0	23.3	23.9	23.2	23.0
35-39	28.3	32.8	35.4	36.6	38.5	38.6	37.3	37.2	35.7	34.2	34.2
≥40	39.7	44.4	48.6	50.2	52.5	51.6	50.4	51.7	51.3	51.4	51.4

* Denominator for total abortion rate is women aged 15-44.
+ Numerator is abortions obtained by girls younger than 15; denominator is number of 14-year-old females.
** Numerator is abortions obtained by women 40 and over; denominator is women aged 40-44.
++ Denominator is live births six months later (to match time of conception with abortions) and abortions.
   Pregnancies exclude miscarriages and stillbirths. Births and abortions are adjusted to age of women at time of conception.
Note: n.a.= unavailable.

SOURCE: Stanley K. Henshaw and Jennifer Van Vort, *Abortion Services in the United States, Each State & Metropolitan Area, 1984–1985* (New York: Alan Guttmacher Institute, 1988), pp. 86–87. © 1988 The Alan Guttmacher Institute.

TABLE 3   Number of abortions, abortion rate per 1,000 women aged 15–44, abortion ratio per 100 known pregnancies, and total abortion rate, by completeness and reliability of data and country

Type of data and country	N‡	Rate	Ratio	Total rate
Statistics believed to be complete				
Australia (1988)	63,200	16.6	20.4	484
Belgium				
In Belgium§ (1985)	10,800	5.1	8.7	u
All** (1985)	15,900	7.5	12.2	u
Bulgaria (1987)	119,900	64.7	50.7	u
Canada				
In Canada (1987)	63,600	10.2	14.7	299
All†† (1985)	74,800	12.1	16.6	u
China (1987)	10,394,500	38.8	31.4	u
Cuba (1988)	155,300	58.0	45.3	u
Czechoslovakia (1987)	156,600	46.7	42.2	1,400
Denmark (1987)	20,800	18.3	27.0	548
England and Wales‡‡ (1987)	156,200	14.2	18.6	413
Finland (1987)	13,000	11.7	18.0	356
German Democratic Republic (1984)	96,200	26.6	29.7	u
Hungary (1987)	84,500	38.2	40.2	1,137
Iceland (1987)	700	12.0	14.0	336
Netherlands ‡‡ (1986)	18,300	5.3	9.0	155
New Zealand (1987)	8,800	11.4	13.6	323
Norway (1987)	15,400	16.8	22.2	493
Scotland §§ (1987)	10,100	9.0	13.2	255
Singapore (1987)	21,200	30.1	32.7	840
Sweden (1987)	34,700	19.8	24.9	600
Tunisia (1988)	23,300	13.6	9.8	u
United States (1985)	1,588,600	28.0	29.7	797
Vietnam (1980)	170,600	14.6	8.2	u
Yugoslavia (1984)	358,300	70.5	48.8	u
Statistics that are incomplete				
Bangladesh (FY 1989)	77,800	3.4	1.6	u
France*† (1987)	161,000	13.3	17.3	406*‡
German Federal Republic				
In country (1987)	88,500	6.7	12.1	197
All** (1986)	92,200	7.0	12.8	u
Hong Kong (1987)	17,600	12.7	20.1	u
India (FY 1987)	588,400	3.0	2.2	u
Ireland*§ (1987)	3,700	4.8	5.9	139
Israel (1987)	15,500	16.2	13.5	u
Italy (1987)	191,500	15.3	25.7	460
Japan (1987)	497,800	18.6	27.0	564
Poland (1987)	122,600	14.9	16.8	u
Romania†* (1983)	421,400	90.9	56.7	u
Soviet Union (1987)	6,818,000	111.9	54.9	u
Estimates based on surveys or other data				
Bangladesh (FY 1986)	241,400	12	5	u
Japan (1975)	2,250,000	84	55	u
South Korea (1984)	528,000	53	43	u
Soviet Union (1982)	11,000,000	181	68	u
Spain (1987)	63,900	8	u	u
Switzerland (1984)	13,500	9	15	u
Turkey (1987)	531,400	46	26	u

survey, which collected data for the two previous years, 3,853 possible providers were identified, including 1,574 hospitals, 990 nonhospital clinics, and 1,289 physicians' offices. Of these, 2,680 were ascertained to have provided abortions in 1985, while 827 had not. An additional 103 facilities that did not respond to the survey but that had reported no abortions in 1982 were assumed not to have performed abortions in 1985. The remaining 203 facilities—64 hospitals, 41 clinics, and 98 physicians—refused to participate in the survey, for a refusal rate of 6 percent.

The AGI data corroborates the CDC report that the number of legal abortions increased until the early 1980s. Since then, it has remained relatively stable at just under 1.6 million per year. Table 2 shows the numbers of abortions, abortion rates, and abortion ratios for the 10-year period 1973–1983, broken down by age, as reported to AGI.

Abortions in Other Countries

Table 3 shows how the numbers, rate, and ratio of abortions in the United States compares with abortions in other countries for which data is available.

Characteristics of Women Obtaining Abortions

Both AGI and CDC have collected considerable data on the characteristics of women who obtain abortions, including age, race, marital status, and parity (number of prior live births). AGI has also collected data on such characteristics as religion, living arrangements, employment, and income.

Table 4 is based on data reported to the CDC. (Although the absolute numbers of abortions reported by the CDC are lower than those reported by the Alan Guttmacher Institute, the percentages are

---

TABLE 3   NOTES

*Known pregnancies are defined as legal abortions plus live births. Births have not been lagged by six months because the necessary birth data are unavailable for most countries.

†The number of abortions that would be experienced by 1,000 women during their reproductive lifetimes, given present age-specific abortion rates.

‡Rounded to the nearest 100 abortions.

§Abortions performed in 17 hospitals and 20 nonhospital facilities, usually illegally.

**Including abortions obtained in the Netherlands and England.

††Including abortions obtained in Canadian clinics and in the United States.   ‡‡Residents only.

§§Including abortions obtained in England.   *†Provisional data.   *‡1986 data.

*§Based on Irish residents who obtained abortions in England.

†*Combining counts of illegal abortions with treated complications and of legal abortions.

Notes: Sources of country data for this table and subsequent tables available from author; u=unavailable.

SOURCE: Stanley K. Henshaw, "Induced Abortion: A World Review, 1990," *Family Planning Perspectives,* Vol. 22, No. 2 (March/April 1990): 78. © 1990 The Alan Guttmacher Institute.

TABLE 4   Characteristics of women obtaining legal abortions, United States, selected years, 1972–1987

Characteristics	1972	1973	1974	1976	1978	1980	1982	1984	1985	1986	1987
Reported number of legal abortions	586,760	615,831	763,476	988,267	1,157,776	1,297,606	1,303,980	1,333,521	1,328,570	1,328,112	1,353,671
Abortion ratio*	180.1	196.3	241.6	312.0	347.3	359.2	354.3	364.1	353.8	354.2	356.1
Abortion rate†	13	14	17	21	23	25	24	24	24	23	24
					Percentage Distribution§						
Residence											
Abortion in-state	56.2	74.8	86.6	90.0	89.3	92.6	92.9	92.0	92.4	92.4	91.7
Abortion out-of-state	43.8	25.2	13.4	10.0	10.7	7.4	7.1	8.0	7.6	7.6	8.3
Age (years)											
≤19	32.6	32.7	32.7	32.1	30.0	29.2	27.1	26.4	26.3	25.3	25.8
20-24	32.5	32.0	31.8	33.3	35.0	35.5	35.1	35.3	34.7	34.0	33.4
≥25	34.9	35.3	35.6	34.6	34.9	35.3	37.8	38.3	39.0	40.7	40.8
Race											
White	77.0	72.5	69.7	66.6	67.0	69.9	68.5	67.4	66.6	67.0	66.4
Black and other	23.0	27.5	30.3	33.4	33.0	30.1	31.5	32.6	33.4	33.0	33.6
Marital Status											
Married	29.7	27.4	27.4	24.6	26.4	23.1	22.0	20.5	19.3	23.5	27.2
Unmarried	70.3	72.6	72.6	75.4	73.6	76.9	78.0	79.5	80.7	76.5	72.8
Number of live births¶											
0	49.4	48.6	47.8	47.7	56.6	58.4	57.8	57.0	56.3	55.1	53.6
1	18.2	18.8	19.6	20.7	19.2	19.5	20.3	20.9	21.6	22.1	22.8
2	13.3	14.2	14.8	15.4	14.1	13.7	13.9	14.4	14.5	14.9	15.5
3	8.7	8.7	8.7	8.3	5.9	5.3	5.1	5.1	5.1	5.3	5.5
≥4	10.4	9.7	9.0	7.9	4.2	3.2	2.9	2.6	2.5	2.6	2.6

TABLE 4 *continued*

Characteristics	1972	1973	1974	1976	1978	1980	1982	1984	1985	1986	1987
Type of procedure											
Curettage	88.6	88.4	89.7	92.8	94.6	95.5	96.4	96.8	97.5	97.0	97.2
Suction	65.2	74.9	77.4	82.6	90.2	89.8	90.6	93.1	94.6	94.5	93.3
Sharp	23.4	13.5	12.3	10.2	4.4	5.7	5.8	3.7	2.9	2.5	3.7
Intrauterine instillation	10.4	10.4	7.8	6.0	3.9	3.1	2.5	1.9	1.7	1.4	1.3
Hysterotomy/ hysterectomy	0.6	0.7	0.6	0.2	0.1	0.1	0.0**	0.0**	0.0**	0.0**	0.0**
Other	0.5	0.6	1.9	0.9	1.4	1.3	1.0	1.3	0.8	1.6	1.5
Weeks of Gestation											
≤8	34.0	36.1	42.6	47.0	52.2	51.7	50.6	50.5	50.3	51.0	50.4
9-10	30.7	29.4	28.7	28.0	26.9	26.2	26.7	26.4	26.6	25.8	26.0
11-12	17.5	17.9	15.4	14.4	12.3	12.2	12.4	12.6	12.5	12.2	12.4
13-15	8.4	6.9	5.5	4.5	4.0	5.2	5.3	5.8	5.9	6.1	6.2
16-20	8.2	8.0	6.5	5.1	3.7	3.9	3.9	3.9	3.9	4.1	4.2
≥21	1.3	1.7	1.2	0.9	0.9	0.9	1.1	0.8	0.8	0.8	0.8

* Abortions per 1,000 live births.
† Abortions per 1,000 females 15-44 years of age.
§ Excludes unknowns. Since the number of states reporting each characteristic varies from year to year, temporal comparisons should be made with caution.
¶ For years 1972-1976, data indicate number of living children.
** <0.05%

SOURCE: Centers for Disease Control, *Morbidity and Mortality Weekly Report: CDC Surveillance Summaries*, Vol. 39, No. SS-2 (June 1990): 28–29.

TABLE 5   Percentage distribution of women having abortions in 1987 and of all women aged 15–44, index of abortion incidence, and age-standardized index, all by selected characteristics

Characteristic	Abortion patients	All women	Index	Index (adj.*)	Characteristic	Abortion patients	All women	Index	Index (adj.*)
Age					**Marital status**				
<15	0.9	u	na	na	Married	18.5	52.1	0.36	0.52
15–17	10.8	9.4	1.15	na	Separated	6.4	3.3	1.94	2.62
18–19	13.8	6.2	2.23	na	Divorced	11.2	8.2	1.37	2.05
20–24	33.1	17.0	1.95	na	Widow	0.6	0.7	0.81	2.01**
25–29	22.3	18.9	1.18	na	Never-married	63.3	35.7	1.77	1.35
30–34	11.7	18.4	0.64	na					
35–39	5.7	16.3	0.35	na	**Living arrangements**				
≥40	1.7	13.7†	0.12	na	Cohabiting††	17.4	3.4	5.12	4.65
					Not cohabiting	82.6	96.6	0.86	0.86
Ethnicity									
Hispanic	12.8	8.4	1.52	1.44	**Employment status**				
Non-Hisp.	87.2	91.6	0.95	0.96	Employed	68.1	64.2	1.06	1.09§
					Not employed	31.9	35.8	0.89	0.81§
Race									
White	68.6	83.3	0.82	0.83	**Family income**				
Nonwhite	31.4	16.7	1.88	1.80	<$11,000	33.1	14.9	2.22	1.99
					$11,000–				
Religion					$24,999	33.8	29.2	1.16	1.10
Protestant	41.9	57.9	0.72	0.74	≥$25,000	33.1	55.9	0.59	0.62
Catholic	31.5	32.1	0.98	0.95					
Jewish	1.4	2.5	0.56	0.69	**Medicaid status**				
Other	2.9	2.0	1.45	2.04	Covered	23.8	9.0	2.64	2.44
None	22.2	5.5	4.04	3.68	Not covered	76.2	91.0	0.84	0.85
Born again/									
Evangelical‡	15.8	32.0	0.49	0.51	**Childbearing intention**				
Not born again	84.2	68.0	1.24	1.23	More children	69.7	61.6	1.13	0.90
					No more	30.3	38.4	0.79	1.32
School enrollment									
Enrolled	31.1	20.5	1.52	1.51§	**Residence status**				
Not enrolled	68.9	79.5	0.87	0.94§	Metro	85.7	77.1	1.11	1.11
					Nonmetro	14.3	22.9	0.62	0.62
Total	100.0	100.0	1.00	1.00	Total	100.0	100.0	1.00	1.00

*Age-standardized.   †Women 40–44 only.   ‡Based on women 18–44.
§Standardized on women 25–44.   ††Among women not currently married.
**Standardized on women 20–44.   Notes: na = not applicable; u = unavailable.

Sources: **Hispanic origin**—U.S. Bureau of the Census, "The Hispanic Population in the United States: March 1986 and 1987 (Advance Report)," *Current Population Reports*, Series P–20, No. 416, 1987, Table 3; ——, "The Hispanic Population in the United States: March 1985," *Current Population Reports*, Series P–20, No. 422, 1988, Table 6. **Race**—U.S. Bureau of the Census, "United States Population Estimates, by Age, Sex, and Race: 1980 to 1987," *Current Population Reports*, Series P–25, No. 1022, 1988, Table 2. **Religion**—Special tabulation of the National Survey of Family Growth (NSFG), Cycle III, 1988. **Born again**—Special tabulations (six Gallup Polls), The Roper Center for Public Opinion Research, Storrs, Conn., 1988. **Marital status and cohabitation**—U.S. Bureau of the Census, "Marital Status and Living Arrangements: March 1987," *Current Population Reports*, Series P–20, No. 423, 1988, Tables 1 and 7. **School enrollment**—R. Bruno, unpublished data, Current Population Survey, Oct. 1986, U.S. Bureau of the Census, May 31, 1988. **Employment status**—U.S. Department of Labor, Bureau of Labor Statistics, "Employment and Unemployment: A Report on 1987," Jan. 1988, Table 3. **Family income**—U.S. Bureau of the Census, unpublished data from Current Population Survey, Table PF1; ——, "Money Income of Households, Families and Persons in the United States: 1985," *Current Population Reports*, Series P–60, No. 156, 1987, Table 18. **Medicaid coverage**—AGI, *The Financing of Maternity Care in the United States*, New York, 1987, Table 105. **Future childbearing intentions**—Special tabulation, NSFG, Cycle III, 1988. **Metropolitan area**—Distributions of the female population by age according to metro status, U.S. Bureau of the Census, 1980 Census, General Population Characteristics PC80–1–B1, U.S. summary, Table 43: updated to 1986 using U.S. Bureau of the Census, *Statistical Abstract of the United States 1988*, U.S. Government Printing Office, Washington, D.C., 1988, Table 30.

SOURCE: Stanley K. Henshaw and Jane Silverman, "The Characteristics and Prior Contraceptive Use of U.S. Abortion Patients," *Family Planning Perspectives*, Vol. 20, No. 4 (July/August 1988): 162. © 1988 The Alan Guttmacher Institute.

very close to those found by AGI. For example, in the year 1982, AGI reported that 57.3 percent of women having abortions were experiencing their first pregnancy; the CDC figure for the same year was 57.8 percent.)

Table 5, which is based on data reported to AGI, provides a more detailed breakdown, comparing the proportion of women who obtained abortions in 1987 with the proportion of all women of child-bearing age by such characteristics as age, ethnicity, marital status, religion, school enrollment, and employment status.

As these tables show, women having abortions range across all socio-demographic categories and all socioeconomic and cultural backgrounds, as well as across all age groups within the child-bearing years.

While the highest *absolute* numbers of abortions are found among women who are between 18 and 25 years old, white, and single, this group of women has the lowest *frequency* of abortions to live births.

Black and Hispanic women are proportionately more likely to have abortions than white women.

Poor women (those with family incomes under $11,000) are proportionately more likely to have abortions than those in the middle class.

The percentage of Catholic women obtaining abortions is comparable to the percentage of Catholics in the general population, while the percentage of Protestant women having abortions is somewhat lower than the percentage of Protestants in the general population, and the percentage of Evangelical Christians having abortions is considerably lower than the percentage of Evangelicals overall.

Teenagers age 15 or younger and women age 40 or older have the highest frequency of abortions to live births, even though the absolute numbers of abortions in these age ranges are small. This is graphically illustrated in Figure 4, produced by the CDC.

Weeks of Gestation

As Table 4 shows, most abortions (89 percent) are performed within the first 12 weeks of pregnancy (as measured since the last menstrual period, or LMP); at least half are performed within the first 8 weeks. Approximately 6 percent are performed between 13 and 15 weeks and

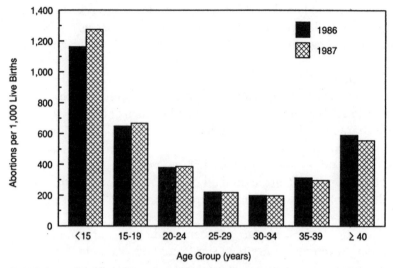

FIGURE 4   Abortion ratios, by age group, United States, 1986 and 1987. *Source: Centers for Disease Control, Morbidity and Mortality Weekly Report: CDC Surveillance Summaries,* Vol. 39, No. SS-2 (June 1990): 56.

4 percent between 16 and 20 weeks. Less than 1 percent of abortions are performed after 20 weeks, and virtually none after 24 weeks.

Type of Abortion Technique Used

As Table 4 shows, the overwhelming majority (97 percent) of abortions are performed by curettage, with most of these being done by suction curettage, or vacuum aspiration. This includes abortions performed by dilatation and evacuation (D&E). Slightly more than 1 percent of abortions are performed using medical induction, and only a tiny fraction by hysterotomy or hysterectomy.

Why Women Have Abortions

In 1987, the Alan Guttmacher Institute conducted a survey of 1,900 abortion patients to determine why they were having abortions. The majority of respondents (93 percent) said they had more than one reason for deciding to have an abortion; the mean number of reasons was just under four. The most commonly cited reason was that having a baby would interfere with work, school, or other responsibilities, followed by not being able to afford a child. About half of the women said that they either were having relationship problems or did not want to become single parents. Table 6 shows the percentages of respondents citing each reason, broken down by age, as well as the percentage of respondents stating that a given reason was the most important.

A number of respondents offered additional details for their reasons for deciding to have abortions; those for the three leading reasons are summarized in Table 7.

Reasons for Having Late Abortions

The AGI survey included several facilities that provided late term abortions; women having abortions at 16 weeks LMP or later were also asked their reasons for delaying the abortion. Most of these women reported that more than two factors were involved in the delay. Nearly three-quarters (71 percent) said that they either had not realized they were pregnant or did not know soon enough how long they had been pregnant. Almost half said that the delay was caused by problems in arranging the abortion, usually because they needed time to raise the money. Tables 8 and 9 show the reasons cited for having late abortions and the percentages of women citing each reason, including detailed breakdowns of the three most cited reasons.

TABLE 6   Percentage of abortion patients reporting that a specific reason contributed to their decision to have an abortion, by age, and percentage saying that each reason was the most important

Reason	Total*	Age†					% most important*
		<18	18–19	20–24	25–29	≥30	
	(N= 1,900)	(N= 275)	(N= 309)	(N= 645)	(N= 337)	(N= 319)	(N= 1,773)
Woman is concerned about how having a baby could change her life	76	92	82	75	72	69	16
Woman can't afford baby now	68	73	73	70	64	58	21
Woman has problems with relationship or wants to avoid single parenthood	51	37	46	56	55	50	12
Woman is unready for responsibility	31	33	40	36	25	18	21
Woman doesn't want others to know she has had sex or is pregnant	31	42	41	35	21	22	1
Woman is not mature enough, or is too young to have a child	30	81	57	28	7	4	11
Woman has all the children she wanted, or has all grown-up children	26	8	12	23	31	51	8
Husband or partner wants woman to have abortion	23	23	29	25	18	20	1
Fetus has possible health problem	13	9	13	12	14	17	3
Woman has health problem	7	3	4	7	8	15	3
Woman's parents want her to have abortion	7	28	12	4	3	2	‡
Woman was victim of rape or incest	1	1	1	1	1	‡	1
Other	6	2	5	8	5	8	3

*Ns are unweighted.

†The Ns upon which the age-breakdowns are based do not add to 1,900 because age was not available for some women.

‡Less than 0.5 percent.

SOURCE: Aida Torres and Jacqueline Darroch Forrest, "Why Do Women Have Abortions?" *Family Planning Perspectives*, Vol. 20, No. 4 (July/August 1988): 170. © 1988 The Alan Guttmacher Institute.

Abortion-Related Deaths

Deaths from Illegal Abortions

Illegal abortions are a leading cause of death for women in many parts of the world. This is true not only in countries where abortion is illegal, but also in countries where legal abortions are too expensive or difficult for poor women to obtain, so that they resort to illegal abortions. Worldwide, about 500,000 maternal deaths occur each year. According to Henshaw (1990), the World Health Organization (WHO) has estimated that 115,000 to 204,000 of these deaths result from

TABLE 7   Percentage of respondents offering various additional details for each of the three leading reasons women gave for having an abortion

Reason	% citing main reason
Unready for how having a baby could change her life (N=1,339)	
A baby would interfere with job, employment or career	67
A baby would interfere with school attendance	49
Children or other people depend on her for care	28
Can't afford baby now (N=856)	
Woman is student or is planning to study	41
Woman is unmarried	22
Woman is unemployed	19
Woman has low-paying job	14
Woman can't leave job	9
Woman is on welfare	7
Woman's husband or partner is unemployed	6
Woman can't afford basic needs	5
Woman receives no support from her husband or partner	4
Problems with relationship or with single parenthood (N=790)	
Woman doesn't want to marry partner	49
Couple may break up soon	32
Partner doesn't want to or can't marry	29
Woman is not in a relationship	25
Woman's husband or partner mistreats respondent or children	6
Woman is unready to commit herself to a relationship	5

SOURCE: Aida Torres and Jacqueline Darroch Forrest, "Why Do Women Have Abortions?" *Family Planning Perspectives*, Vol. 20, No. 4 (July/August 1988): 172. © 1988 The Alan Guttmacher Institute.

complications of illegal abortions performed by unqualified practitioners. A more conservative estimate, derived from hospital studies suggesting that, on average, 20–25 percent of maternal mortality is attributable to abortion, is that 100,000 to 125,000 women die each year from illegal abortions.

WHO estimates that more than half of the deaths from illegal abortions occur in South and Southeast Asia, with the next largest proportion occurring in Sub-Saharan Africa (Henshaw, 1990, p. 81). According to Hartmann (1987), in Latin America, where abortion is mostly illegal, one-fifth to one-half of maternal deaths are due to illegal abortion. In Bolivia, complications from illegal abortions account for over 60 percent of the country's obstetrical and gynecological expenses.

In the United States, the number of abortion-related deaths has declined dramatically since abortion became legal in 1973. The number of deaths from illegal abortions prior to 1973 is impossible to ascertain, and estimates vary. Although abortion rights groups tend to talk in terms of "thousands" of deaths, a few hundred per year is probably

TABLE 8   Percentage of women who reported that various reasons contributed to their having a late abortion and who cited specific reasons as accounting for the longest delay

Reasons	All (N=399)	Longest Delay (N=311)
Woman did not recognize that she was pregnant or misjudged gestation	71	31
Woman found it hard to make arrangements for abortion	48	27
Woman was afraid to tell her partner or parents	33	14
Woman took time to decide to have abortion	24	9
Woman waited for her relationship to change	8	4
Someone pressured woman not to have abortion	8	2
Something changed after woman became pregnant	6	1
Woman didn't know timing is important	6	*
Woman didn't know she could get an abortion	5	2
A fetal problem was diagnosed late in pregnancy	2	1
Other	11	9

*Less than 0.05 percent

SOURCE: Aida Torres and Jacqueline Darroch Forrest, "Why Do Women Have Abortions?" Family Planning Perspectives, Vol. 20, No. 4 (July/August 1988): 174. © 1988 The Alan Guttmacher Institute.

TABLE 9   Among women who provided information relating to three specific reasons for having abortions at 16 or more weeks gestation, percentage who gave various detailed reasons for delay

Reason	%
Woman failed to recognize pregnancy or misjudged gestation (N=277)	
She didn't feel physical changes	50
She hoped she was not pregnant	50
She had irregular periods	33
She thought she had had her period	32
Her MD underestimated gestation	20
She was practicing contraception	20
Her pregnancy test was negative	9
She didn't know where or how to get a pregnancy test	7
Woman found it hard to make arrangements for an abortion (N=185)	
She needed time to raise money	60
She tried to get an abortion from a different clinic or MD	32
She had to arrange transportation because there was no nearby provider	26
She didn't know where to get an abortion	20
She couldn't get an earlier appointment	16
She took time to notify her parents or get their consent	11
She needed child care or a Medicaid card	9
She needed time to obtain court permission	0
Woman took time to decide to have an abortion (N=74)	
She found having an abortion to be a difficult decision	78
She had religious or moral reasons for waiting	19
She talked with her parents/husband/partner	11

SOURCE: Aida Torres and Jacqueline Darroch Forrest, "Why Do Women Have Abortions?" *Family Planning Perspectives,* Vol. 20, No. 4 (July/August 1988): 175. © 1988 The Alan Guttmacher Institute.

more accurate. Seaman and Seaman, from *Women and the Crisis in Sex Hormones* (cited in Hartmann, 1987), state that before 1973, deaths in the United States from induced abortion averaged 292 a year. Table 10, which is based on CDC figures, shows a decline from an average of 359 deaths per year from 1958 to 1962 to 11 per year in 1981 and 18 in 1982.

Deaths from Legal Abortions

In countries where abortion is both legal and relatively available, abortion mortality is very low, averaging less than 1 death per 100,000 abortions (Henshaw, 1990, p. 81). This is true in the United States. However, complication and death-to-case rates vary according to gestational age of the fetus and the method used, with the risks rising with

TABLE 10   Number of deaths associated with abortion, by type of abortion, United States, 1958–1982

Year or average	Type of abortion All types	Legally induced[1]	Other than legal Total	Illegally induced[2]	Spontaneous
1958–62[3,4]	364	5	359	na	na
1963–67	276	4	272	na	na
1968–69	164	4	160	111	49
1970	168	36	132	109	23
1971	143	54	89	65	24
1972[5]	90	24	66	41 (2)	25
1973	57	25	32	22 (3)	10
1974	54	26	28	7 (1)	21
1975	48	29	19	5 (1)	14
1976	27	11	16	3 (1)	13
1977	37	17	20	4	16
1978	25	9	16	7	9
1979	26	18	8	0	8
1980	17	9	8	2 (1)	6
1981	11	7	4	1	3
1982	18	11	7	1	6

Note: na = data not available.

1. Excludes 10 deaths during 1973-79 that occurred shortly after legal abortion was attempted and that are attributed to ectopic pregnancy.
2. Numbers in parentheses are deaths classified as unknown by the CDC.
3. Figures for 1958-69 are annual averages.
4. Estimates for 1958-71 are based on deaths attributed to abortion inflated to comparability with data for later years.
5. For 1972-82 figures represent deaths reported by the CDC (excluding ectopic-related deaths). The number of deaths has been updated and may be more than previously reported (United States, 1985a, 1986b).

SOURCE: Christopher Tietze and Stanley K. Henshaw, *Induced Abortion: A World Review, 1986* (New York: Alan Guttmacher Institute, 1986), p. 131. © 1986 The Alan Guttmacher Institute.

each additional week of gestation. Estimates of the increase in the maternal mortality rate for abortion range from 30 percent to 50 percent with each additional week of gestation after the twelfth week. (Weeks are measured as weeks since the start of the last menstrual period, or LMP. Since fertilization generally takes place midway through the menstrual cycle, gestational age is about two weeks less than the number of weeks LMP.)

In the United States, from 1981 to 1985, the number of deaths per 100,000 legal abortions was 0.2 at 8 or fewer weeks LMP, 0.3 at 9–10 weeks, 0.6 at 11–12 weeks, 3.7 at 16–20 weeks, and 12.7 at 21 weeks or more (Henshaw, 1990, p. 81). As noted above, however, 90 percent of abortions in the United States are performed within the first 12 weeks, and the vast majority of these are performed by instrumental evacuation, including vacuum aspiration and curettage. The death-to-case rate for these is about 1 per million (0.1 per 100,000) (Hern, 1984, p. 28).

According to Hern (1984), most abortion-related deaths result from anesthesia complications. A CDC review of death-to-case rates for general versus local anesthesia for first trimester abortions (from 1972 to 1977) found a two to four times greater risk of death for general anesthesia. Another study found that general anesthesia was twice as likely to be associated with uterine perforation and cervical injury, while the relative risks of blood transfusion, cervical suture, and major surgery were 3.9, 2.1, and 7.6, respectively, for general as compared with local anesthesia (Hern, pp. 35–37).

Comparing the Risk of Abortion with Term Pregnancy and Use of Contraceptives

From 1981 to 1985, the maternal mortality rate, excluding deaths from abortion and ectopic pregnancies, was 6.6 deaths per 100,000 live births—a rate more than 30 times as high as that for abortions up to 8 weeks LMP, and twice as high as for abortions performed between 16 and 20 weeks; after 20 weeks the death rate for abortion is higher. In studying comparative mortality risks of term pregnancy, contraception, and induced abortion, Tietze and Henshaw (1986) concluded that "reliance on barrier methods, with early abortion as a backup, is the safest reversible regimen of fertility regulation at any age" (p. 115).

Ory (1983) lists the mortality risks in ascending order:

Barrier methods backed by abortion

Barrier methods alone

Abortion alone

IUD only

Oral contraceptives only in women who do not smoke

The highest risk is for women age 35 or over who smoke and use oral contraceptives.

Abortion Providers in the United States

According to Jaffe (1981), in 1973, half of all legal abortions were performed in New York and California. Few or none were performed in Louisiana, Mississippi, North Dakota, Utah, or West Virginia. One in 4 women had to leave their home states to obtain legal abortions. By 1977, 3 out of every 10 abortions were performed in New York and California, and only 1 woman in 11 had to travel outside her home state to find a legal abortion (p. 10). Over the last decade the number of facilities (including hospitals, free-standing clinics, and physicians' offices) providing abortion has declined, at least partly due to pressure from anti-abortion groups. Nine out of every 10 U.S. counties currently have no facilities that provide abortion services.

Table 11 shows a state-by-state breakdown of the number and percentage distribution of abortions and abortion providers by type— hospitals, nonhospitals performing more than 400 abortions, and non-hospitals performing less than 400 abortions.

Abortion Techniques

In the following descriptions, length of pregnancy is measured by the number of weeks since the last menstrual period, referred to as weeks LMP. Since fertilization generally takes place midway through the menstrual cycle, gestational age is about two weeks less than the number of weeks LMP. Weeks LMP is the method of measurement used by most medical professionals.

Instrumental Techniques

Menstrual Extraction

Menstrual extraction is the extraction of uterine contents before confirmation of pregnancy. It is defined by Edelman and Berger (in Hodgson, 1981) as "any procedure used to terminate a suspected

TABLE 11   Number and percentage distribution of reported abortions and providers by type of facility (hospitals, nonhospitals performing more than 400 abortions, and nonhospitals performing less than 400 abortions) and by state

State and Type of Provider	Number of Abortions				Number of Providers			
	1984		1985		1984		1985	
	Number	Percent	Number	Percent	Number	Percent	Number	Percent
Alabama	19,210	100	19,380	100	27	100	27	100
Hospital	470	2	490	3	11	41	11	41
Nonhospital 400+	18,470	96	18,620	96	12	44	12	44
Nonhospital <400	270	1	270	1	4	15	4	15
Alaska	3,170	100	3,450	100	15	100	13	100
Hospital	340	11	370	11	6	40	4	31
Nonhospital 400+	1,850	58	2,100	61	2	13	2	15
Nonhospital <400	980	31	980	28	7	47	7	54
Arizona	21,190	100	22,330	100	32	100	32	100
Hospital	360	2	320	1	3	9	3	9
Nonhospital 400+	19,020	90	20,210	91	11	34	11	34
Nonhospital <400	1,810	9	1,800	8	18	56	18	56
Arkansas	4,680	100	5,420	100	13	100	13	100
Hospital	70	1	80	1	6	46	6	46
Nonhospital 400+	3,900	83	4,510	83	4	31	4	31
Nonhospital <400	710	15	830	15	3	23	3	23
California	297,730	100	304,130	100	583	100	571	100
Hospital	60,030	20	57,200	19	300	51	292	51
Nonhospital 400+	218,580	73	226,020	74	113	19	108	19
Nonhospital <400	19,120	6	20,910	7	170	29	171	30

	No.	%	No.	%	No.	%	No.	%
Colorado								
Hospital	24,600	100	24,350	100	70	100	71	100
Nonhospital 400+	3,180	13	1,670	7	25	36	24	34
Nonhospital <400	18,050	73	19,240	79	16	23	17	24
	3,370	14	3,440	14	29	41	30	42
Connecticut								
Hospital	21,490	100	21,850	100	47	100	47	100
Nonhospital 400+	6,220	29	5,570	25	19	40	19	40
Nonhospital <400	13,820	64	14,850	68	10	21	10	21
	1,450	7	1,430	7	18	38	18	38
Delaware	4,710	100	4,590	100	8	100	8	100
District of Columbia								
Hospital	23,690	100	23,910	100	15	100	16	100
Nonhospital 400+	4,610	19	4,790	20	7	47	7	44
Nonhospital <400	18,920	80	18,870	79	6	40	6	38
	160	1	250	1	2	13	3	19
Florida								
Hospital	75,800	100	76,650	100	125	100	127	100
Nonhospital 400+	3,920	5	3,510	5	46	37	47	37
Nonhospital <400	68,940	91	70,890	92	56	45	59	46
	2,940	4	2,250	3	23	18	21	17
Georgia								
Hospital	38,710	100	38,340	100	66	100	65	100
Nonhospital 400+	7,570	20	7,700	20	43	65	41	63
Nonhospital <400	29,650	77	29,630	77	11	17	13	20
	1,490	4	1,010	3	12	18	11	17
Hawaii								
Hospital	10,430	100	11,160	100	50	100	53	100
Nonhospital 400+	4,550	44	4,480	40	13	26	13	25
Nonhospital <400	3,260	31	3,490	31	4	8	4	8
	2,620	25	3,190	29	33	66	36	68
Idaho								
Hospital	2,740*	100	2,660*	100	11	100	11	100
Nonhospital 400+	0*	0	0	0	1	9	1	9
Nonhospital <400	1,350	49	1,050	39	3	27	2	18
	1,390	51	1,610	61	7	64	8	73

TABLE 11 *continued*

State and Type of Provider	Number of Abortions				Number of Providers			
	1984		1985		1984		1985	
	Number	Percent	Number	Percent	Number	Percent	Number	Percent
Illinois	65,940	100	64,960	100	50	100	48	100
Hospital	3,450	5	2,820	4	27	54	26	54
Nonhospital 400+	62,170	94	62,110	96	20	40	20	42
Nonhospital <400	320	0	30	0	3	6	2	4
Indiana	16,070	100	16,090	100	30	100	28	100
Hospital	1,680	10	2,030	13	17	57	16	57
Nonhospital 400+	13,780	86	13,180	82	9	30	8	29
Nonhospital <400	610	4	880	5	4	13	4	14
Iowa	10,430	100	9,930	100	23	100	21	100
Hospital	2,230	21	1,910	19	10	43	8	38
Nonhospital 400+	7,170	69	7,110	72	6	26	6	29
Nonhospital <400	1,030	10	910	9	7	30	7	33
Kansas	12,420	100	10,150	100	18	100	18	100
Hospital	1,180	10	1,150	11	7	39	7	39
Nonhospital 400+	10,350	83	8,210	81	5	28	5	28
Nonhospital <400	890	7	790	8	6	33	6	33
Kentucky	10,090	100	9,820	100	12	100	12	100
Hospital	60	1	50	1	3	25	3	25
Nonhospital 400+	9,420	93	9,250	94	5	42	5	42
Nonhospital <400	610	6	520	5	4	33	4	33

	No.	%	No.	%	No.	%	No.	%
Louisiana	20,730*	100	19,240*	100	16	100	15	100
Hospital	0	0	0	0	2	13	2	13
Nonhospital 400+	20,210	97	18,510	96	11	69	10	67
Nonhospital <400	520	3	730	4	3	19	3	20
Maine	5,180	100	4,960	100	25	100	24	100
Hospital	240	5	260	5	14	56	13	54
Nonhospital 400+	3,660	71	3,170	64	3	12	2	8
Nonhospital <400	1,280	25	1,530	31	8	32	9	38
Maryland	29,120	100	29,480	100	48	100	48	100
Hospital	5,530	19	5,930	20	28	58	27	56
Nonhospital 400+	22,460	77	22,320	76	11	23	12	25
Nonhospital <400	1,130	4	1,230	4	9	19	9	19
Massachusetts	36,340	100	40,310	100	80	100	77	100
Hospital	5,560	15	5,300	13	38	48	35	45
Nonhospital 400+	28,990	80	32,900	82	11	14	9	12
Nonhospital <400	1,790	5	2,110	5	31	39	33	43
Michigan	66,010	100	64,390	100	81	100	83	100
Hospital	14,970	23	13,360	21	32	40	35	42
Nonhospital 400+	50,230	76	50,170	78	39	48	38	46
Nonhospital <400	810	1	860	1	10	12	10	12
Minnesota	17,410	100	16,850	100	18	100	18	100
Hospital	2,090	12	1,710	10	10	56	10	56
Nonhospital 400+	15,220	87	15,010	89	6	33	6	33
Nonhospital <400	100	1	130	1	2	11	2	11
Mississippi	5,490	100	5,890	100	9	100	8	100
Hospital	50	1	30	1	3	33	3	38
Nonhospital 400+	5,220	95	5,860	99	4	44	5	63
Nonhospital <400	220	4	0	0	2	22	0	0

TABLE 11   *continued*

State and Type of Provider	Number of Abortions				Number of Providers			
	1984		1985		1984		1985	
	Number	Percent	Number	Percent	Number	Percent	Number	Percent
Missouri	22,140	100	20,100	100	26	100	25	100
Hospital	1,200	5	870	4	9	35	9	36
Nonhospital 400+	20,490	93	18,950	94	11	42	11	44
Nonhospital <400	450	2	280	1	6	23	5	20
Montana	3,880	100	3,710	100	15	100	14	100
Hospital	30	1	20	1	3	20	3	21
Nonhospital 400+	2,230	57	2,120	57	2	13	2	14
Nonhospital <400	1,620	42	1,570	42	10	67	9	64
Nebraska	6,730	100	6,680	100	8	100	9	100
Hospital	110	2	20	0	3	38	4	44
Nonhospital 400+	6,460	96	6,470	97	3	38	3	33
Nonhospital <400	160	2	190	3	2	25	2	22
Nevada	9,370	100	9,910	100	25	100	25	100
Hospital	80	1	90	1	4	16	4	16
Nonhospital 400+	7,700	82	8,200	83	3	12	3	12
Nonhospital <400	1,590	17	1,620	16	18	72	18	72
New Hampshire	6,740	100	7,030	100	20	100	20	100
Hospital	300	4	270	4	6	30	5	25
Nonhospital 400+	5,150	76	5,650	80	5	25	5	25
Nonhospital <400	1,290	19	1,110	16	9	45	10	50

New Jersey	65,860	100	69,190	100	101	100	102	100
Hospital	10,250	16	9,510	14	42	42	42	41
Nonhospital 400+	52,420	80	56,140	81	28	28	27	26
Nonhospital <400	3,190	5	3,540	5	31	31	33	32
New Mexico	5,380	100	6,110	100	25	100	28	100
Hospital	580	11	600	10	7	28	7	25
Nonhospital 400+	3,110	58	3,810	62	3	12	5	18
Nonhospital <400	1,690	31	1,700	28	15	60	16	57
New York	192,020	100	195,120	100	301	100	299	100
Hospital	41,530	22	40,680	21	153	51	148	49
Nonhospital 400+	140,150	73	143,560	74	59	20	58	19
Nonhospital <400	10,340	5	10,880	6	89	30	93	31
North Carolina	35,800	100	34,180	100	110	100	108	100
Hospital	3,830	11	3,020	9	71	65	67	62
Nonhospital 400+	29,700	83	29,130	85	18	16	19	18
Nonhospital <400	2,270	6	2,030	6	21	19	22	20
North Dakota	2,940	100	2,850	100	3	100	3	100
Hospital	0	0	0	0	0	0	0	0
Nonhospital	2,940	100	2,850	100	3	100	3	100
Ohio	58,040	100	57,360	100	54	100	54	100
Hospital	1,860	3	1,920	3	21	39	21	39
Nonhospital 400+	55,410	95	54,740	95	25	46	25	46
Nonhospital <400	770	1	700	1	8	15	8	15
Oklahoma	12,630	100	13,100	100	16	100	16	100
Hospital	120	1	120	1	4	25	4	25
Nonhospital 400+	12,220	97	12,220	97	6	38	6	38
Nonhospital <400	290	2	300	2	6	38	6	38

TABLE 11   *continued*

State and Type of Provider	Number of Abortions				Number of Providers			
	1984		1985		1984		1985	
	Number	Percent	Number	Percent	Number	Percent	Number	Percent
Oregon	15,310	100	15,230	100	52	100	50	100
Hospital	6,990	46	6,820	45	22	42	21	42
Nonhospital 400+	6,500	42	6,820	45	7	13	7	14
Nonhospital <400	1,820	12	1,590	10	23	44	22	44
Pennsylvania	60,680	100	57,370	100	105	100	101	100
Hospital	12,720	21	10,600	18	63	60	60	59
Nonhospital 400+	44,870	74	44,410	77	15	14	17	17
Nonhospital <400	3,090	5	2,360	4	27	26	24	24
Rhode Island	7,450	100	7,770	100	6	100	6	100
South Carolina	11,280	100	11,200	100	12	100	12	100
Hospital	100	1	120	1	3	25	3	25
Nonhospital	11,180	99	11,080	99	9	75	9	75
South Dakota	1,770	100	1,650	100	2	100	2	100
Tennessee	22,570	100	22,350	100	40	100	41	100
Hospital	1,230	5	730	3	20	50	21	51
Nonhospital 400+	20,240	90	20,550	92	12	30	11	27
Nonhospital <400	1,100	5	1,070	5	8	20	9	22
Texas	99,960	100	100,820	100	102	100	102	100
Hospital	1,170	1	1,150	1	19	19	19	19
Nonhospital 400+	94,730	95	95,600	95	50	49	51	50
Nonhospital <400	4,060	4	4,070	4	33	32	32	31

Utah	4,240	100	4,440	100	7	100	7	100
Hospital	70	2	70	2	2	29	2	29
Nonhospital	4,170	98	4,370	98	5	72	5	71
Vermont	3,450	100	3,430	100	16	100	16	100
Hospital	60	2	60	2	4	25	4	25
Nonhospital	3,390	99	3,370	98	12	75	12	76
Virginia	31,670	100	34,180	100	65	100	61	100
Hospital	3,150	10	3,100	9	45	69	41	67
Nonhospital 400+	27,640	87	30,190	88	11	17	11	18
Nonhospital <400	880	3	890	3	9	14	9	15
Washington	29,510	100	30,990	100	84	100	83	100
Hospital	3,500	12	3,370	11	32	38	33	40
Nonhospital 400+	21,500	73	23,480	76	17	20	18	22
Nonhospital <400	4,510	15	4,140	13	35	42	32	39
West Virginia	4,680	100	4,590	100	9	100	9	100
Hospital	180	4	120	3	3	33	3	33
Nonhospital 400+	4,460	95	4,430	97	4	44	4	44
Nonhospital <400	40	1	40	1	2	22	2	22
Wisconsin	18,640	100	17,830	100	26	100	25	100
Hospital	660	4	620	3	7	27	6	24
Nonhospital 400+	17,320	93	16,430	92	11	42	11	44
Nonhospital <400	660	4	780	4	8	31	8	32
Wyoming	1,060	100	1,070	100	8	100	8	100
Hospital	80	8	80	7	4	50	4	50
Nonhospital 400+	0	0	0	0	0	0	0	0
Nonhospital <400	980	92	990	93	4	50	4	50

* Providers of 1–4 abortions are rounded to zero.

Note: Percentages may not add to 100 due to rounding.   Some provider types are omitted to preserve confidentiality.

SOURCE: Stanley K. Henshaw and Jennifer Van Vort, Abortion Services in the United States, Each State & Metropolitan Area, 1984–1985 (New York: Alan Guttmacher Institute, 1988), pp. 100–105. © 1988 The Alan Guttmacher Institute.

pregnancy no later than 14 days after the expected onset of a menstrual period" (i.e., 6 weeks LMP). According to Hern (1984, p. 121) it is a controversial practice for several reasons:

There is a higher incidence of continued pregnancy—in other words, the embryo may be too small and may be missed.

Some studies have shown a higher incidence of complications for abortions performed at less than 7 weeks LMP.

A high proportion of menstrual extraction patients turn out not to be pregnant, and thus have exposed themselves to unnecessary risks.

Menstrual extraction has a higher retained tissue rate than for later procedures.

Statistical studies and clinical experience indicate that very early abortions may be more difficult and hazardous than those performed after the sixth week of pregnancy.

It allows denial of pregnancy, which "may not assist the patient in dealing positively with the need for contraception to prevent future unplanned pregnancy or in dealing realistically with the sense of loss and grief that many women experience at the time of pregnancy termination" (pp. 121–122).

On the other hand, menstrual extraction offers advantages (cited by Hern, p. 121):

It is simple to do, and can be performed with a small, flexible cannula and a hand suction device such as a syringe, without the need for dilatation or anesthesia. It can, in fact, be self-administered.

It allows a woman to avoid the trauma of knowing for certain that she is pregnant.

It reduces the likelihood of persecution or prosecution where abortion is illegal.

Vacuum Aspiration (Suction Curettage)

The vast majority of legal abortions performed in the United States (96 percent) use the vacuum aspiration technique, which may be used up to about 14 weeks LMP. Vacuum aspiration is also used in later dilatation and evacuation (D&E) abortions to supplement the use of forceps and sharp curettage (see "Dilatation and Evacuation," below).

The use of vacuum aspiration was reported in Communist China as early as 1958, but was not recognized in this country until 1967, when *Obstetrics and Gynecology* published two articles on the technique. Following the legalization of abortion in New York in 1970 and the development of more sophisticated suction equipment, the technique rapidly gained popularity, largely replacing the traditional D&C (dilatation and sharp curettage) procedure.

Vacuum aspiration may be performed under either local or general anesthetic, though local is usually preferred for several reasons:

It is safer. Hern (1984, pp. 35–37) notes that most abortion deaths result from anesthesia complications. A Centers for Disease Control review of death-to-case rates for general versus local anesthesia for first trimester abortions from 1972 to 1977 found a two to four times greater risk of death for general anesthesia. Another study found that general anesthesia was twice as likely to be associated with uterine perforation and cervical injury, while the relative risks of blood transfusion, cervical suture, and major surgery were 3.9, 2.1, and 7.6, respectively, for general as compared with local anesthesia.

The risks of perforating the uterus are lower. With general anesthetic, the uterus is softer and thus more easily perforated (Hodgson, 1981, p. 257).

A conscious, alert patient can report unusual pain or other symptoms, increasing the likelihood of quick diagnosis and correction of any problems. Also, notes Hern (1984), "the use of general anesthesia eliminates physician-patient interaction during the abortion and insulates the physician from the patient's emotional experience. This is a serious loss for physicians and may make it extremely difficult for them to relate to the emotional problems encountered by abortion patients. It does nothing to enhance the physician's empathy for the abortion patient's dilemma or the physician's understanding of the importance of this experience for the patient's life" (p. 120).

The vacuum aspiration technique consists of two steps. First the cervix is dilated, which is usually done one of two ways:

With tapered metal rods called dilators, which are progressively larger in diameter. These are inserted in the cervix one at a time, each time using a slightly larger size, until the cervix is dilated enough to insert the vacuum cannula.

With laminaria tents. These are sticks made from the stems of a kind of seaweed. As the sticks absorb moisture, they swell from two to three times their original size. The tents are inserted into the cervix and left for anywhere from a few hours to overnight. As the tent swells, the cervix is gradually dilated. Laminaria tents are commonly used for later (D&E) abortions, but some practitioners prefer them over forcible dilatation even for early abortions, since the gradual dilatation decreases the need for local anesthetic.

Other methods of dilatation include plastic dilators; plastic foam sponges that, like laminaria, swell when wet; and prostaglandin suppositories, which cause the cervix to soften and make dilatation easier.

When the cervix is adequately dilated, the operator inserts a transparent hollow tube, or cannula, into the uterine cavity. The cannula, which may be either metal or plastic, is attached to a suction device, which is usually electrical but may be hand operated. The vacuum pump is then started and the cannula is gently rotated to empty the uterus. In many cases, the operator then uses a small, sharp curette, or spoon-shaped instrument, to check for any residual tissue. The average time for the procedure is less than five minutes. In the earlier stages of pregnancy (up to about 12 weeks), the cannula is about the diameter of a drinking straw.

Dilatation and Curettage

Until the mid-1970s, dilatation and sharp curettage, or D&C, was the most common method for performing early abortions. In this procedure the cervix is dilated using manual dilators and a sharp curette is used to scrape out the uterine contents. The procedure is usually performed under general anesthetic. According to Hodgson (1981, p. 229) the advantages of vacuum aspiration over D&C are:

Less time required

More complete removal of tissue

Less blood loss

Fewer major complications

More adaptable to local anesthesia

Dilatation and Evacuation

Since the late 1970s, dilatation and evacuation (D&E) has become the preferred method for abortions performed from about 13 to 20 weeks of pregnancy, rather than the more hazardous and traumatic saline or prostaglandin induction methods (see below). In most cases D&E is a two-stage process, because the cervix must be dilated more than in early abortions. The procedure varies according to the clinic and operator, but usually laminaria are used to dilate the cervix. These are inserted and left for anywhere from several hours to overnight, depending on the length of pregnancy. Sometimes manual dilators are also used.

Once the cervix is dilated, the physician removes the fetus and placenta using a combination of vacuum suction, forceps, and sharp curettage. This may be done either under general anesthesia, spinal or epidural anesthesia, or a paracervical block. For pregnancies up to about 16 weeks, it is possible to use large cannula that will remove all of the uterine contents with suction. For later pregnancies and in cases where large cannula are not available, forceps are used to crush and dismember the fetus and withdraw it through the cervix.

Possible complications include perforation of the uterus, cervical laceration, hemorrhage, incomplete abortion, and infection. Dilatation and evacuation is generally agreed to be safer and more effective than instillation methods, and it is less traumatic for the patient. However, it is more upsetting for the physician and assistants, particularly in later pregnancies where the fetus must be crushed and dismembered before it can be removed.

Medical Induction Techniques

Intraamniotic Instillation

Until recently, amnioinfusion with a saline solution was the most common method for abortions performed at 16 weeks or later LMP, but it has been largely replaced by dilatation and evacuation (see above) for pregnancies of 20 weeks or less. Saline abortions usually require hospitalization. Under local anesthetic, a large needle inserted into the uterus is used to withdraw 100–200 milliliters of amniotic fluid. A similar amount of 20 percent hypertonic saline solution is then infused into the uterine cavity. In most cases, the fetal heartbeat stops within about 1.5 hours, and the woman goes into labor and delivers the dead fetus within 24 to 72 hours. The time between the injection and the abortion may be reduced by the insertion of laminaria at least 6 hours prior to the infusion; this also reduces the risk of cervical injury.

\

Oxytocin is also often used to stimulate uterine contractions and shorten the injection to abortion time. A hyperosmolar urea solution may be used in place of saline. This may not be as effective as saline, but it is safer.

Saline abortions carry a higher risk of complications than D&E abortions. Occasionally, though rarely, the fetus is born alive. Other possible complications include accidental injection of saline solution into a vein, hypernatremia (an increase in blood sodium levels), blood coagulation disorders, water intoxication, cervical injuries, infection, hemorrhage, and incomplete abortion. Instillation abortions can also be traumatic for the woman, who must endure a long and painful labor and the delivery of a dead, immature fetus.

Prostaglandins

Prostaglandins are naturally occurring hormones or hormone-like substances that have proved effective in causing uterine contractions and expulsion of the fetus. They may be administered intravenously, intramuscularly, vaginally (through suppositories), or into the uterus itself, either extraamniotically (between the fetal membranes and the uterine wall) or intraamniotically (directly into the amniotic sac). Laminaria may be used to facilitate cervical dilatation and decrease the number of contractions needed to expel the fetus, as well as to shorten the instillation to abortion time. In some cases oxytocin is also used. Sometimes saline and prostaglandins may be used together.

Prostaglandins compare favorably in safety with saline for inducing second trimester abortions; blood clotting is considerably less likely and there is no risk of hypernatremia. Also, the instillation to abortion time is generally shorter. Because prostaglandins act on the musculature of the gastrointestinal tract as well as the uterus, they can cause severe gastrointestinal side effects. Other possible complications include a higher incidence of retained placenta, as well as cervical trauma, infection, hemorrhage, and sudden death; also up to 7 percent of fetuses will show brief signs of life (Hern, 1984, and Tietze and Henshaw, 1986).

According to Hern (1984), a comparison of complication rates for saline instillation versus prostaglandin abortions from 1972 to 1978 showed higher risks for prostaglandin. The actual number of deaths, however, was low—a total of 136 from 1972 to 1978. Of these, the highest number, 47, was for abortions done from the sixteenth to the twentieth week. The fewest complications were for D&E abortions performed from 13 through 16 weeks.

Prostaglandins may also be combined with RU 486 (see below) to induce abortions up to seven weeks LMP.

Surgical Techniques

Hysterotomy and Hysterectomy

Hysterotomy resembles a caesarean section. An incision is made in the abdomen and the uterus, and the fetus is removed. If done early in the second trimester, a hysterotomy may be done vaginally. Because it carries high risks compared to other techniques, hysterotomy is rarely used unless other abortion techniques have failed, usually repeatedly, or if the patient's medical condition makes other procedures unworkable. Sometimes hysterotomy is performed in conjunction with sterilization. Even more rarely, a hysterectomy (removal of the uterus) is performed—almost always only in cases where a hysterectomy is already indicated, as in the case of a malignant tumor. Both hysterotomy and hysterectomy are performed under general anesthesia.

Folk Methods

For thousands of years women have tried various methods to induce abortion. These range from the innocuous—and ineffective—such as taking very hot baths, to the dangerous, such as swallowing poison or having someone jump on one's abdomen. Perhaps the most common method is inserting some kind of foreign object into the uterus, such as a twig, a catheter, or the infamous coathanger. Another common technique is the injection of soapy water or household disinfectants into the uterus. These methods often kill the woman as well as the fetus, or at the least lead to serious infection and often sterility.

RU 486: The French "Abortion Pill"

In September 1988, the French government approved RU 486 for marketing. By mid-1990, it had been used in more than 50,000 abortions. Currently the drug and its manufacturer, Roussel-UCLAF, are the center of a heated tug-of-war that pits anti-abortion groups against abortion rights supporters who want to see RU 486 marketed in the United States.

How It Works

RU 486 is a progesterone antagonist, or an "anti-progesterone." Progesterone, a hormone that is produced by a woman's body midway through her menstrual cycle, signals the uterus to develop the lining that can receive and nourish a fertilized egg. If the egg is not fertilized, progesterone production ceases and the egg, along with the uterine lining, is shed during menstruation. If fertilization occurs, progesterone levels increase, preventing the shedding of the lining as well as ovulation and the start of a new cycle. Progesterone also aids in the development of the placenta and inhibits the production of natural prostaglandins, hormones that cause uterine contractions and make the cervix softer and more pliable.

RU 486 appears to work by inhibiting or halting the production of progesterone, causing the uterus to slough off its lining. Also in the absence of progesterone, production of prostaglandins increases, softening the cervix and causing the uterus to contract, thereby facilitating the dislodging and expulsion of the embryo. Taken alone, RU 486 is about 90 percent effective in inducing abortion during very early pregnancy. If the dose of RU 486 is followed with either an injection or a vaginal suppository containing a synthetic prostaglandin one to two days later, the effectiveness is increased to 96 percent through the seventh week LMP. The use of prostaglandin also speeds the process. With RU 486 alone, it took seven to ten days, and in some cases longer, for the abortion to be complete. With the combination of RU 486 and prostaglandin, the time is reduced to a few hours after the administration of the prostaglandin.

RU 486 appears to produce few serious side effects, the main one being sustained bleeding, similar to a heavy menstrual period, which may last up to two weeks. Hemorrhage occurs in a few cases; 1 in 1,000 women may require a transfusion. Many women also report other side effects such as cramps and nausea, which may have been caused by the pregnancy itself rather than the drug. RU 486 has not been shown to have any effect on subsequent pregnancies. No anesthesia is required, and, because there is no instrumental intervention, there is no risk of cervical injury or uterine perforation. Nevertheless, it is important that the drug be taken under medical supervision. Currently the process in France requires at least three visits—one for pregnancy testing and counseling and to sign a consent form, the second to take the oral dose of RU 486, and the third to receive either an injection of the prostaglandin sulprostone or a vaginal suppository of gemeprost. A fourth visit a week later is strongly encouraged, to make sure the abortion is complete and to check for serious side effects. It is not foreseeable that women will simply be able to obtain a prescription and swallow a pill at home. This fact has severe implications should the drug end up being sold on the black market.

A concern raised by anti-abortion groups is the possible effect on a fetus should the pregnancy continue, although there is no evidence of problems to date. In Britain, three women who stopped treatment after the first step later delivered healthy babies.

Where It Stands

As of this writing, in addition to France, where it accounts for one-quarter to one-third of abortions, RU 486 is slated for release in Great Britain, Holland, the Scandinavian countries, and possibly China and India. Although Roussel-UCLAF has said that it will not market the drug in the United States, a number of alternatives are being explored by private investors and groups such as Planned Parenthood on possible ways to bring the drug to this country. A major obstacle is the federal Food and Drug Administration (FDA), which would have to approve not only RU 486 but also the synthetic prostaglandin used with it, which is not currently available in the United States. Before its research was halted by Roussel-UCLAF's refusal to continue supplying the drug, the Los Angeles County–University of Southern California Medical Center's Women's Hospital had conducted clinical trials with 400 women; still, it is expected that it will take at least three years and as much as $50 million to win FDA approval.

The campaign to introduce RU 486 in the United States may be boosted by the fact that the drug has a number of other promising applications, including treatment for such diseases as breast and prostate cancer, brain tumors, glaucoma, and Cushing's syndrome, as well as aiding in term deliveries that might otherwise require caesarean sections. It may also provide a safe, effective means of birth control when taken, for example, on a weekly basis to prevent ovulation or once a month to induce menstruation.

For further information on RU 486, see:

Klitsch, Michael, *RU 486: The Science and the Politics* (New York: Alan Guttmacher Institute, 1989). Available from AGI, 111 Fifth Avenue, New York, NY 10003-1089, (212) 254-5656.

Lake, Alice, "The New French Pill," *McCalls* (March 1990): 58–63.

Ulmann, Andre, Georges Teutsch, and Daniel Philibert, "RU 486," *Scientific American*, Vol. 262, No. 6 (June 1990): 42–48.

Abortion Complications and Long-Term Impact

According to Hern (1984, p. 175), abortion complications tend to fall into five categories:

Failure of dilatation

Failure to completely empty the uterus

Error in the estimate of length of gestation

Trauma to the uterus, cervix, or other pelvic structures due to the operator's failure to exercise sufficient caution

Developmental or functional abnormalities

The risks associated with abortion increase with length of gestation. According to Cates and Grimes (in Hodgson, 1981), the lowest risk of complications is at seven to eight weeks of pregnancy. After eight weeks gestation, the risk of major complications appears to rise 15 to 30 percent for each week of delay. The risk of complications also varies with the type of procedure used, as noted in the procedure descriptions above. Other variables affecting complications include the patient's age, race, gravidity, parity, and socioeconomic status, as well as pre-existing conditions such as sickle-cell anemia or heart conditions.

The use of prophylactic antibiotics, development of safer techniques such as vacuum aspiration, and increased experience among physicians performing abortions has greatly reduced the incidence of abortion complications. Also, where abortion is legal, women tend to get abortions earlier, when the procedure is less risky, and any complications that do develop are more likely to receive prompt treatment. Overall, compared to other surgical procedures, abortion has a very low death-to-case rate, carrying approximately half the risk of death as a routine tonsillectomy.

Opponents of abortion dispute these statistics, claiming that many deaths and complications are "covered up" or are not reported as being due to abortion. The bulk of the evidence supporting the claim that abortion is medically hazardous, however, is based on case studies by individual physicians or individual accounts reported to such organizations as Women Exploited by Abortion (WEBA) and American Rights Coalition (see Chapter 4). It is worth noting in this context that abortion is currently the most performed surgical procedure in the United States, and even a minute percentage of complications can translate to several thousand individuals per year.

Problems in Determining Long-Term Risks of Abortion

The subject of long-term risks of abortion is a matter of considerable controversy. Although abortion opponents claim that abortions may lead to subsequent fertility problems, including sterility, premature birth, low birth weight, and miscarriages, researchers attempting to study such effects run into serious methodological problems. Among these are the following:

Abortion techniques used now are safer than those used 20 years ago. This fact confounds statistics on morbidity, mortality, and risks to subsequent pregnancies, since statistics on repeat abortions often include abortions by older methods that are no longer used.

Many studies also do not indicate at what gestational age the abortions were performed, and later abortions carry much higher risks for both short-term complications and long-term effects.

Many women are reluctant to admit to prior abortions, so data on "first abortions" often are not reliable.

Many earlier studies failed to control for background factors, such as age, parity, ethnicity, socioeconomic status, and smoking habits, that might cause such pregnancy problems as low birth weight, premature birth, or miscarriage.

According to Tietze and Henshaw (1986), based on the best available data, "There can be no doubt that any adverse effects of terminating the first pregnancy by suction curettage must be quite small. . . . The few available evaluations of secondary sterility or reduced ability to conceive lead to the same conclusion. . . . This is also true for complications of labor and delivery." They go on to state, "The absolute risk attributable to the termination of the first pregnancy by suction curettage abortion . . . was negative for subsequent spontaneous midtrimester abortion, virtually zero for premature delivery and less than one per 100 live births for low birth weight" (p. 99).

Studies following the long-term effects of abortions done by surgical curettage seem to indicate a somewhat higher risk of adverse effects on subsequent pregnancies, but "it is not clear to what extent these higher risks reflect greater traumatization by the method or the manner in which it was used, inadequate correction for confounding variables or other biological or social factors associated with geography. No consistent pattern was found in the few sites where both methods of abortion were used and studied" (Tietze and Henshaw, p. 99).

For more detailed discussions of the risks and the long-term impact of abortion, see the following (see Chapter 5 for more detailed information):

Committee on Government Operations, 101st Congress, *The Federal Role in Determining the Medical and Psychological Impact of Abortion on Women* (Washington, DC: U.S. Government Printing Office, 1989).

Hern, Warren, *Abortion Practice* (Philadelphia: J. B. Lippincott, 1984).

Hilgiers, Thomas W., M.D., Dennis J. Horan, and David Mall, eds., *New Perspectives on Human Abortion* (Frederick, MD: University Publications of America, 1981).

Hodgson, Jane E., ed., *Abortion and Sterilization: Medical and Social Aspects* (London: Academic Press, 1981).

Reardon, David C., *Aborted Women: Silent No More* (Chicago: Loyola University Press, 1987).

Tietze, Christopher, and Stanley K. Henshaw, *Induced Abortion: A World Review, 1986* (New York: Alan Guttmacher Institute, 1986).

Psychological Effects of Abortion

The issue of psychological effects is one of the most hotly contested subtopics in the overall debate about abortion. Proponents of legal abortion, including a majority (though not all) of the members of such organizations as the American Medical Association and the American Psychological Association (APA), point to research indicating that the primary emotion experienced by the majority of women after undergoing an abortion is relief. A report released by the APA in 1990 (Adler et al.) concluded that "although there may be sensations of regret, sadness, or guilt, the weight of the evidence from the best scientific studies indicates that legal abortion of an unwanted pregnancy in the first trimester does not constitute a psychological hazard for most women" (p. 4).

The APA report goes on to note that "although the vast majority of women do not experience negative psychological experiences after abortion, case studies document some negative experiences" (p. 6); these are most likely to occur in cases where the decision to abort was difficult or conflicted, where the woman did not perceive support for her decision, or where the pregnancy was personally meaningful. Rates of distress were also higher for women who had abortions later in pregnancy. The report notes that, although these case studies have established that some women do experience "severe distress or psychopathology" after undergoing an abortion and that "such responses can be overwhelming to a given individual," they represent a small minority of the total number of abortion patients. For most women, the report concludes, distress is greatest immediately *preceding* an abortion. The report does go on to describe "weaknesses and gaps" in existing studies that "provide challenges for further research." Among these are a lack of information on subjects who chose not to participate, the necessary limitation of studies to volunteer subjects, and the lack of long-term follow-ups.

Much of the information supporting the belief that abortion is psychologically harmful is based on case studies and individual accounts reported to such organizations as Women Exploited by Abortion (WEBA) and Victims of Choice (see Chapter 4). A growing number of lay and professional counselors and physicians describe a condition labeled "post-abortion syndrome" (PAS) or "post-abortion stress syndrome" (PASS), which includes such symptoms as severe depression, suicidal thoughts, anxiety, intense rage, and extreme passivity. Self-help and counseling services for PAS are appearing in many areas around the country; WEBA reports that it gets "hundreds of calls" every week. It is worth noting in this context that even 1 percent of abortion patients suffering serious psychological effects would represent some 15,000 women each year.

In 1989, researchers James Rogers, George Stoms, and James Phifer compiled a report that painstakingly analyzed 76 empirical studies on the psychological sequelae of abortion with respect to such factors as study type, demographics, reporting outcome, and methodological limitations. The authors conclude that "Both advocates and opponents of abortion can prove their points by judiciously referencing only articles supporting their political agenda" and cite their efforts as an aid to a "reliable method [for deciding] how much confidence to place in statements seemingly supported by quantitative references from this literature" (p. 370).

For further information and discussions on this issue, see the references cited under "Abortion Complications and Long-term Impact," above, plus the following (see Chapter 5 for additional information):

Adler, Nancy E., Henry P. David, Brenda N. Major, Susan H. Roth, Nancy F. Russo, and Gail E. Wyatt, "Psychological Responses after Abortion," published in *Science* (April 6, 1990): 41–44.

American Psychological Association, *Testimony on the Psychological Sequelae of Abortion* (Washington, DC: American Psychological Association, 1987).

Rogers, James L., George B. Stoms, and James L. Phifer, "Psychological Impact of Abortion: Methodological and Outcomes Summary of Empirical Research between 1966 and 1988," published in *Health Care for Women International*, 10 (1989): 347–376.

Overview of Embryonic and Fetal Development

1. Fertilization (2 weeks LMP)

This is the union of sperm and egg, which takes place around the middle of the menstrual cycle—about 2 weeks since the last menstrual period, or 2 weeks LMP—within one of the woman's Fallopian tubes. About 20 hours after a single sperm (out of several hundred million released during ejaculation) succeeds in penetrating the fertile ovum, the nuclei of the sperm and egg fuse, forming a single cell, called a zygote, which contains the full human complement of 46 chromosomes. About 12 hours later, the zygote begins to divide. As cell division continues, the zygote begins to travel down the tube toward the uterus. If it fails to reach the uterus, implanting instead in the Fallopian tube itself, an ectopic pregnancy results.

2. Implantation (3–4 weeks LMP)

About four or five days after fertilization, the still-dividing cells have formed a hollow, fluid-filled sphere called a blastocyst, which is about one-hundredth of an inch in diameter. The blastocyst floats around the uterine cavity for several days before attaching itself to the inner lining of the uterus. There it begins producing a hormone that signals the ovaries to make progesterone, which in turn signals the woman's pituitary that she is pregnant and stops the uterine lining from being shed through menstruation. By the twelfth day after fertilization, the dividing cells have begun to specialize: some of them will begin to form the embryo, while the rest will become the placenta. It is important to note that as many as four out of ten fertilized eggs never make it to this stage, and of those that do, many more will not survive much longer. For reasons not yet fully understood, it is estimated that at least 50 percent of fertilized eggs never fully develop into babies (this is not counting induced abortions).

3. Embryonic Development (5–8 weeks LMP)

At the start of the fifth week, the embryo is about one millimeter, or 78 thousandths of an inch, long. It floats in the embryonic sac, which is about two-thirds of an inch in diameter. Its cells have begun to differentiate and to form the rudiments of organs, bones, muscles, and blood vessels—a process known as organogenesis. The primitive streak, which will become the spine, forms.

By the end of the fifth week, the vertebrae, spinal cord, and nervous system are beginning to form, as is the brain. The tubular, S-shaped primitive heart has begun to beat, allowing the growing organism to circulate nutrients and waste products and exchange them through the placenta. Rudiments of eyes have formed. The embryo is now about one-quarter inch long. It has a separate blood system from its mother, to whom it is connected through the placenta.

During the sixth week, the head begins to form. The beating heart is still located outside the body. The intestinal tract starts to form from the mouth cavity downward. At this stage the embryo, which has a rudimentary tail, is visually indistinguishable from the embryos of many other species, including mice, chickens, pigs, and elephants.

By the end of the sixth week, the backbone is formed and the spinal cord has closed over. The brain is growing rapidly, but its neurons have not yet begun to form synapses, or connections, with one another. Tiny buds indicate the beginning of arms and legs, and depressions show where eyes and ears will form. Germ cells that will develop into either ovaries or testes have formed. The embryo is about one-half inch long.

By the end of the seventh week, the chest and abdomen have formed and the heart is now contained in the chest cavity. External ears are perceptible, and the face is starting to flatten. Big toes have appeared on the paddle-like feet. The tail is nearly gone. Lung buds have started to form, and the mouth opens. The embryo is about five-eighths of an inch long and weighs one-hundredth of an ounce; its heart beats about 150 times a minute.

During the eighth week, the face and features begin to form, along with the teeth and facial muscles. Rudimentary fingers and toes appear, and in male embryos the penis begins to appear as well. The cartilage and bone of the skeleton are beginning to form, and neurons are beginning to establish connections with one another through synapses. The fetus is now about three-quarters of an inch long and weighs three-hundredths of an ounce.

If even a small defect occurs during this stage of development, a miscarriage is likely to result.

4. Fetal Development (9–40 weeks LMP)

The growing organism is now referred to as a fetus. By the end of the ninth week its face is completely formed, and the arms, legs, hands, and feet are partially formed, with stubby toes and fingers. The eyes have developed lenses, corneas, and irises. If female, the fetus begins to develop a clitoris. The fetus is now recognizably human, looking much like a tiny infant. It is, however, structurally immature and functionally quite limited. It is a little over an inch long and weighs about one-tenth of an ounce.

During the tenth week, the eyes begin to move from the sides of the head to the front, and the face begins to look human. The heart is beginning to form four chambers, and major blood vessels are developed. The heart beats about 120 to 160 times per minute. The head is very large in proportion to the body. The number of synapses in the neural system increases rapidly, and the fetus begins to display reflexive movements such as hiccuping and moving its arms and legs. It is about 1.6 inches long.

At 13½ weeks, the arms, legs, hands, feet, fingers, toes, and ears are completely formed. Fingernails and toenails appear. External genital organs begin to differentiate. The fetus kicks, curls its toes, bends its arms, forms fists, squints closed eyes, and opens its mouth. It may swallow amniotic fluid and urinate. All of these movements, however, are reflexive; the brain is not yet well enough organized to control movements or form even the most basic perceptions. The fetus is now about three inches long and weighs one ounce.

At 18 weeks, the sex of the fetus is clearly distinguishable. The fetus's movements can be felt by the mother ("quickening") and the heartbeat can be heard with a stethoscope. The skin is covered with fine, downy hair, and eyebrows and eyelashes have begun to appear. The fetus is about 8.5 inches long and weighs 6 ounces.

At 20 to 22 weeks, the first synapses begin to form among neurons in the cortex, the part of the brain that deals with thought and perception. By 23 weeks, hair has begun to appear on the head. The fetus is about 12 inches long and weighs as much as a pound. A fetus born at this stage may live very briefly, but will almost certainly not survive, even with intensive care.

At 27 weeks, the skin is wrinkled and covered with a cheeselike secretion called vernix caseosa. The eyes are open. The neurons of the cortex begin to synapse with neurons in the thalamus and to develop the branchy structure characteristic of the adult brain. The brain wave patterns become more regular; over the next few weeks they will begin to resemble the waking and sleeping states of the adult brain. The fetus is now about 14 inches long and weighs about 2 pounds. If born at this stage, a fetus has a two-out-of-three chance of survival with expert care, although it may suffer moderate to severe abnormalities.

By the end of 32 weeks, the fetus is well enough developed so that, if born, it has an 85 percent chance of survival. It is about 16 inches long and weighs well over 3 pounds. Thereafter the chances of survival increase with each day of development.

At about 40 weeks, the fetus is ready to be born. Although it can now survive outside its mother with proper care, it will take months before the newborn's nervous system and brain have developed enough for it to sit up, several months more before it can stand and walk, and years before it can function and survive on its own.

References and suggestions for further reading (starred item is described in Chapter 5):

*Grobstein, Clifford, *Science and the Unborn: Choosing Human Futures* (New York: Basic Books, 1988).

Guttmacher, Alan, *Pregnancy, Birth and Family Planning*, rev. by Irwin H. Kaiser (New York: New American Library, 1987).

Nilsson, Lennart, *A Child Is Born* (New York: Delacorte Press, 1990). Excerpted in "The First Days of Creation," *Life*, Vol. 13, No. 10 (August 1990): 26–46.

Harassment of Abortion Providers

An increasing issue in the United States is the harassment of abortion providers, as some individuals and groups seek to decrease or stop abortion services by direct means. Besides legal tactics such as demonstrations, picketing, and "sidewalk counseling," an increasing number of clinics report such events as vandalism, death threats, and jamming of telephone lines. In addition, a number of clinics have sustained severe damage or even been destroyed by arson and bombings. In some cases these actions have succeeded in closing the facilities. In other cases, the actions have resulted in increased costs for security and legal services, increased need for security personnel, and problems in hiring staff.

Recent surveys of abortion providers by the Alan Guttmacher Institute (AGI) have included questions about anti-abortion activity. Tables 12 and 13 are based on 1985 data.

TABLE 12   Percentage of large nonhospital facilities (those providing 400 or more abortions) that experienced harassment in 1985, percentage of affected facilities reporting multiple episodes of harassment, and percentage of affected facilities reporting an increase over 1984, by type of activity

Type of activity	All facilities (N=501)	≥5 times	≥20 times	Increase from 1984
Picketing	80	82	68	50
Literature distributed inside facility	48	42	22	59
Bomb threats	48	15	3	58
Physical contact with or blocking of patients by picketers	47	62	34	56
Mass scheduling of no-show appointments	46	73	48	46
Demonstrations loud enough to be heard in patient areas	42	60	38	65
Invasion of facility by demonstrators	29	14	4	60
Vandalism	28	12	5	53
Jamming of telephone lines	22	54	41	66
Death threats	19	18	4	65
Tracing of patients' license plates	16	41	21	63
Picketing of homes of staff members	16	27	8	73

SOURCE: Jacqueline Darroch Forrest and Stanley K. Henshaw, "The Harassment of U.S. Abortion Providers," in *Abortion Services in the United States, Each State & Metropolitan Area, 1984–1985* (New York: Alan Guttmacher Institute, 1988), p. 29. © 1988 The Alan Guttmacher Institute.

Additionally, the National Abortion Federation has tracked successful and attempted bombings and arsons at abortion facilities since 1977. Table 14 shows a state-by-state breakdown of such activity, the estimated dollar amount of damage, and convictions resulting from the activity; Table 15 contains a summary of incidents of extreme violence for 1990.

Public Opinion and Abortion

Measuring public opinion about abortion is a difficult task, not only because of the intense emotionalism associated with the issue but also because of the problems in shaping questions so as to get objective results. Further, many so-called polls, such as "reader surveys" published by popular magazines, are methodologically flawed—the respondents are self-selected, rather than random, and there are no

TABLE 13   Percentage of large nonhospital facilities that reported anti-abortion harassment and, among those reporting harassment, average number of types of activity reported, by characteristic of facility, 1985

Characteristic	Percent	Number of types of activity	Characteristic	Percent	Number of types of activity
All facilities	88	5.0	**Percent of visits for abortions**		
Type			≥75	96	5.5
Clinic	92	5.3	50–74	87	5.7
MD's office	68	3.4	25–49	89	5.1
			10–24	85	4.5
Region			<10	68	3.1
Midwest	95	5.7			
South	93	5.4			
East	84	4.4			
West	76	4.3			

SOURCE: Jacqueline Darroch Forrest and Stanley K. Henshaw, "The Harassment of U.S. Abortion Providers," in *Abortion Services in the United States, Each State & Metropolitan Area, 1984–1985* (New York: Alan Guttmacher Institute, 1988), p. 29. © 1988 The Alan Guttmacher Institute.

safeguards against individuals submitting multiple responses, to mention just two problems.

Despite these difficulties, numerous attempts have been made to determine what Americans think and feel about abortion. At their most basic, most polls seem to indicate that a minority of people subscribe to either extreme viewpoint—about 12 to 15 percent believe abortion should be legal in all circumstances, and a similar number believe it should be illegal in all circumstances—while the majority are somewhere in the middle. Beyond these simplistic answers are many shades of subtlety and a host of surrounding issues, many related to basic values and outlooks. Dealing with such complexities is well beyond the scope of this book.

Readers who wish to pursue this path further are referred to the major polling organizations, including Gallup and Louis Harris and Associates, both of which have conducted opinion polls at various times regarding abortion. Another excellent source is the National Opinion Research Center (NORC) at the University of Chicago, which has asked questions on abortion as part of its General Social Survey (GSS) since 1972.

Gallup Organization
P.O. Box 628
Princeton, NJ 08542
(609) 924-9600

Louis Harris and Associates
630 Fifth Avenue
New York, NY 10020
(212) 975-1600

NORC
University of Chicago
1155 East Sixtieth Street
Chicago, IL 60637
(312) 702-1213; 702-1014; 702-1200

References

Adler, Nancy E., Henry P. David, Brenda N. Major, Susan H. Roth, Nancy F. Russo, and Gail E. Wyatt, "Psychological Responses after Abortion," published in *Science* (April 6, 1990): 41–44.

Centers for Disease Control, *Morbidity and Mortality Weekly Report: CDC Surveillance Summaries*, Vol. 39, No. SS-2 (June 1990).

Guttmacher, Alan, *Pregnancy, Birth and Family Planning*, rev. by Irwin H. Kaiser (New York: New American Library, 1987).

Hartmann, Betsy, *Reproductive Rights and Wrongs: The Global Politics of Population Control and Contraceptive Choice* (New York: Harper and Row, 1987).

Henshaw, Stanley K., "Induced Abortion: A World Review, 1990," *Family Planning Perspectives*, Vol. 22, No. 2 (March/April 1990): 76–89.

Hern, Warren, *Abortion Practice* (Philadelphia: J. B. Lippincott, 1984).

Hodgson, Jane, ed., *Abortion and Sterilization: Medical and Social Aspects* (London: Academic Press, 1981).

Jaffe, Frederick S., Barbara L. Lindheim, and Philip R. Lee, *Abortion Politics: Private Morality and Public Policy* (New York: McGraw-Hill, 1981).

Klitsch, Michael, *RU 486: The Science and the Politics* (New York: Alan Guttmacher Institute, 1989).

Lake, Alice, "The New French Pill," *McCalls* (March 1990): 58–63.

Ory, H. W., "Mortality Associated with Fertility and Fertility Control," *Family Planning Perspectives*, Vol. 15, No. 57 (1983).

Rogers, James L., George B. Stoms, and James L. Phifer, "Psychological Impact of Abortion: Methodological and Outcomes Summary of Empirical Research between 1966 and 1988," *Health Care for Women International*, Vol. 10 (1989): 347–376.

Smolowe, Jill, "Gagging the Clinics," *Time*, Vol. 37, No. 22 (June 3, 1991): 16–17.

Tietze, Christopher, and Stanley K. Henshaw, *Induced Abortion: A World Review, 1986* (New York: Alan Guttmacher Institute, 1986).

Tribe, Laurence H., *Abortion: The Clash of Absolutes* (New York: W. W. Norton and Company, 1990).

Ulmann, Andre, Georges Teutsch, and Daniel Philibert, "RU 486," *Scientific American*, Vol. 262, No. 6 (June 1990): 42–48.

TABLE 14   Anti-abortion violence: incidents of arsons, bombings, and attempts, 1977–1990

	Date	Name of Facility	Description of Incident	Estimated Damages	Convicted Perpetrator(s)
SOUTH					
ALABAMA					
Montgomery	12/87	Beacon Women's Center	Attempted arson. Molotov cocktail cracked window, caused smoke damage.	$500	
ARKANSAS					
Fayetteville	7/85	Fayetteville Women's Clinic	Arson. Damaged window frame and side walls. Previous picketing and break-ins.	$1,500	
FLORIDA					
Ocala	3/89	All Women's Health Center of Ocala	Arson. Partially destroyed clinic.	$60,000	
Ocala	4/89	All Women's Health Center of Ocala	Arson. Completely destroyed clinic. Second arson in one week. See 3/89 incident.	$190,000	
Ft. Myers	4/89	Ft. Myers Women's Health Center	Arson. Set at the same time as All Women's incident. Partially destroyed clinic.	$50,000	
Pensacola	5/88	Ladies Center	Attempted bomb. No damage.	None	Brockhoeft[1]
Pensacola	12/84	Ladies Center	Bomb. 3:30 AM.	$100,000	Goldsby, Simmons, Simmons & Wiggins[2]
Pensacola	12/84	West Florida Women's Clinic	Bomb. Destroyed building, 3:30 AM.	$225,000	Goldsby, Simmons, Simmons & Wiggins[2]
Pensacola	12/84	Office of Dr. Bagenholm	Bomb. Picketing prior to bombing, 3:30 AM.	$100,000	Goldsby, Simmons, Simmons & Wiggins[2]
Pensacola	6/84	Ladies Center	Bomb. Destroyed building, 3:50 AM.	$200,000	Goldsby, Simmons, Simmons & Wiggins[2]
St. Petersburg	3/84	Ladies Choice Clinic	Bomb. Destroyed clinic, 4:30 PM.	$60,000	
St. Petersburg	5/82	St. Petersburg Women's Health Center	Firebomb. Destroyed clinic. "Army of God" claimed responsibility.	$122,000	Anderson & Moore[3]
Clearwater	5/82	Bread and Roses Clinic	Arson. Fire and heavy smoke damage. "Army of God" claimed responsibility.	$340,000	Anderson & Moore[3]

TABLE 14   *continued*

	Date	Name of Facility	Description of Incident	Estimated Damages	Convicted Perpetrator(s)
GEORGIA					
Marietta	9/84	Planned Parenthood of Atlanta, Cobb County	**Firebomb. Device thrown through window, destroyed waiting room; extensive smoke damage. Clinic does not do abortions.**	$8,000	
Atlanta	9/84	Northside Family Planning	Bomb. Device thrown through window, damaged waiting room.	$5,000	
LOUISIANA					
New Orleans	1/89	Delta Women's Clinic	**Attempted bomb. Device set to explode at 11:30 AM. No warning by perpetrators to evacuate.**	None	
Baton Rouge	3/86	Acadian Women's Center	**Attempted arson.**	None	Braud, Jarreau, Cheshire & Newchurch[4]
Baton Rouge	10/85	Delta Women's Clinic-West	**Arson.** Damaged reception and waiting room, 3:00 AM. Burglar alarm had sounded at time of River City Woman's Clinic fire three days before.	$120,000	Cheshire & Newchurch[4]
Baton Rouge	10/85	River City Woman's Clinic	**Arson.** Destroyed clinic; 3:00 AM.	$300,000	Braud & Jarreau[4]
Baton Rouge	3/85	Delta Women's Clinic-West	**Attempted arson.** Building soaked with gasoline but did not ignite.	None	Cheshire & Newchurch[4]
NORTH CAROLINA					
Charlotte	10/85	Hallmark Clinic	**Arson.** Damaged supply room and sterilization area, 9:00 PM.	$75,000	
TEXAS					
Dallas	12/88	Metro-Plex GYN Group	**Arson. 1:00 AM.**	$2,000	
Dallas	12/88	Fairmount Center	**Arson. 1:00 AM.**	$75,000	
Dallas	12/88	North Dallas Women's Clinic	**Arson. 1:00 AM.**	$25,000	
Mesquite	2/85	Women's Clinic of Mesquite	**Arson.** Gasoline-Ignited fire destroyed entire shopping center, 10:30 PM. Two firefighters injured.	$1,500,000	
Houston	11/84	Alameda Medical Square	**Arson.** Extensive smoke damage to office of two doctors, one of whom works at abortion clinic next door, 9:40 AM.	$400,000	
Webster	9/84	Clear Lake Women's Center	**Arson.** Perpetrators entered through skylight, kicked in clinic wall.	$120,000	
Houston	9/84	Women's Outpatient Clinic	**Bomb.** Thrown through side window, destroyed front room, extensive smoke damage.	$10,000	
Houston	9/84	West Loop Clinic	**Bomb.** Molotov Cocktail thrown through side window.	$90,000	
Houston	8/84	Cyprus-Fairbanks Family Planning	**Arson.**	$30,000	

VIRGINIA

City	Date	Clinic	Description	Damage	Reference
Norfolk	2/84	Hillcrest Clinic	Attempted firebomb. Only one of seven pipe bombs exploded. Destroyed bank building windows. "Army of God" claimed responsibility.	$1,000	Bray, Shields & Spinks[5]
Norfolk	5/83	Hillcrest Clinic	Firebomb. Partially destroyed two procedure rooms and waiting area, 5:30 AM.	$250,000	Grace[6]

WEST

CALIFORNIA

City	Date	Clinic	Description	Damage	Reference
Concord	9/90	Planned Parenthood of Shasta Diablo	Arson. Fires, set to cover up burglary, destroyed one-third of clinic. Brian Martin has been charged in state court; proceedings delayed pending psychiatric evaluation.	$50,000	
Redding	10/89	Redding Feminist Women's Health Center	Arson. Fire started in crawlspace under building, damaging floor and melting pipes. Liquid from the burst pipes extinguished the fire. Local investigators determined that the fire was deliberately set.	$7,000	
Long Beach	10/88	Women's Family Planning Abortion Counseling Clinic	Arson. Shannon Taylor charged in state court after confessing to 6/88 and 10/88 arson incidents in Long Beach.	$70,000	
Long Beach	6/88	Women's Family Planning Abortion Counseling Clinic	Attempted arson. See 10/88 Long Beach incident for details.		
San Diego	7/87	Family Planning Associates — Alvarado Medical Center	Attempted bomb.	None	Owens, Kreipel, Sullenger, Sullenger, Harmon, Harmon & Svelmoe[7]
Riverside	12/86	Planned Parenthood of San Diego and Riverside Counties	Arson. Fire started in kitchen; clinic partially destroyed.	$75,000	Tipps[8]
San Diego	3/85	Birth Control Institute	Bomb. Molotov Cocktail thrown through lobby window.	$10,000	Cameron[9]
Pomona	2/85	Planned Parenthood of Los Angeles, Pomona Chapter	Attempted bomb. Device improperly made.	None	
Santa Ana	12/84	Planned Parenthood of Orange County	Attempted arson. Set outside building; clinic does not do abortions.	Minimal	
Eureka	11/84	Planned Parenthood Assoc. of Humboldt County	Attempted arson. 8:00 AM.	Minimal	
Eureka	10/84	Planned Parenthood Assoc. of Humboldt County	Attempted arson. Box of debris ignited at back of clinic.	None	
San Diego	9/84	Birth Control Institute	Bomb. 4:00 AM.	$125,000	

TABLE 14 *continued*

Date	Name of Facility	Description of Incident	Estimated Damages	Convicted Perpetrator(s)
COLORADO				
1/82	Boulder Valley Clinic	**Attempted arson.**	Minimal	
OREGON				
5/90	Lovejoy Surgicenter	**Arson.** Gasoline poured through window and ignited. Daniel J. Carver, indicted by the state on 6/1/90, is a fugitive as of 12/31/90.	$15,000	
12/85	Portland Feminist Women's Health Ctr.	**Package bomb.** Designed to explode when opened, intercepted at PFWHC; similar packages found at Post Office addressed to three other centers. See below.	None	
12/85	Bours Health Center	**Attempted package bomb.** Intercepted at local post office.[10]	None	
12/85	Planned Parenthood Assoc.	**Attempted package bomb.** Intercepted at local post office.[10]	None	
12/85	Lovejoy Surgi-Center	**Attempted package bomb.** Intercepted at local post office.[10]	None	
8/85	Lovejoy Surgi-Center	**Bomb.** Exploded outside concrete building.	Minimal	
5/84	Bours Birth & Surgery Center	**Attempted arson.** Two devices attached to outside of building.	$1,000	
12/82	Lovejoy Surgi-Center	**Attempted firebomb.** Molotov Cocktail thrown through window. Second attempt failed the following week.	$500	
WASHINGTON				
1/88	Planned Parenthood of Everett	**Attempted arson.**	None	
4/84	Everett Feminist Women's Health Center	**Arson.** Gasoline-ignited, 9:40 PM.	$50-75,000	Beseda[11]
3/84	Everett Feminist Women's Health Center	**Arson.** Damaged counseling room, 2:58 AM.	$10,000	Beseda[11]
3/84	Bellingham Family Practice	**Firebomb.** Extensive smoke damage, previous vandalism. 8:30 PM.	$70,000	Beseda[11]
12/83	Everett Feminist Women's Health Center	**Firebomb.**	$40,000	Beseda[11]

Note: The state names COLORADO, OREGON, and WASHINGTON appear with city names Boulder; Portland (Portland, Forest Grove, Portland, Portland, Portland, Forest Grove, Portland); and Everett (Everett, Everett, Bellingham, Everett) respectively.

MIDWEST

ILLINOIS

City	Date	Clinic	Incident	Damage	Suspect
Rockford	1/87	Northern Illinois Women's Center	Arson. Door burned.	Minimal	Holman[12]
Rockford	12/86	Northern Illinois Women's Center	Arson.	Minimal	Holman[12]
Rockford	11/86	Northern Illinois Women's Center	Arson.	Minimal	Holman[12]
Rockford	10/86	Northern Illinois Women's Center	Arson.	Minimal	Holman[12]
Rockford	5/86	Northern Illinois Women's Center	Attempted arson.	None	Holman[12]
Granite City	4/85	Hope Clinic for Women	Attempted arson. Guard alerted police who made arrest.	None	Lanning[13]
Granite City	1/82	Hope Clinic for Women	Arson. Extensive damage.	Unavailable	

INDIANA

City	Date	Clinic	Incident	Damage	Suspect
Fort Wayne	11/90	Fort Wayne Women's Health Organization	Arson. Damage confined to stairs by fire doors.	$10,000	
Indianapolis	2/87	Clinic for Women	Attempted bomb. Local antiabortion activist tried for soliciting others to commit act.	None	Kefauver[14]

IOWA

City	Date	Clinic	Incident	Damage	Suspect
Iowa City	6/78	Emma Goldman Clinic for Women	Firebomb.	Unavailable	

KANSAS

City	Date	Clinic	Incident	Damage	Suspect
Kansas City	1/90	Aid for Women	Attempted Arson.	None	
Wichita	6/86	Women's Health Care Services	Bomb. Placed in clinic doorway. Exploded close to midnight.	$100,000	Two Juveniles

MICHIGAN

City	Date	Clinic	Incident	Damage	Suspect
Kalamazoo	9/89	Planned Parenthood Kalamazoo	Bomb. Moderate damage.	$5,000	
Lathrup Village	12/86	Women's Care Clinic	Attempted bomb. Device found in dumpster.	None	
Kalamazoo	12/86	Planned Parenthood Kalamazoo	Arson. Completely destroyed clinic.	$750,000	
Saginaw	4/81	Women's Health Services	Arson. Limited to hallway.	$30,000	

TABLE 14 *continued*

	Date	Name of Facility	Description of Incident	Estimated Damages	Convicted Perpetrator(s)
MINNESOTA					
St. Paul	10/87	Planned Parenthood of Minnesota	Attempted arson. Gasoline poured on grounds and ignited.	$1,500	
Robbinsdale	9/87	The Robbinsdale Clinic	Arson. Flammable liquid thrown through window.	$5,000	
St. Paul	9/87	Planned Parenthood of Minnesota	Attempted bomb. Device found on roof.	None	
St. Paul	9/87	Planned Parenthood of Minnesota	Attempted bomb. Device found smouldering outside building.	None	
Minneapolis	1/87	Midwest Health Center for Women	Arson. Suspect Mark J. Bundlle confessed. Declared incompetent to stand trial. Committed to state institution indefinitely.	$1,500	
Minneapolis	10/81	Meadowbrook Women's Clinic	Attempted bomb. Man entered with bomb in briefcase and was arrested.	None	
St. Paul	2/77	Planned Parenthood Clinic	Arson. Destroyed administrative floor above clinic. Water and smoke damage in clinic.	$250,000	
MISSOURI					
Independence	12/89	Planned Parenthood of Greater Kansas City	Bomb. 4:00 AM. Extensive damage to a contraceptive clinic.	$100,000	Filley & Spohr[15]
Manchester	6/86	Reproductive Health Services	Arson.	$100,000	
NEBRASKA					
Omaha	8/77	Ladies Clinic	Arson.	$35,000	
NORTH DAKOTA					
Fargo	8/87	Fargo Women's Health Organization	Arson. Unnamed juvenile also being charged in state court.	$500	Garman[16]
OHIO					
Toledo	6/87	Toledo Medical Services	Arson. Pro-Life Action Network activist Marjorie Reed awaiting trial for 6/87 (Toledo Medical Services), 5/86 (Center for Choice) and 10/89 (North Jersey Women's Health) incidents.[17]	$1,000	

City	Date	Facility	Incident	Damage	Perpetrator
Toledo	3/87	Toledo Medical Services	**Attempted arson.**	None	
Cincinnati	2/87	Margaret Sanger Center	**Attempted bomb.**	None	
Toledo	5/86	Center for Choice	**Arson.** Extensive damage. 5:00 AM. Pro–Life Action Network activist Marjorie Reed awaiting trial. See 6/87 incident above.[17]	$200,000	
Cincinnati	2/87	Margaret Sanger Center	**Attempted bomb.**	None	
Toledo	12/85	Toledo Medical Services	**Arson.** Damage from fire and smoke. 1:30 AM.	$20,000	
Cincinnati	12/85	Margaret Sanger Center of Planned Parenthood Assoc. of Cincinnati	**Arson.** Gutted surgery floor. Followed major demonstration organized by Americans Against Abortion.	$100,000+	
Cincinnati	12/85	Women's Center of Cincinnati	**Arson.**	$100,000	
Toledo	8/85	Toledo Medical Services	**Arson.** Gasoline-ignited fire damaged procedure room. Burglar alarm sounded at 5:09 AM, fire alarm at 5:14.	Unavailable	
Columbus	2/85	Founder's Clinic	**Attempted bomb.** Device malfunctioned.	None	
Columbus	6/78	Founder's Clinic	**Firebomb.** Device tossed through window of clinic.	Unavailable	
Akron	2/78	Akron Women's Clinic	**Arson.** Fire set in bathroom off reception area; staff and three patients present.	Unavailable	
Cincinnati	2/78	Women for Women of Cincinnati, Inc.	**Chemical bomb.** Device thrown into clinic.	$3,000	
Columbus	2/78	Northwest Women's Center	**Arson.**	$200,000	
Cleveland	2/78	Concerned Women's Clinic	**Arson.** Perpetrator entered during open hours when clinic was full of patients; blinded technician with chemical and set fire. Clinic destroyed.	Unavailable	
Cincinnati	11/77	Margaret Sanger Clinic	**Attempted firebomb.** Device hit outside of air conditioner and failed to explode.	None	
Cincinnati	11/77	Planned Parenthood of Cincinnati	**Arson.**	$4,000	

MID-ATLANTIC

DELAWARE

City	Date	Facility	Incident	Damage	Perpetrator
Dover	1/84	Reproductive Care Center	**Arson.** Clinic destroyed. 7:30 AM.	$100,000	Bray, Shields & Spinks[5]

MARYLAND

City	Date	Facility	Incident	Damage	Perpetrator
Annapolis	7/84	Planned Parenthood of Maryland	**Bomb.** Extensive damage. 1:00 AM.	$50,000	Bray, Shields & Spinks[5]

TABLE 14   *continued*

	Date	Name of Facility	Description of Incident	Estimated Damages	Convicted Perpetrator(s)
NEW JERSEY					
Fairfield	10/89	North Jersey Women's Health	**Attempted arson.** Pro-Life Action Network activist Marjorie Reed awaiting trail on this and two additional incidents in Toledo, Ohio (5/89 & 6/87).[17]	$5,000	
Cherry Hill	10/82	Cherry Hill Women's Clinic	**Arson.** Gas thrown through window and ignited. Clinic destroyed.	Unavailable	
PENNSYLVANIA					
Pittsburgh	9/89	Allegheny Reproductive Health Services	**Arson.** "Army of God" claimed responsibility.	$10,000	
WASHINGTON, DC METROPOLITAN AREA					
Washington, DC	1/85	Hillcrest Women's Surgi-Center	**Bomb.** Extensive damage to clinic and broke 250 windows in buildings across street. 12:00 AM.	$100,000	Bray, Shields & Spinks[5]
Suitland, MD	12/84	Metropolitan Family Planning	**Bomb.** Damaged hair salon and IRS office, no damage to clinic on 5th floor. 4:26 AM.	$100–200,000	Bray, Shields & Spinks[5]
Wheaton, MD	11/84	Metro Medical and Women's Center	**Firebomb.** Clinic destroyed. Covenant Life Christian Community pickets every Saturday.	$300,000	Bray, Shields & Spinks[5]
Rockville, MD	11/84	Planned Parenthood Randolph Medical Clinic	**Bomb.** 6:30 AM.	$50,000	Bray, Shields & Spinks[5]
Washington, DC	11/84	American Civil Liberties Union	**Small bomb.** Damaged door and wall. Employee present.	Minimal	Bray, Shields & Spinks[5]
Washington, DC	7/84	National Abortion Federation	**Propane bomb.** Extensive damage. Second bomb attached. 11:50 PM.	$40,000	Bray, Shields & Spinks[5]
Hyattsville, MD	2/84	Prince George's County Reproductive Health Services	**Firebomb.** "Army of God" claimed responsibility. 1:30 AM.	$100,000	Bray, Shields & Spinks[5]
Arlington, VA	6/82	Arlington-Fairfax Medical Clinic	**Pipe bombs.** Exploded when door of clinic was opened. Extensive damage. "Army of God" claimed responsibility.	$18,000+	Anderson[18]

NORTHEAST

MASSACHUSETTS

City	Date	Facility	Description	Damage	Reference
Worcester	9/90	Planned Parenthood of Central Massachusetts	Arson. 6:30 AM. Man shattered clinic door, fled when spotted by cleaning woman. Left ignited molotov cocktail, and material for two more bombs.	$500	
Boston	7/83	New England Women's Services & Co.	Firebomb. Destroyed clinic, 3:00 AM.	Unavailable	

NEW HAMPSHIRE

City	Date	Facility	Description	Damage	Reference
Concord	7/89	Concord Feminist Women's Health Center	Arson. Damaged files on eight-year research project on cervical cap. 2:00 AM.	$5,000+	

NEW YORK

City	Date	Facility	Description	Damage	Reference
Syracuse	5/90	Planned Parenthood	Arson. Small fire started at building's foundation. Shari DiNicola, arrested on site and indicted, is awaiting trial on state charges for three Syracuse incidents.	$1,000	
Syracuse	5/90	Planned Parenthood	Attempted Arson. See above.	Minimal	
Syracuse	5/90	Planned Parenthood	Attempted Arson. See above.	Minimal	
New York	12/86	Planned Parenthood of New York City	Attempted bomb. Perpetrator handcuffed realtor in building, then left bomb with 15 sticks of dynamite in clinic. Realtor escaped. Extensive damage from sprinkler system.	$30,000	[Malvasi, Cenera, Wright & Pryor][19]
Queens	11/86	Women's Medical Office	Attempted bomb. Two sticks of dynamite and a timing device were found under cushion in waiting room.	None	Malvasi, Cenera, Wright & Pryor[19]
New York	10/86	Eastern Women's Center	Bomb. Exploded in waiting room. Two passersby injured. 1:30 AM.	$15,000	Malvasi, Cenera, Wright & Pryor[19]
New York	12/85	Manhattan Women's Medical Center	Bomb. Exploded in clinic bathroom during office hours. Police had been alerted; evacuated clinic minutes before explosion.	Minimal	[Malvasi, Cenera, Wright & Pryor][19]
Coram	10/85	Coram Women's Center	Bomb. Device thrown through window, damaged reception and record-keeping area. Clinic on 2nd floor of 3-story office building. 6:00 AM.	Unavailable	
Hempstead	2/79	Bill Baird Clinic	Arson. During business hours; perpetrator injured; later found not guilty by reason of insanity.	$100,000+	

VERMONT

City	Date	Facility	Description	Damage	Reference
Burlington	5/78	Vermont Women's Health Center	Firebomb. Damage to front porch and door.	Unavailable	
Burlington	5/77	Vermont Women's Health Center	Arson. Destroyed building.	Unavailable	

TABLE 14   *continued*

CANADA

Date	Name of Facility	Description of Incident	Estimated Damages	Convicted Perpetrator(s)
QUEBEC				
Montreal				
7/83	Morgentaler Clinic	Firebomb. Destroyed bookstore below clinic.	Unavailable	

[1] JOHN BROCKHOEFT. Sentenced to 30 months prison, 3 months probation, and $150 in fines for 5/88 bombing attempt in Pensacola, FL.

[2] MATTHEW GOLDSBY and JAMES SIMMONS. Arrested but not prosecuted for 6/84 bombing; convicted in U.S. District Court for Christmas day bombings in Pensacola: sentenced to 10 years, $353,073 in fines. KATHREN SIMMONS and KAYE WIGGINS. Convicted in U.S. District Court for conspiracy: sentenced to 5 years probation, $2,000 in fines.

[3] DON BENNY ANDERSON and MATTHEW MOORE. Pled guilty and convicted in state court: sentenced to 30 years to be served consecutively with 30-year sentence for kidnapping and extortion of abortion doctor in Granite City, IL.

[4] BRENT PAUL BRAUD, DERRICK JAMES JARREAU, CHARLES ALBERT CHESHIRE, and JOHN DAVID NEWCHURCH. Convicted in U.S. District Court after pleading guilty to conspiracy charges. Braud and Jarreau sentenced to 2 years and $50 special assessment. Newchurch sentenced to 5 years subject to review after psychiatric exam. Cheshire sentenced to 5 years and $314,000 in restitution.

[5] MICHAEL BRAY. Convicted in U.S. District Court, sentenced to 10 years and ordered to pay $43,782 in restitution. Conviction overturned in November 1986 on a jury selection technicality. In subsequent charges and plea bargaining, sentenced to 6 years, with credit for time served. Paroled in 1989 after serving 3 years. KENNETH SHIELDS and THOMAS SPINKS. Pled guilty to conspiracy, convicted in U.S. District Court, sentenced to 2 and 15 years respectively. Spinks ordered to pay $55,000 in restitution.

[6] JOSEPH GRACE. Convicted in state court, sentenced to 10-20 years.

[7] REVEREND DORMAN OWENS, JOANN KREIPEL, CHERYL SULLENGER, RANDY SULLENGER, CHRIS HARMON, ROBIN HARMON, ERIC SVELMOE. Sentenced, respectively, to: 21 months; 15 months; 3 years; 18 months; 5 years; 1 year; and 149 days with 5 years probation; for conspiracy in 7/87 attempted bombing in San Diego, CA.

[8] FREDERICK GORDON TIPPS. Pled guilty to conspiracy, convicted in U.S. District Court, sentenced to 10-20 years.

[9] SHANE CAMERON. Arrested for 3/85 bombing in San Diego, CA; convicted on unrelated arson.

[10]RICHARD DUANE BATSON. Convicted and sentenced on another bombing charge. Circumstantial evidence linking Batson to the three December 1985 package-mail bomb attempts in Portland and Forest Grove, Oregon was presented but the charges were dropped.

[11]CURTIS BESEDA. Convicted in U.S. District Court: sentenced to 2 consecutive 10-year terms and 5 years probation; ordered to pay $295,000 restitution.

[12]DAVID HOLMAN. Pled guilty, sentenced to 18 months imprisonment and 3 years probation.

[13]WILLIAM H. LANNING. Pled guilty and convicted in U.S. District Court: serving 10 years.

[14]WALTER KAFAUVER. Sentenced to 5 years for attempted solicitation to commit bombing. Following 90 day psychiatric investigation, sentence reduced to 90 days time served and $1,500 fine.

[15]JASON FILLEY and DAVID SPOHR. Both 17 at the time of the incident, they confessed to arson of Planned Parenthood of Greater Kansas City, MO. They could be charged as adults under Missouri law for the Planned Parenthood arson. Convicted of felony arson, Filley and Spohr were sentenced to 5 years. They served 3 months during the summer of 1990, are serving the remainder on probation.

[16]SCOTT GARMAN. Sentenced to 2 months in prison, 2 years probation and $215 in fines for 8/87 arson in Fargo, North Dakota.

[17]MARJORIE REED. Pro-Life Action Network activist was convicted and sentenced to the maximum penalty of 10 years imprisonment for assaulting a federal officer with her car. Currently awaiting trial for three clinic arson incidents (5/86 & 6/87 in Toledo, Ohio, and 10/89 in Fairfield, New Jersey).

[18]DON BENNY ANDERSON. Convicted in U.S. District Court: sentenced to 12 years to be served consecutively with other sentence.

[19]DENNIS JOHN MALVASI. Pled guilty to planting explosives, sentenced to 7 years. Others sentenced in connection with preparation or transport of explosives were: CARL CENERA pled guilty, sentenced to 3 years; FRANK WRIGHT, JR. pled guilty, sentenced to 2 years; DONALD C. PRYOR, JR. pled guilty, died prior to sentencing. [Bracketed incidents: charges on these incidents were dropped in connection with plea bargains and convictions on other New York incidents.]

*NAF wishes to thank the Federal Bureau of Alcohol, Tobacco & Firearms (BATF) for its assistance in compiling this data.

SOURCE: National Abortion Federation. Reprinted with the permission of the National Abortion Federation. Copyright 1991.

TABLE 15   Summary of extreme violence—1990

```
ARSON......................................4
BOMB ......................................0
ATTEMPTED ARSON/BOMB.......................4
SEVERE VANDALISM  (see reverse)...........8
ASSAULT.......... (see reverse)...........1

TOTAL # OF EXTREME INCIDENTS.............17
```

ARSON AND BOMBING INCIDENTS - REPORTED 1990

DATE	FACILITY	CITY/STATE	INCIDENT	ESTIMATED $ DAMAGE
1/90	Aid For Women	Kansas City, KS	1 attempted arson	0
5/90	Lovejoy Surgicenter	Portland, OR	1 arson	$ 15,000
5/90	Planned Parenthood of Syracuse	Syracuse, NY	1 arson; 2 attempted arsons	570
9/90	Planned Parenthood of Central Mass.	Worcester, MA	1 attempted bombing	500
9/90	Planned Parenthood of Shasta Diablo	Concord, CA	1 arson	90,000
11/90	Fort Wayne Women's Health Organization	Fort Wayne, IN	1 arson	10,000

```
                                TOTAL:    $116,070
               TOTAL FROM OTHER SIDE:       72,900

          TOTAL $ DAMAGE TO CLINICS - -   $188,970
```

TABLE 15   *continued*

OTHER INCIDENTS OF SERIOUS VIOLENCE - REPORTED 1990

DATE	FACILITY	CITY/STATE	INCIDENT	ESTIMATED $ DAMAGE
1/90	Memphis Center for Reproductive Health	Memphis, TN	concrete block thrown through window	$ 3,000
5/90	West End Women's Medical Group	Reno, NV	antichoice slogans painted on wall; stairs destroyed	1,400
5/90	Allegheny Reproductive Health Service	Pittsburgh, PA	roof of clinic damaged with ax	50,000
6/90	Planned Parenthood of Minnesota	St. Paul, MN	director assaulted at clinic	Unavailable
7/90	Atlanta Surgi Center	Atlanta, GA	noxious chemical poured into ventilation system	2,000
10/90	Women's Health Services	Pittsburgh, PA	noxious chemical flushed into clinic with water from floor above	12,000
10/90	Northeast Women's Center	Phila., PA	safety glass on front door broken	1,500
12/90	Women's Pavilion	South Bend, IN	roof vandalized	3,000*
			TOTAL:	$72,900

*preliminary estimate

See NAF's Violence and Disruption Fact Sheet for more information and totals of all incidents.

TABLE 15   *continued*

INCIDENTS OF VIOLENCE & DISRUPTION AGAINST ABORTION PROVIDERS

VIOLENCE: (# of Incidents)	1977-83	1984	1985	1986	1987	1988	1989	1990	TOTAL
BOMBING	8	18	4	2	0	0	2	0	34
ARSON	13	6	8	7	4	4	6	4	52
ATTEMPTED BOMBING OR ARSON	5	6	10	5	8	3	2	4	43
INVASION	68	34	47	53	14	6	25	19	266
VANDALISM	35	35	49	43	29	29	24	25	269
ASSAULT & BATTERY	11	7	7	11	5	5	12	6	64
DEATH THREAT	4	23	22	7	5	4	5	7	77
KIDNAPPING	2	0	0	0	0	0	0	0	2
BURGLARY	3	2	2	5	7	1	0	2	22
TOTAL #INCIDENTS REPORTED	149	131	149	133	72	52	76	67	829

NOTE: Statistics represent incidents reported to NAF: actual number may be higher.

TABLE 15   *continued*

INCIDENTS OF VIOLENCE & DISRUPTION AGAINST ABORTION PROVIDERS (cont.)

DISRUPTION: (# of Clinics)	1977-83	1984	1985	1986	1987	1988	1989	1990	TOTAL
HATE MAIL & HARASSING CALLS	9	17	32	53	32	19	30	21	--
BOMB THREATS	9	32	75	51	28	21	21	11	--
PICKETING	107	160	139	141	77	151	72	45	--
CLINIC BLOCKADES*									
# Clinics	0	0	0	0	2	138	103	21	--
# Incidents	0	0	0	0	2	182	201	34	419
# Arrests	0	0	0	0	290	11732	12358	1363	26357

*   "CLINIC BLOCKADES" are protests during which groups of demonstrators physically block the doors to reproductive healthcare facilities to prevent patient access.

Despite claims to be nonviolent, many "blockaders" are arrested for assault, trespass and invasion. NOTE: The "# Arrests" represents the total number of arrests, not the total number of persons arrested -- many blockaders are arrested repeatedly.

NOTE: Due to clinic duplication, totals for "# Clinics" are not applicable. Statistics represent incidents reported to NAF: actual number may be higher.

SOURCE: National Abortion Federation. Reprinted with the permission of the National Abortion Federation. Copyright 1991.

4

Directory of Organizations

Alan Guttmacher Institute
111 Fifth Avenue
New York, NY 10003
(212) 254-5656; FAX (212) 254-9891

The Alan Guttmacher Institute (AGI) is an independent, nonprofit corporation that performs research, public policy analysis, and public education related to reproductive health issues. AGI's underlying goal is to "enhance and defend the reproductive rights of all women and men, with particular attention to and concern for those who may be disadvantaged because of age, race, poverty, education or geographical location." The institute seeks to provide information and influence public policies and attitudes in order to:

Prevent unplanned, unwanted pregnancies

Achieve wanted pregnancies

Preserve the freedom to terminate unwanted pregnancies

Preserve women's health and well-being throughout pregnancy and childbirth

Ensure the birth of healthy infants

AGI conducts research and disseminates information both in the United States and abroad; it is probably the primary source for statistical and factual information on reproductive health issues, including abortion.

PUBLICATIONS: *Family Planning Perspectives,* a bimonthly journal; *International Family Planning Perspectives,* a quarterly journal that includes Spanish- and French-language summaries of each article; *Washington Memo,* a biweekly newsletter analyzing federal policy developments; *State Reproductive Health*

Monitor, a quarterly compilation of state legislation related to reproductive health. Books and other materials on reproductive health issues include *Abortion and Women's Health: A Turning Point for America?,* a look at the effects of current and potential state restrictions on abortion; *Abortion Services in the United States, Each State & Metropolitan Area, 1987–1988,* which includes information on government funding, availability of services, abortion rates, patient characteristics, and clinic harassment; *Induced Abortion, A World Review: 1986* and *Induced Abortion, A World Review: 1990 Supplement,* the "single most authoritative source of information on worldwide abortion services, laws and policies"; plus fact sheets and public policy analyses. Call or write for catalog.

Alternatives to Abortion International/Women's Health and Education Foundation
1213½ S. James Road
Columbus, OH 43227-1801
(614) 239-9433

Alternatives to Abortion International/Women's Health and Education Foundation (AAI/WHEF) is a federation of emergency pregnancy centers and individuals dedicated to offering alternatives to abortion through "education, action and creative services." Affiliates include pregnancy service centers, residential centers, hotlines, and support services, including post-abortion support and counseling services. AAI/WHEF offers its affiliates and members the following:

An annual academy featuring a variety of speakers and workshops on topics of interest to service providers

Networking opportunities

An information clearinghouse, with a continuously updated list of brochures, educational handouts, manuals, posters, etc.

Consulting services

Certificates of affiliation

A periodically updated directory of organizations worldwide offering alternatives to abortion

AAI/WHEF also responds to requests from the public for educational material on abortion alternatives.

Membership is $35.00 per year.

PUBLICATION: *Heartbeat,* quarterly newsletter (included with membership).

American Academy of Pro-Life Pediatricians
2160 First Avenue
Maywood, IL 60153
(312) 531-3334

The American Academy of Pro-Life Pediatricians (AAPP) is composed of members of the American Academy of Pediatrics who have organized to promote the awareness of pro-life issues, including those related to abortion, defective newborn children, sterilization of the retarded, and "threats to family integrity and freedom" among medical professionals whose practice is devoted to the care of children. AAPP, which supports the position that human life should be protected from the moment of conception, currently has about 510 members.

PUBLICATIONS: Position papers "Abortion and Personhood" and "Clarification of the Goals Statement Re: 'Every Child Should Be Born Wanted.'"

American Association of Pro Life Obstetricians and Gynecologists
4701 N. Federal Highway, Suite B4
Ft. Lauderdale, FL 33308-4663
(305) 771-9242; (305) 772-1853

The American Association of Pro Life Obstetricians and Gynecologists was founded in 1973 by Dr. Matthew J. Bulfin to "meet the needs of women who were pregnant and who did not want to have their babies delivered by doctors who performed or arranged abortions." The organization also works to educate the public about abortion and to "persuade our pro-abortion colleagues to return with us to the traditional role of the obstetrician, protecting both the mother and her unborn, perfect or imperfect." Membership is open to all physicians who are either members of the American College of Obstetricians and Gynecologists (ACOG) or Board Certified or Board Eligible by the American Board of Obstetricians and Gynecologists. Once elected, members agree not to perform abortions or to promote abortions either directly or indirectly. The association meets once each year, usually in conjunction with the annual ACOG meeting. Dues are $50.00 per year; retired members pay $10.00 and residents pay $5.00 a year.

American Civil Liberties Union
Reproductive Freedom Project
132 W. 43rd Street
New York, NY 10036
(212) 944-9800, ext. 515; FAX (212) 730-4652

The Reproductive Freedom Project (ACLU-RFP) is a special project of the American Civil Liberties Union, with its own staff of attorneys, paralegals, and support personnel. Its goal is to protect the constitutional right of privacy, particularly with regard to issues of reproductive choice, including "the right to choose between childbirth and abortion; the right to obtain and use contraceptives regardless of age; and the right to choose between sterilization and fertility." The project pursues its goals through:

> Public education, including sponsorship of and participation in conferences, meetings, and rallies; media campaigns; public speeches, articles, and media interviews by staff attorneys; research projects; and pro bono training programs

> Legislative advocacy at the state and federal levels, including technical assistance; development of model briefing papers, analyses, and strategies for countering anti-abortion arguments

> Litigation, including blocking the implementation of federal, state, and local laws and federal administrative actions designed to restrict access to reproductive rights; providing legal and technical assistance for attorneys and organizations litigating reproductive rights cases; filing of and coordination of amicus curiae briefs; and presentation of arguments in state and federal Supreme Court cases

An important focus of the ACLU-RFP is building coalitions with organizations and individuals who are forwarding the women of color reproductive rights movement.

PUBLICATIONS: *Reproductive Rights Update,* biweekly newsletter; *Legal Docket,* annual summary of issues and status of current reproductive rights cases; *Reproductive Freedom: The Rights of Minors,* briefing paper; *Parental Notice Laws: Their Catastrophic Impact on Teenagers' Right to Abortion,* pamphlet; and *The Case against a Constitutional Convention on Abortion,* pamphlet; plus a video, *In Defense of Roe,* showing highlights of the 1990 conference "In Defense of Roe," a cooperative project of the ACLU Reproductive Freedom Project and its Women of Color partnership program.

American College of Obstetricians and Gynecologists (ACOG)
409 12th Street, SW
Washington, DC 20024-2188
(202) 638-5577

With more than 29,000 members—approximately 90 percent of American obstetricians and gynecologists—ACOG is the leading organization for medical professionals involved in women's health care. ACOG concentrates its efforts in four major areas: (1) serving as an advocate for quality health care for women; (2) maintaining high standards of clinical practice and continuing education for its members; (3) promoting patient education and stimulating patient understanding of, and involvement in, medical care; and (4) increasing awareness among its members and the public of the changing issues facing women's health care. ACOG supports legal, safe, readily available, publicly funded abortion services for all women who desire them and works actively toward this end, including working to educate legislators and other government officials and filing amicus curiae briefs. To qualify for ACOG membership, physicians must be certified by the American Board of Obstetrics and Gynecology, must have limited their practice to obstetrics and gynecology for at least five years, and must demonstrate high moral and ethical standards.

PUBLICATIONS: *Public Health Policy Implications of Abortion: A Government Relations Handbook for Health Professionals* (1990), a "resource document designed to assist the health professional in responding to new legislative and public policy initiatives on abortion"; also "Important Medical Facts about Induced Abortion," patient education brochure.

American Collegians for Life (ACL)
P.O. Box 1112
Washington, DC 20013

Established in 1987, American Collegians for Life currently boasts 600 affiliate groups around the country. The only requirement for membership is to be a pro-life college student. ACL supports the "right to life from conception through natural death." ACL's goals are:

To network and unify existing campus pro-life groups

To help members start new groups

To help organize state and regional networks of pro-life college students and groups

To provide experience, educational, and support resources to educate all college students on pro-life issues

Dues are $5.00 per year.

PUBLICATIONS: *VITA,* a monthly newsletter; "Project Manuals" with how-to information on starting a state network, public relations, recruiting new members, and other activities; and an educational reprint series.

American Life League, Inc.
P.O. Box 1350
Stafford, VA 22554-1350
(703) 659-4171

Lobbying office:
Director of Legislative Affairs
American Life Lobby
1 Farragut Square, NW, 9th Floor
Washington, DC 20006
(202) 347-5394

American Life League (ALL) was founded in the late 1970s by Judie Brown, who felt that most pro-life organizations had failed to "attack the anti-life ethic at its roots rather than battle its symptoms." Following Judie's vision, ALL has grown into an umbrella organization that includes a full range of educational, research, and political activities. ALL's primary focus is on educating the public on "life issues," among them abortion, contraception, euthanasia, school-based clinics, and medical ethics, including the treatment of handicapped newborns. To promote its "no-compromise" message, ALL produces and distributes a wide variety of publications, conducts training seminars, and is involved in a variety of other activities including nonviolent protests at abortion clinics, "sidewalk counseling," crisis pregnancy counseling, post-abortion counseling, and adoption referrals. ALL and its affiliate groups have a membership of 250,000. Affiliate groups include:

> American Life League Advocates, a legal research and advisory group

> American Life League Affiliates, which consists of local and state groups involved in various pro-life activities

> Athletes for Life, an organization of professional athletes

> Castello Institute of Stafford, a research and educational group that has published numerous studies and "refutations of pro-death literature"

> Executives for Life, a group of pro-life business leaders

> Teen American Life League (TALL), a peer-support group for 11- to 18-year-olds "who wish to say 'NO' to promiscuity, abortion and other life-threatening temptations facing young Americans today"

> American Life Lobby, ALL's political arm, which with its internal political action committee, ALLPAC, works actively to lobby for a human life amendment and to promote total prohibition of abortion, as well as campaigning against euthanasia, sex education and school-based clinics, and taxpayer funding of "anti-life" programs (i.e., organizations such as Planned Parenthood and the American Civil Liberties Union)

Dues are $20.00 per year.

PUBLICATIONS: *All About Issues,* magazine published nine times per year ($24.95 per year); wide variety of books, manuals, booklets, pamphlets; *ALL NEWS*, biweekly news bulletin of American Life Lobby ($29.95 per year).

American Pro Life Council
1612 S. Prospect Avenue
Park Ridge, IL 60068
(312) 692-2183

The American Pro Life Council is a nonprofit, voluntary association of pro-life organizations. It functions as a service organization to facilitate the work of pro-life organizations throughout the country and to provide various types of assistance to both individuals and groups involved in the pro-life movement. Through its affiliates, the council offers a variety of services to members, which include a credit union, a nonprofit pro-life insurance company, a national mail-order pharmacy offering discount prescriptions to members, and a custom check printing company. Other programs include:

Support for a church-related home for teenage unwed mothers

Support for counseling services designed to encourage and assist prospective mothers to give birth to and provide for their babies

Support for legal services for persons arrested demonstrating for pro-life concerns or for women who have legal problems arising from a decision to carry a child to term rather than to abort

Additional legal services, public relations services, guidance in grant writing, and other practical and legal assistance to new and existing pro-life organizations

American Rights Coalition
P.O. Box 487
Chattanooga, TN 37401
(615) 698-7960; hotline (800) 634-2224

American Rights Coalition (ARC) is a Christian, pro-life organization ministering to women who have been hurt physically and/or emotionally by abortion. This assistance includes helping women pursue legal options where malpractice, misrepresentation, and fraud are indicated. Women who contact ARC are referred to local volunteer "support teams" who assist them in finding medical help if necessary, act as liaisons with ARC in determining whether legal action is indicated and channel the women to the appropriate resources if it is, and provide sympathetic support. Women are also encouraged to join Christian post-abortion healing groups and to attend church. Wherever possible, support team participants are persons who have had personal experience with abortion. ARC also seeks to fight abortion through legislative action, working with local regulatory boards, and exposing abuses by abortion providers.

PUBLICATIONS: *The Abortion Injury Report,* a monthly bulletin featuring reprints of news stories about women who have been injured by abortions, abortion-related lawsuits and convictions, clinic closings, etc.; *ARC Manual,* information for grass-roots organizers; *The Abortion Busters Manual,* on exposing abortion abuses; an ARC video, with founder and president Charlie Wysong; plus billboard posters and business cards with the ARC 800 number.

Americans United for Life
Legal Defense Fund

343 S. Dearborn Street
Suite 1804
Chicago, IL 60604
(312) 786-9494

Americans United for Life (AUL) Legal Defense Fund is a nonprofit, nonsectarian public interest law firm serving as the legal arm of the pro-life movement. Founded in 1971, AUL was the first national pro-life organization. It is committed to "defending human life through vigorous judicial, legislative and educational efforts." Funded by 7,500 private contributors, AUL has a 24-person board whose members include congressmen Henry Hyde and Christopher Smith, Northwestern University law professor Victor Rosenblum, and Harvard University's Arthur Dyck. Its staff of 30 includes 7 attorneys. AUL has participated in more than 20 Supreme Court cases, including *Roe v. Wade* and all subsequent abortion-related cases, as well as "right-to-die" cases and the Adolescent Family Life Act, which set up programs encouraging sexual abstinence by teenagers and the promotion of adoption over abortion. AUL's activities include:

> Drafting model legislation to be used at the state level
>
> Writing and filing amicus curiae briefs before the Supreme Court and lower courts
>
> Providing legal counsel to parties defending pro-life laws
>
> Representing key parties in the federal courts; providing legal counsel to state legislators and lobbyists
>
> Providing expert testimony during hearings in support of pro-life legislation
>
> Conducting quantitative research and publishing law review articles, books, and periodicals
>
> Sponsoring educational activities, including periodic forums, conferences, and workshops
>
> Conducting media relations campaigns, including appearances by spokespersons on network and local television and radio broadcasts

PUBLICATIONS: *Life Docket,* a monthly pro-life legal news summary sent to reporters and "public policy influencers"; *Lex Vitae,* a quarterly report on key pro-life litigation and legislation around the country; *AUL Studies in Law, Medicine and Society,* a monograph series of law review and other scholarly articles relating to abortion and euthanasia; *AUL Forum,* a quarterly newsletter for AUL friends and supporters; *AUL Insights,* periodic in-depth analyses of pertinent court cases and legislation. Also available is a set of videos from the 1989 AUL Legislative Educational Conference.

Association of Reproductive Health Professionals (ARHP)

409 12th Street, SW
Washington, DC 20024-2188
(202) 863-2475

The Association of Reproductive Health Professionals was founded in 1963 by Dr. Alan Guttmacher, then president of the Planned Parenthood Federation of America. ARHP started as a society of physicians who practiced at Planned Parenthood affiliates; its original objective was to provide a forum for these professionals to discuss practical and clinical aspects of family planning. The organization has since broadened to include scientists, educators, and health professionals in reproductive health as well as physicians. Its principal objectives are to educate the public and health care professionals on matters pertaining to reproductive health, including sexuality, contraception, prevention of sexually transmitted disease, family planning, and abortion. ARHP supports the United Nations World Population Plan of Action, which states that "all couples and individuals share the basic human right to decide freely and responsibly the number and spacing of their children, and to have the information, education and means to do so." ARHP activities include:

Consumer education campaigns

An annual scientific conference and various independent scientific meetings and seminars

Collaboration on reproductive health issues with other professional organizations, government agencies, nonprofit organizations, and corporations

Promotion of pro-choice public policies through support of judicial challenges to restrictive laws

Various information exchange, networking, and liaison activities

Membership is open to any individual with an interest and expertise in reproductive health. Annual dues are $100.00 for physicians and $60.00 for nonphysicians.

PUBLICATIONS: *American Journal of Gynecologic Health,* a bimonthly journal; quarterly newsletter; various scientific papers; and other materials in the field of reproductive health.

Birthright, Inc.

686 N. Broad Street
Woodbury, NJ 08096
(609) 848-1818; (609) 848-1819; for clients (800) 848-LOVE;
in Canada (800) 328-LOVE

Birthright is a nonprofit, interdenominational volunteer organization that operates a network of some 600 crisis pregnancy centers throughout the United States and Canada, as well as centers in South Africa, Ghana, Nigeria, Hong Kong, the Philippines, Colombia, Britain, and Germany. Founded in Toronto, Canada, in 1968 by Louise Summerhill, Birthright operates on the beliefs that women are driven to abortion by such problems as financial crisis, physical or emotional illness, or "social quandaries" created by extramarital or pre-marital conception and that "there is no reason why a woman who is guided and assisted through a difficult pregnancy cannot love and accept her child." It therefore attempts to offer women sympathy and friendship as well as the resources to cope with their problems so that they will not have to resort to abortion. The centers offer a full array of services to women with unplanned pregnancies, including pregnancy testing, counseling, housing, medical care, legal assistance, adoption referral, maternity and baby clothing, and job placement assistance. To receive help, pregnant women may call a toll-free number that operates from 8:00 A.M. to midnight (Eastern time) every day, or they may call local centers, which are listed in telephone directories.

Boston Women's Health Book Collective

240A Elm Street
Box 192
Somerville, MA 02144
Information requests (617) 625-0271; administration (617) 625-0277;
FAX (617) 625-0294

The Boston Women's Health Book Collective (BWHBC) is probably best known for its bestselling book *Our Bodies, Ourselves* and other publications on women's health issues. The nonprofit collective also serves as a health educa-tion, advocacy, and consulting organization whose purpose is to "help indi-viduals and groups to make informed personal and political decisions about issues affecting health and medical care, especially as they relate to women." BWHBC supports the belief that "women's health issues must be addressed in an economic, political and social context, and that women should have a much greater role in health policy decisions." All royalties from *Our Bodies, Ourselves* go to support women's health projects, including:

Publication and distribution of a Spanish-language edition of *Our Bodies, Ourselves*

Formation and ongoing support of Amigas Latinas en Acción por Salud (ALAS), a group of Latina women that creates and disseminates Spanish-language health information, including videos relevant to the specific conditions of Latina women in the United States

The Women's Health Information Center, which maintains an extensive collection of women's health information and annually responds to thousands of letters and calls from women, community groups, educators, and others regarding women and health

Media and community outreach, including radio and television appearances and a speaker's bureau

PUBLICATIONS: *The New Our Bodies, Ourselves,* including a chapter on abortion; *Abortion,* a packet of articles and abstracts from published and unpublished sources; plus books, bibliographies, pamphlets, and literature packets on a wide range of women's health topics.

Catholics for a Free Choice
1436 U Street, NW, Suite 301
Washington, DC 20009-3916
(202) 638-1706; FAX (202) 332-7995

Established in 1973, Catholics for a Free Choice (CFFC) is an international educational organization that supports the right to legal reproductive health care, especially in family planning and abortion. CFFC also works to reduce the incidence of abortion and to increase women's choices in child-bearing and child-rearing through advocacy of social and economic programs for women, children, and families. In the United States, CFFC works to counter efforts by the Roman Catholic hierarchy to overturn *Roe v. Wade* and implement a ban on all abortions. A Latin American affiliate, Católicas por el Derecho a Decider (CDD), is working to shape the emerging debate about legal abortion in "a way that is both pro-choice and sensitive to the Catholic traditions of the region." CFFC is especially concerned with working with the "middle ground"—the more than 50 percent of the public that holds uncertain or seemingly contradictory views about the legality and morality of various reproductive issues including abortion. CFFC's goal is to further dialogue on these issues to assist the policy process and work toward national consensus. Its activities include:

Maintaining an education and communications program, including electronic and print media exposure, public speaking, seminars, and conferences

Researching, producing, and disseminating publications and educational materials

Conducting a national public affairs program for policymakers

Stimulating grass-roots education in targeted states and regions

Networking with Catholic and secular women and groups in Latin America and the Caribbean in support of reproductive rights and U.S. international family planning assistance (in conjunction with CDD)

Working with pro-choice and Catholic organizations to "increase the level of concern and responsiveness to the moral and ethical dimensions of pro-choice issues"

Associate dues of $25.00 per year include a subscription to *Conscience*.

PUBLICATIONS: *Conscience*, a bimonthly news journal; *Abortion: A Guide to Making Ethical Choices; Bishop's Watch Reports*, series of monographs including an in-depth analysis of surveys on Catholics' opinions and practices in the areas of family planning, abortion, and teenage sexuality; *Currents*, an occasional series on ethics and public policy that includes original articles and reprints; *Abortion in Good Faith Series*, series of monographs including one on the history of abortion in the Catholic Church; *Guide for Pro-Choice Catholics: The Church, the State, and Abortion Politics*, report on church-sponsored sanctions or directives limiting the participation of pro-choice policymakers in religious life; plus several Spanish-language publications, brochures, booklets, and stickers. Write or call for catalog.

Catholics United for Life
New Hope, KY 40052
(502) 325-3061

Catholics United for Life (CUL) was founded by Elasah Drogin, who converted to Catholicism from Judaism and became opposed to abortion following her own illegal abortion in Mexico in 1968. CUL is primarily dedicated to preventing abortions through "sidewalk counseling"—standing outside abortion clinics and attempting to dissuade women from going through with their abortions. CUL is opposed to contraception and "the promise of the liberation of sex from pregnancy" and teaches that abortion is murder and a mortal sin. To aid "sidewalk counselors," CUL produces and/or distributes a large selection of pamphlets, brochures, tapes, and other materials, as well as a free monthly newsletter.

PUBLICATIONS: *Margaret Sanger: Father of Modern Society*, by Elasah Drogin, plus a large variety of booklets, pamphlets, brochures, audiotapes and videotapes, bumper stickers, and visual aids.

Center for Constitutional Rights
666 Broadway
New York, NY 10012
(212) 614-6464; FAX (212) 614-6499

The Center for Constitutional Rights (CCR) was founded in 1967 to "preserve the Constitution as a living document belonging to all the people" and to fight against "those who ignore the Constitution's mandate and twist its meanings to deny freedom and equality to those less privileged and powerful than themselves." The original focus of the nonprofit group was to provide legal defense to poor blacks and others arrested during the civil rights movement; it has since broadened to encompass a variety of progressive causes. CCR has two offices, one in New York City and another in Mississippi, and nine staff attorneys. It provides legal assistance, amicus curiae briefs, and public education in support of a wide range of freedoms and rights that it believes are explicit or implicit under the U.S. Constitution, among them freedom of speech; racial, ethnic, and sexual equality; and reproductive rights, including the right to abortion. CCR's amicus curiae brief in the 1989 Supreme Court case *Webster v. Reproductive Health Services* was the only brief devoted exclusively to young and poor women and women of color—"the women most affected but least talked about."

PUBLICATIONS: *Birth Control Confidential 1987,* a newspaper format pamphlet containing information on legal rights of teenagers to birth control and abortion in Texas, Arkansas, Mississippi, Missouri, and Oklahoma that includes articles written by teenagers; *Movement Support Network News,* quarterly newsletter; *The Center for Constitutional Rights Looks at the Constitution;* collection of essays; annual docket report.

Center for Population Options
1025 Vermont Avenue, NW, Suite 210
Washington, DC 20005
(202) 347-5700; FAX (202) 347-2263

Founded in 1980, the Center for Population Options (CPO) is an educational and advocacy organization devoted specifically to preventing teen pregnancy and HIV infection and improving access to reproductive health care for adolescents. CPO also works to enhance opportunities for young people in key areas such as continuing education, planning their families, and preparing for and obtaining productive employment. Based on the belief that young people can more satisfactorily complete their education and prepare for employment if they delay parenthood, CPO advocates assisting teenagers in making decisions to delay sexual activity or practice contraception; providing them with information about sexuality, birth control, and abortion; and providing them with ready access to family planning and reproductive health services. CPO also supports providing comprehensive health services to help adolescents remain mentally, emotionally, and physically healthy through school-based or school-linked or other conveniently located clinics. CPO's activities include:

A partnership program, in which it acts as a resource and advocate for national youth-serving agencies

A policy project that includes filing of amicus curiae briefs, educating policymakers about teen pregnancy prevention, and serving as a watchdog group

Promotion of school-based clinics, including providing resources, consulting, and training to build and strengthen such clinics

A research program that provides program evaluation, information systems technology, and statistical analysis for the organization's project areas

A media project aimed at encouraging the positive portrayal of sexuality and family planning issues in the media

The International Clearinghouse on Adolescent Fertility, which maintains an information clearinghouse, produces practical materials, and administers a grant program for innovative adolescent fertility projects in developing countries

A Public Education and Resources Center, a library stocked with domestic and international periodicals, books, videos, curricula, and reports related to adolescent fertility and open to the general public

PUBLICATIONS: *Options,* a quarterly newsletter; fact sheet series, including "Adolescents and Abortion"; *Life Planning Education,* curriculum guide; plus a variety of books, booklets, brochures, and monographs.

Christian Action Council
101 W. Broad Street, Suite 500
Falls Church, VA 22046
(703) 237-2100

The Christian Action Council (CAC) was formed in 1975 by the Reverend Billy Graham and others to "defend the sanctity of human life, to resist abortion and related practices that kill innocent people, and to provide biblical alternatives to abortion, infanticide and euthanasia." CAC activities include lobbying for pro-life laws and public policy, educating the public about abortion, and ministering to women with crisis pregnancies. Local affiliate CACs receive extensive support and assistance from the national council, including training and educational materials, newsletters, and legislative alerts, as well as national conferences, regional planning meetings, and onsite leadership training. Local groups work to "[identify] the reasons abortion is accepted within [their communities]" and to challenge those reasons through clinic protests, working with public officials, and encouraging alternatives to abortion. CAC also provides extensive assistance and guidance for planning, implementing, and operating crisis pregnancy centers (CPCs).

PUBLICATIONS: *Action Line,* newsletter, plus a wide selection of books, manuals (including *How To Start a Local CAC, How To Start a CPC, Abortion Debaters Manual, CAC Media Manual,* and others), educational brochures, booklets, bulletin inserts and handouts, fact sheets, and videotapes. Call or write for list.

Dads for Life
908 Thorn Street
Princeton, WV 24740
(304) 487-1644

The primary goal of Dads for Life is to obtain, through legislation and judicial action, legal rights for men in cases of unplanned or "unwanted" (by the woman) pregnancy and to involve more men in the pro-life movement. While it is not a support service as such, the organization provides counseling referrals for men dealing with the experience of an unwanted abortion and works to educate crisis pregnancy centers and the public about how abortion affects men. At the time of this writing, Dads for Life was in the process of incorporating and establishing chapters in a number of states and major cities around the country.

Doctors for Life
11511 Tivoli Lane
St. Louis, MO 63146

Doctors for Life is an organization of physicians who believe that human life begins at fertilization and who have vowed to uphold the portion of the Hippocratic oath specifying that a doctor will not participate in, assist, or condone either euthanasia or abortion. The recently formed organization seeks to complement other pro-life groups by providing educational materials and assistance in developing programs, as well as working to form a Pro-Life Caucus within the American Medical Association. Members of the Doctors for Life Advisory Board include such well-known pro-life physicians as Matthew Bulfin, Thomas Hilgiers, Mildred Jefferson, Carolyn Gerster, Bernard Nathanson, Joseph Stanton, and John Willke. Doctors for Life is an affiliate of the World Federation of Doctors Who Respect Human Life.

EMILY's List
1112 16th Street, NW, Suite 750
Washington, DC 20036
(202) 887-1957; FAX (202) 452-1997

EMILY's List is a political donor network for pro-choice, pro-ERA Democratic women who are campaigning for gubernatorial or congressional office. Founded in 1985, EMILY's List (the acronym stands for Early Money Is Like Yeast) targets races; recruits, recommends, and trains candidates; and raises money early in the election cycle to fund initial campaign efforts, including staffing, fundraising, research, and other components "essential to establishing a candidate as credible and capable of winning." Donor members receive profiles of each recommended candidate. They then decide which candidates they wish to support and write checks directly to those candidates. EMILY's List also conducts research and analysis on topics that concern women candidates, such as the problems women may encounter when running for public office and the impact of the pro-choice issue on Democratic candidates. Membership requires a minimum donation of $100.00, plus a promise to consider donations of at least $100.00 each to two or more of the recommended candidates.

PUBLICATIONS: *Notes from EMILY,* quarterly newsletter, plus candidate profiles and various white papers and reports.

Federation of Feminist Women's Health Centers
6221 Wilshire Boulevard, Suite 419-A
Los Angeles, CA 90048
(213) 930-2512

The Federation of Feminist Women's Health Centers is a nonprofit, tax-exempt association of women's health projects and their supporters who provide health services to women, including abortion, well-woman care, and birth control. The federation's goals are to secure reproductive rights for women and men, to educate women about the healthy functioning of their bodies, and to improve the quality of women's health care. The federation currently has six affiliate centers on the West Coast and in Georgia that work together to foster close communication, share resources, and achieve common goals. Particular emphasis is placed on teaching and facilitating self-care. Federation activities include:

An annual political education session

Coordination of participation at conferences for national and local organizations, including the National Abortion Federation, the American Public Health Association, and the National Organization for Women

Networking among women's health activists for participation in federation projects

Education of public policymakers on women's health issues

Consultation, loans, and grants to members, usually for the purpose of promoting communication and networking

Consultation and referrals to group and individual members on concerns shared by women's health clinics, including malpractice insurance, internal organization, administration, clinic protocols and standards, and harassment of clinics by anti-abortion activists

Individual memberships are available on a sliding scale; contact the federation for information on categories of group membership.

PUBLICATIONS: *When Birth Control Fails . . . ,* a guide to self-abortion techniques; *A New View of a Woman's Body; How To Stay Out of the Gynecologist's Office;* plus a video, *No Going Back,* on self-abortion techniques.

The Feminist Majority

The Fund for the Feminist Majority
1600 Wilson Boulevard, Suite 704
Arlington, VA 22209
(703) 522-2214; FAX (703) 522-2219

8105 W. 3rd Street, Suite 1
Los Angeles, CA 90048
(213) 651-0495; FAX (213) 653-2689

The Feminist Majority Foundation
186 South Street
Boston, MA 02111
(617) 695-9688

The Feminist Majority was founded by former National Organization for Women president Eleanor Smeal with the goal of involving more women in "areas of power," i.e., politics, business, and government. Abortion rights activities play a large part in the organization's ongoing "Feminization of Power" campaign, a nationwide effort "to inspire unprecedented numbers of feminists to seek leadership positions, to promote a National Feminist Agenda, and to heighten awareness and visibility of the feminist majority." The organization consists of two separate groups, the Fund for the Feminist Majority and the Feminist Majority Foundation.

The Fund for the Feminist Majority (FFM) is a lobbying and political advocacy group whose current activities include the Becky Bell–Rosie Jimenez campaign, which has three goals:

To repeal the "Mexico City policy," which forbids nations and groups receiving U.S. funding from providing or even discussing abortion as part of family planning services

To end parental notification/consent laws, which pro-choice groups believe were responsible for the death of Becky Bell, an Indiana teenager who had an illegal abortion rather than tell her parents she was pregnant

To repeal the Hyde Amendment, which prohibits federal funding for abortions, forcing women like Rosie Jimenez, its "first known victim" to seek illegal abortions because they cannot afford legal ones

FFM also spearheads the Clinic Defense Project, which aims to counter anti-abortion activities such as clinic blockades by mobilizing supporters to keep the clinics open.

The Feminist Majority Foundation is the organization's research and education arm, which, in addition to developing educational materials and activities, pursues projects on the use of initiatives and referenda for women's rights and contraceptive research and development. Activities include collecting election rules for states that allow the initiative process and analyzing former campaigns waged for ballot measures on abortion rights, the Equal Rights Amendment, and pay equity in order to develop model language, strategies, and implementation plans for future referenda and initiatives on these and other issues of importance to women. The foundation is also waging a campaign to bring the French "abortion pill," RU 486, into the United States through petition drives and other activities.

PUBLICATIONS: *Feminist Majority Report,* quarterly newsletter; *The Feminization of Power,* photos and biographies of women in political office and public life in the United States and abroad who "made a feminist difference"; plus two videos, *Abortion: For Survival* and *Abortion Denied: Shattering Young Women's Lives,* each with an optional viewer guide.

Feminists for Life of America

811 E. 47th Street
Kansas City, MO 64110
(816) 753-2130; hotline (816) 561-1365

Feminists for Life (FFL) is a national organization of women and men who believe that abortion violates the basic principles of feminism—justice, fairness, equality, nonviolence, and respect for life. They see a connection between "denying personhood and basic human rights to women and others and denying these same rights to unborn children" and believe that abortion simply helps to perpetuate patriarchal policies of male ownership of women and children, violence as a way of dealing with problems, and competitive individualism rather than mutual cooperation, support, and respect. Accordingly, FFL and a growing number of state and local chapters work on a variety of fronts to stop abortion, including:

Participating in demonstrations and protests at abortion clinics

Lobbying

Participating in debates and television and radio appearances

The Feminists for Life Education Project, which produces radio spots and magazine ads and conducts other public education activities

The Feminists for Life Law Project, which prepares amicus curiae briefs for abortion-related court cases

A national hotline with recorded three-minute messages on current abortion news (updated each Friday)

Membership is $10.00 per year, or $15.00 to belong to a local chapter, which includes national dues.

PUBLICATIONS: *Sisterlife,* quarterly newsletter (free to members); *Prolife Feminism: Different Voices,* an anthology; plus several brochures. Some local chapters produce their own newsletters.

Focus on the Family
Pomona, CA 91799
(714) 620-8500

Focus on the Family is a nonprofit Christian organization "whose only reason for existence is to contribute to the stability of the family in our society" by providing parents with resources that will help them "fortify" their homes through the transmission and practice of Judeo-Christian values. Focus on the Family broadcasts several radio programs, which are heard on stations throughout the United States and Canada. Broadcasts include "Focus on the Family," hosted by founder Dr. James Dobson and heard Monday through Saturday (also Sunday in some areas); "Adventures in Odyssey," a children's radio drama; "Family News in Focus," a news program; and "Enfoque a la Familia," a Spanish-language program [call (800) A-FAMILY for a listing of stations airing these programs]. The ministry also works to help women find alternatives to abortion and supports educational and national outreach efforts to stop abortion.

PUBLICATIONS: *Focus on the Family,* monthly magazine; *Focus on the Family Physician,* bimonthly magazine addressing the pressures doctors face in their professional and personal lives; *Washington Watch,* monthly newsletter focusing on congressional, federal court, and White House activities affecting families; *Family Policy,* bimonthly newsletter offering in-depth analysis of major concerns affecting the family, with each issue focusing on a specific topic such as abortion or child care; the videotapes *A Question of Worth* and *Your Crisis Pregnancy,* about and for crisis pregnancy centers; a variety of audiotapes on crisis pregnancies, abortion, and the pro-life movement; and assorted booklets. Call or write for a complete list of materials.

Human Life Center
University of Steubenville
Steubenville, OH 43952
(614) 282-9953

The Human Life Center maintains a library of information on some 1,200 topics, including abortion, and answers information requests from individuals and organizations from all over the country. The library consists mostly of vertical files made up of articles from newspapers, periodicals, and organization newsletters. Files are kept on individuals (e.g., Judge Robert Bork and Supreme Court Justice Harry Blackmun) and organizations as well as topics and subtopics ranging from AIDS and animal rights to sterilization and "verbal engineering." Begun in Minnesota in 1972, the center moved to Ohio in 1986. Information is provided free of charge, although donations are welcome (the center is supported entirely by private donations). The Human Life Center also serves as the base organization for the International Anti-Euthanasia Task Force.

PUBLICATIONS: *International Review* (originally *Natural Family Planning*), the "only English-language journal on natural family planning," it also contains articles on subjects such as abortion, euthanasia, and reproductive technology.

Human Life International
7845-E Airpark Road
Gaithersburg, MD 20879
(301) 670-7884; FAX (301) 869-7363

Human Life International (HLI) is a missionary organization that works to stop abortion and euthanasia and to promote "chastity, sound marriage preparation, and modern natural family planning," primarily through education. Founded in 1980 by activist Father Paul Marx, HLI distributes pro-life, pro-family literature, films, videos, and teaching aids to people in 109 countries. Representing HLI, Father Marx travels worldwide speaking and organizing against legalized abortion, contraception, and euthanasia. HLI sponsors international pro-life conferences to educate and train activists, including the first such conferences held in Africa and in a Communist country. HLI also founded Prolife Seminarians International, an educational group "helping to prepare a zealous, well-informed future clergy." HLI has an international board of advisors and branch offices in 22 countries.

PUBLICATIONS: *Special Report,* monthly newsletter on Father Marx's mission journeys; *¡Escoge la Vida!* Spanish-language newsletter published six times/year; *HLI Reports,* monthly newsletter including foreign reports, facts, and statistics (Canadian edition also available); *ANFA,* News Agency for the Family, free news service for Hispanic media; *Sorrow's Reward,* newsletter for "aborted mothers and people in post-abortion healing ministries"; *Seminarians for Life International Newsletter,* quarterly newsletter by and for those studying for the priesthood; Prolife/Family Parish Notes, monthly collections of inserts for church bulletins, petitions, and daily homily topics; plus a wide assortment of books, pamphlets, tracts, reprints, videotapes and audiotapes, paintings, pictures, posters, and postcards on abortion and related topics, many also available in Spanish. Write or call for catalog.

International Life Services, Inc.
2606½ W. 8th Street
Los Angeles, CA 90057
(213) 382-2156

International Life Services, Inc. (ILSI) is a nonprofit, nonsectarian organization that works to promote the right to life for human beings from the moment of conception to natural death. It consists of three divisions:

The Education Division sponsors a variety of educational activities, including the Annual Learning Center, a week-long program providing instructions on everything from fundraising and handling the media to crisis pregnancy and post-abortion counseling; workshops held throughout the United States and abroad; a series of videotape trainings for counselors; and production of various publications.

The Scholl Institute of Bioethics, a group of doctors, nurses, lawyers, and citizens concerned about the growing acceptance of euthanasia. The institute's activities include producing educational materials and training speakers.

The Counseling Division, which consists of nine Pregnancy Help Centers located throughout southern California. The centers provide information, counseling, assistance, and referrals at no cost to pregnant women; they also provide post-abortion counseling.

PUBLICATIONS: *Pro-Life Resource Directory*, listing more than 3,000 pregnancy service centers and more than 1,000 pro-life education and social action groups throughout the United States; *Living World*, a quarterly magazine covering topics such as abortion, teenage sexuality, medical ethics, and family life; a variety of brochures and pamphlets. ILSI also offers *Pro-Life Counseling Educational Tapes*, consisting of three series: Series I is a five-tape training course for beginners in crisis pregnancy counseling; Series II (four tapes) is designed for experienced counselors and gives advice on specialized counseling problems; and Series III is a five-tape series providing training in post-abortion counseling.

Latinas for Reproductive Choice
P.O. Box 7567
1900 Fruitvale Avenue
Oakland, CA 94601
(415) 534-1362

Latinas for Reproductive Choice is a project of Organización Nacional de La Salud de La Mujer Latina, or National Latina Health Organization (NLHO). NLHO was founded in March 1986 to "raise Latina consciousness about our health and health problems, so that we can begin to take control of our health and our lives." NLHO is committed to working toward the goal of bilingual access to quality health care and the self-empowerment of Latinas through educational programs, outreach, and research. While reproductive issues have been a major focus of NLHO since its inception, in early 1990 the organization created Latinas for Reproductive Choice with several major goals:

To break the silence on reproductive rights within the Latino community and provide a platform for open discussion

To ensure that Latina voices are heard in the debate over abortion and other reproductive health issues by promoting Latinas on the boards of mainstream reproductive rights groups

To mobilize Latinas in the struggle for full reproductive freedom, including access to culturally relevant, quality health care and information, prenatal care, freedom from sterilization abuses, education about sexuality and contraception for young Latina women, and access to alternative forms of birth control

To debunk the myths surrounding Latinas through public education

To monitor elected officials who represent Latino communities with respect to their votes on reproductive rights legislation

To advocate and pressure elected officials, organizations, and individuals to support reproductive choice for Latinas

In 1988 the NLHO held the first National Conference on Latina Health Issues, with over 350 women attending, including several from Puerto Rico and Mexico. Since 1988 the organization has also conducted a workshop series, "Latina Health Issues . . . Better Health through Self-Empowerment," covering such topics as mental health, patients' rights, teen pregnancy, and AIDS. Write or call for information about current projects and activities.

Liberty Godparent Foundation
P.O. Box 27000
Lynchburg, VA 24506
(804) 384-3043;
24-hour hotline (800) 368-3336

Liberty Godparent Foundation was founded on January 22, 1982 (the anniversary of the *Roe v. Wade* decision), to provide information and assistance to pregnant women seeking alternatives to abortion. The core of the ministry is the Liberty Godparent Home, a maternity care residence that provides housing, meals, prenatal and obstetrical care, schooling, counseling, adoption referral, and other services for up to 66 women at a time. Services are provided at no cost to the women, though medical insurance payments are gladly accepted. Women are accepted without regard to age, race, religion, or ability to pay; however, the program is Christian-focused and includes regular church attendance, weekly Bible studies, and daily devotions. As part of a national outreach program, the foundation has also developed a Human Life Sunday seminar for use by churches and is seeking 10,000 churches willing to open and administer similar maternity home facilities around the country. The foundation currently has over 900 affiliate centers on a national referral network, ranging from crisis pregnancy centers through full-scale facilities containing maternity homes and adoption agencies.

PUBLICATIONS: Descriptive booklet.

Lutherans for Life
2717 E. 42nd Street
Minneapolis, MN 55406
(612) 721-3037

Lutherans for Life (LFL) is a national organization of laity and pastors that works to stop abortion and euthanasia. LFL has about 200 local chapters in 30 states; it also participates in pro-life efforts in Germany, Norway, Australia, Canada, and elsewhere. Activities include:

Annual national convention

Regional workshops

Development of models for crisis pregnancy and post-abortion outreach, chastity, and youth pro-life programs, among others

Production of educational materials for youth and adults, including videos, brochures, and pamphlets

Suggested annual membership donation is $20.00; those who cannot afford that amount are asked to give what they can.

PUBLICATIONS: *Lifedate,* a newsletter; *Living,* a quarterly magazine; plus various brochures and pamphlets.

March for Life
P.O. Box 90300
Washington, DC 20090
(202) 547-6721

March for Life is best known as the force behind the pro-life march held in Washington, D.C., each January 22, the anniversary of the Supreme Court *Roe v. Wade* decision. The force behind March for Life is Nellie Gray, a lawyer and devout Catholic who quit her job after the 1973 *Roe v. Wade* decision to become a full-time pro-life lobbyist and organizer. March for Life is dedicated to obtaining the passage of the Paramount Human Life Amendment, which would guarantee the right to life of each human being from the moment of fertilization, with absolutely no exceptions or compromises.

National Abortion Federation
1436 U Street, NW, Suite 103
Washington, DC 20009
(202) 667-5881; FAX (202) 667-5890;
consumer hotline (800) 772-9100

Founded in 1977, the National Abortion Federation (NAF) is an association of abortion service providers and supporters dedicated to making safe, legal abortions accessible to all women. Institutional members include proprietary clinics, nonprofit clinics, feminist clinics, Planned Parenthood affiliates, doctors' offices, and services affiliated with hospitals, as well as other health care providers and national organizations such as the National Abortion Rights Action League, the Planned Parenthood Federation of America, the Alan Guttmacher Institute, and other foundations and research organizations.

Individual memberships are also available. The primary functions of the NAF are:

> To provide standards, guidelines, training, and education to help providers offer the best possible care and services to patients. This includes reviewing membership applications; conducting onsite evaluations; investigating consumer complaints; and providing assistance and professional training on a variety of topics, including nursing, counseling, public affairs, political education, public relations, management, medical and legal issues, and prevention and management of complications.

> To provide information on the variety and quality of services available in abortion facilities to legislative bodies, public policy organizations, medical groups, concerned citizens, and women with unwanted pregnancies.

> To monitor and participate in public policy developments affecting reproductive health care.

> To provide public education, including publications, workshops, and a toll-free consumer education hotline.

In response to attacks on abortion clinics, the NAF also has a Clinic Defense Project that keeps track of harassment and acts of violence around the country; works with providers and local law enforcement officials; and provides technical assistance and training regarding clinic security, protection of staff and patients, and organizing community resources to stop the violence.

PUBLICATIONS: *Update,* quarterly newsletter; *The Truth about Abortion,* a fact sheet series that includes fact sheets on violence against abortion clinics and public support for abortion; *Celebrating Roe v. Wade: Dramatic Improvements in American Health; Consumer's Guide to Abortion Services/Guia sobre servicios de aborto,* with information in both English and Spanish; *Standards for Abortion Care,* covering obligatory and recommended standards for NAF member facilities, including ethical aspects, counseling and informed consent, nursing care, administrative procedures, advertising, reporting, and referral.

National Abortion Rights Action League (NARAL)
1101 14th Street, NW
Washington, DC 20005
(202) 371-0779

With more than 350,000 current members, NARAL is the largest organization in the country working expressly to defend abortion rights. It is also one of the most politically active and visible pro-choice organizations. Founded in 1969 as the National Association to Repeal Abortion Laws, the organization changed its name to the National Abortion Rights Action League following the 1973 *Roe v. Wade* Supreme Court decision. NARAL and its network of 30 affiliate state organizations work on a variety of fronts to "counteract the new and continued threats to reproductive freedom through political and grassroots organizing." The NARAL Foundation, established in 1977, supports a variety of legal, research, public education, and training programs, including:

Providing national, regional, and local training for affiliate directors, board members, and volunteers in such areas as organizational skills, phone banking, fundraising, and strategic planning

Providing information on abortion-related cases and legislative information on both the state and federal levels to elected officials, members of the press, affiliates, and field activists

Conducting public opinion research and analysis

Providing educational materials to pro-choice student groups on college campuses

Sponsoring petition drives

Engaging in lobbying activities

Conducting media campaigns, rallies, and other public education efforts

Providing legal assistance and filing amicus curiae briefs in abortion-related court cases

Affiliate activities include sponsoring counter-demonstrations at pro-life protests, escorting women into abortion clinics, fundraising, and responding to media inquiries.

PUBLICATIONS: *Who Decides? A State by State Review of Abortion Rights in America,* analysis of abortion laws, recent legislative action, recent litigation, and political climate in each state, updated annually; *Reproductive Rights: A Status Report* (1989); *The Voices of Women: Abortion: In Their Own Words,* letters from women who had illegal abortions prior to 1973; *Choice: Legal Abortion: Arguments Pro and Con; Who Decides? A Reproductive Rights Issues Manual; NARAL News,* quarterly newsletter; *NARAL Campus Newsletter,* quarterly newsletter; plus two videos, *Voices*—which features women who had illegal abortions, a doctor whose hospital cared for women who had had illegal abortions, and various elected and NARAL officials—and *One Year Later*—a response to the *Webster* decision.

National Black Women's Health Project
175 Trinity Avenue S.W., 2nd Floor
Atlanta, GA 30303
(404) 681-4554

Public Policy/Education Office
1133 15th Street, NW, Suite 550
Washington, DC 20005
(202) 835-0117; FAX (202) 835-0118

The National Black Women's Health Project (NBWHP) is a self-help and health advocacy organization dedicated to improving the overall health of black women. Begun in 1981 as a pilot program of the National Women's Health Project, NBWHP was incorporated as a nonprofit organization in 1984. Its approach is based on "the understanding that Black women's health problems are aggravated by the extreme stress caused by socioeconomic factors such as poverty, racism, and the increasing rates of crime in the communities in which they live." The NBWHP seeks to empower black women to reach and maintain full health through informal support groups that enable them to share their concerns and problems and learn how to cope with health issues effectively. Currently over 2,000 members are participating in more than 130 self-help chapters in 22 states.

Among NBWHP programs is the Reproductive Health Education Program, a national initiative that includes workshops stressing the need for a full range of reproductive services, including contraceptive choices and prenatal care. In June 1990, the organization sponsored a national Reproductive Rights Conference for African-American Women, where leaders of national African-American organizations met to plan strategies for active participation in the pro-choice movement. Additionally, the NBWHP recently opened a public policy/education office in Washington, D.C., which will focus primarily on reproductive health and rights, including the right to safe, legal, affordable abortion. The purpose of the office is to provide a "national forum to share the information, data and perspectives of the NBWHP self-help networks in a way that will ensure an impact on policy discussions regarding African-American women's health issues" and to ensure that African-American women will be able to "express their own agenda in their own voices with regard to these rights."

**National Committee for a
Human Life Amendment**
1511 K Street, NW, Suite 335
Washington, DC 20005
(202) 393-0703; FAX (202) 347-1383

The National Committee for a Human Life Amendment (NCHLA) was founded in 1974 by the National Conference of Catholic Bishops. It is a grass-roots organization primarily concerned with the development of legislative advocacy programs within congressional districts, through the formation and support of legislative committees consisting of members from the parishes, lay groups, and church institutions within the boundaries of each congressional district. NCHLA's current legislative goals are to maintain existing government policies related to abortion funding, including restrictions on the use of government funds to pay for abortions and denial of tax dollars to organizations that support coercive abortion or promote abortion-on-demand in other countries. An example of NCHLA's cooperative projects was a recent national letter-writing campaign, Project Life, which was aimed at securing and maintaining majority support for pro-life legislation within the House of Representatives.

National Council of Jewish Women
NCJW Choice Campaign

53 W. 23rd Street
New York, NY 10010
(212) 645-4048; telex 9100000085 NCJUQ;
FAX (212) 645-7466

Founded in 1893, the National Council of Jewish Women (NCJW) is the oldest Jewish women's volunteer organization in the country. NCJW's more than 100,000 members "dedicate themselves, in the spirit of Judaism, to advancing human welfare and the democratic way of life" through social action, education, and community service. NCJW activities focus on children and youth, the aging, Jewish life, and women's issues, including reproductive rights.

The NCJW Choice Campaign began in January 1989, in anticipation of the Supreme Court *Webster* decision. The campaign is a "nationwide, locally tailored mobilization designed to generate widespread public demand for women's reproductive freedom." To this end, NCJW maintains a communications network consisting of its State Public Affairs Network and 200 affiliate sections, each of which has a local network that includes not only NCJW members but also coalition partners and state and national elected officials. NCJW also provides extensive information, technical assistance, and guidance for local pro-choice efforts, including community educational programs, letter-writing and media campaigns, state legislative advocacy efforts, and development of local coalitions. The major component of this assistance is a set of six guide packets, each focusing on a different aspect of pro-choice strategy and containing a variety of materials, including handouts, sample letters, and strategy and activity guidelines:

Guide 1 includes general background and historical information about NCJW and reproductive rights

Guide 2 provides ideas and how-tos for organizing public education programs

Guide 3 offers strategies for social action and community service

Guide 4 covers public relations strategies

Guide 5 discusses membership recruitment and retention

Guide 6 presents fundraising strategies

Although the packets are geared to Jewish groups, much of the material they contain would be useful to other pro-choice groups as well. Other materials, including buttons and placards, are also available. NCJW Choice Campaign also offers local groups individualized strategy consultations as well as planning and technical seminars. Membership dues are $25.00 per year (lifetime membership $250.00).

PUBLICATIONS: *Abortion: Challenges Ahead,* summary of a roundtable discussion sponsored by NCJW; Choice background papers, including "NCJW: The Choice Organization," "A Brief History of Reproductive Rights in America," "Background Information on Recent Attacks on Abortion Rights," "Advocacy Activity for Non-profit Tax Exempt Organizations," and "The Language of Choice"; *Choice Update,* periodic reports on court decisions, legislation, etc., concerning reproductive rights; plus the six guide packets described above.

National Organization for Women
P.O. Box 7813
Washington, DC 20044
(202) 331-0066

NOW Legal Defense and Education Fund
99 Hudson Street
New York, NY 10013
(212) 925-6635; FAX (212) 226-1066

The National Organization for Women (NOW) was founded in 1966 to further "true equality for all women in America [and] a fully equal partnership of the sexes, as part of the world-wide revolution of human rights now taking place within and beyond our national borders." Support for reproductive freedom, including access to safe, legal abortion, has been a major focus of NOW since its inception. Since the 1989 *Webster* Supreme Court decision, NOW has stepped up its activity in support of abortion rights and has experienced a dramatic increase in membership, with more than 275,000 members and approximately 800 chapters nationwide. During 1990, NOW sponsored the Freedom Caravan for Women's Lives, a state-by-state campaign to recruit volunteers and promote pro-choice candidates for the 1990 elections. Other activities include letter-writing campaigns and demonstrations. Affiliated groups include the NOW Political Action Committee (NOWPAC) and the NOW Legal Defense and Education Fund. National dues are $25.00 per year.

PUBLICATIONS: *National NOW Times,* quarterly newspaper. A number of materials related to abortion and reproductive rights are also available through the NOW Legal Defense and Education Fund (NOWLDEF). These include *Legal Resource Kit—Reproductive Rights,* which includes an annotated bibliography and resource list and an analysis of public opinion polls on reproductive rights issues; *Attorney Referral Services List,* addresses and telephone numbers of organizations that make attorney referrals; *Facts on Reproductive*

Rights, a manual on the medical, legal, and social issues involved; *Protecting Young Women's Right to Abortion: A Guide to Parental Notification and Consent Laws,* an analysis of reproductive rights in light of recent Supreme Court decisions; and copies of briefs and complaints filed by NOWLDEF in various related court cases.

National Organization of Episcopalians for Life (NOEL)
10523 Main Street
Fairfax, VA 22030
(703) 591-NOEL (591-6635)

The National Organization of Episcopalians for Life was formed in 1966 as Episcopalians for Life and incorporated in 1984 under its present name. NOEL is an educational foundation whose purpose is "to promote the Biblical view of the sanctity of human life at every stage of biological development and to seek to influence our church and culture to embody this Biblical attitude morally, legally, and in practice." Accordingly, NOEL is opposed to infanticide and euthanasia as well as abortion. In addition to publishing and distributing informative pamphlets and videotapes, NOEL recently funded the first of what it hopes will be many NOEL Houses, Christian homes where single mothers and their babies may live for up to one year while the mothers develop parenting and living skills and pursue educational and vocational goals that will lead to independence. Currently about 20,000 people receive NOEL's quarterly newsletter, and the organization has 115 chapters located around the country.

PUBLICATIONS: *NOEL NEWS,* quarterly newsletter, plus various pamphlets, cassette tapes, and cassette tape albums.

National Right to Life Committee (NRLC)
419 7th Street, NW, Suite 500
Washington, DC 20004-2293
(202) 626-8800; FAX (202) 737-9189 or (202) 347-5907;
legislative update line (202) 393-LIFE

The National Right to Life Committee is the largest and best-known pro-life organization in the country, with more than 1,800 local chapters. The NRLC has a representative structure, with local chapters represented at the state level and each state and the District of Columbia electing a director to the national board. Additionally, three at-large directors are elected by the membership. The NRLC was founded in June 1973 in response to the *Roe v. Wade* Supreme Court decision legalizing abortion. NRLC is a nonsectarian organization with members across the religious and political spectrum. In conjunction with the National Right to Life Trust Fund (NRLTF), the NRLC is involved in a broad range of education, outreach, citizen action, and lobbying efforts aimed at stopping abortion, infanticide, and euthanasia. Affiliate groups include:

National Right to Life Political Action Committee (NRLPAC), formed in 1980 to support pro-life candidates of either party running for federal office, through volunteers, endorsements, advertisements, and campaign contributions.

American Victims of Abortion (AVA), an educational outreach program that provides information and speakers on post-abortion issues and concerns. Focusing on legislators and the media, AVA seeks to "heighten awareness of the problems faced by individuals after abortion"; it is particularly active in the areas of ensuring informed consent, fathers' rights, and parental notification.

Black Americans for Life, founded in 1985 to reach out to black communities.

National Teens for Life, founded in 1985 for junior high and high school youth, offering conventions, seminars, fundraisers, services for unwed teenage mothers, and opportunities for political involvement.

NRLC's many projects include a voter identification project, a religious outreach program, and a nationally syndicated five-minute radio program, *Pro-Life Perspective,* aired daily on some 300 stations.

PUBLICATIONS: *National Right to Life News,* semimonthly newspaper; set of booklets containing key abortion-related roll call votes in Congress, 1983–1989; fact sheets on various topics, including legislative updates and abortion statistics; plus a wide variety of books, pamphlets, videos, audiovisual programs, reprints, brochures, and booklets. Call or write for a complete list of materials.

National Women's Health Network
1325 G Street, NW
Washington, DC 20005
(202) 347-1140

National Women's Health Network (NWHN) is "the only national public-interest organization devoted solely to women and health." The nonprofit organization works to promote more accessible, responsible, and humane health care for women and to give women a greater voice in the health care system in the United States. NWHN works to educate people to become better informed health care consumers and monitors health-related legislation to protect women's health rights. As part of its support for legal, safe, affordable abortion, NWHN maintains a visible presence at national pro-choice events, provides speakers for local and regional activities, and acts as an information source for women wanting to contact women-controlled clinics or to have an overview of pro-choice issues and organizations. NWHN is also active in monitoring information and issues related to RU 486, the French "abortion pill." The NWHN operates the Women's Health Information Service, a clearinghouse that provides information on a wide variety of topics related to women's health issues. Membership dues are $25.00 per year for individuals, $35.00 per year for women's health or consumer groups, and $50.00 per year for businesses and institutions.

PUBLICATIONS: *Network News*, newsletter published six times/year; *Abortion Then and Now: Creative Responses to Restricted Access*, a compilation of articles detailing past and present strategies for "[making] reproductive choice available without government restrictions."

National Women's Law Center
1616 P Street, NW
Washington, DC 20036
(202) 328-5160; FAX (202) 328-5137

The National Women's Law Center (NWLC) began in 1972 as the Women's Rights Project of the Center for Law and Social Policy, becoming independent in 1981. It serves as a national resource for persons committed to advancing the status of women through the law. NWLC works both to develop and protect women's rights by "[affecting] public and private sector policies to better reflect the needs and rights of women." NWLC concentrates its efforts in areas of primary concern to women, especially poor women, including employment, education, child and adult dependent care, child support enforcement, public assistance, Social Security, and reproductive rights and health. With respect to reproductive rights, NWLC's work is divided into three components:

Legal and public policy leadership, including chairmanship of a national Pro-Choice Coalition charged with monitoring state and federal abortion-related legislation and contributions to amicus curiae briefs in court cases affecting abortion

Grass-roots education, technical assistance, and mobilization, including providing information to congressional leaders and state and local groups

Public education

PUBLICATIONS: *National Women's Law Center Update*, quarterly newsletter; plus a wide assortment of publications on issues related to women's rights, including "Abortion Rights: Crisis and Opportunity," "Abortion Rights, Legal Available Protections in the States," "Anti-abortion Amendments on Legislation," "Summary of Abortion-related Legislation Considered by Congress, First Session, 101st Congress," "The Supreme Court and Abortion: Parental Notification Laws," and "The Supreme Court and the Threat to Abortion Rights."

The Nurturing Network
910 Main Street, Suite 360
P.O. Box 2050
Boise, ID 83701
(208) 344-7200;
FAX (208) 344-4447;
toll-free (800) TNN-4MOM

The Nurturing Network (TNN) is a nonsectarian, nonprofit organization dedicated to making sure that the "freedom to choose" includes the choice to carry an unplanned pregnancy to term. The Nurturing Network takes no position on the legality or morality of abortion; instead it seeks to "discover the vast common ground that can nurture the seeds of mutual understanding." Its primary concern is meeting the needs of women facing unplanned and unwanted pregnancies, with particular emphasis on those who are most often overlooked—young, middle-class, college-educated and career-oriented women who tend to feel that they have too much to lose by continuing their pregnancies and who lack the resources and support for choosing to give birth rather than to have an abortion. The network consists of more than 7,000 volunteers who are active in all 50 states. Services are aimed at providing counseling and practical support so that "the birth alternative may become more attractive, feasible and available to more women." Services include:

A counselor network made up of degreed and licensed professional nurses, counselors, and social workers

Nurturing Homes, private families who open their homes to prospective mothers

A medical network of doctors and nurses who provide prenatal and obstetrical care and nutritional guidance

An education network, through which women can arrange temporary transfers from one college to another of comparable academic standing so that they can continue their education during pregnancy without violating confidentiality

An employer network, which assists clients in designing a workplan and which provides a woman with the option of relocating and working "in a challenging professional environment for an employer who understands her needs at this particular time"

Adoption counseling and assistance

Financial assistance

Classes and workshops in parenting and child care

All services are provided without charge to client women. Funding is provided through individual, corporate, and foundation donations. Strict confidentiality is also maintained for all clients, and services are provided without regard to race, religion, or creed.

PUBLICATIONS: Descriptive brochures.

Operation Rescue
P.O. Box 1180
Binghamton, NY 13902
(607) 723-4012

Operation Rescue (OR) grew out of a frustration with the slowness of political approaches to stopping abortion. OR is a grass-roots organization based on the principles of civil disobedience and a belief that "when man's laws conflict with God's laws, God's laws must be obeyed." Accordingly, OR's primary focus is on "rescue missions" in which members attempt to temporarily shut down abortion clinics by creating human blockades of singing, praying "rescuers." The missions are usually carried out in conjunction with pro-life counselors, who take advantage of the blocked access to attempt to persuade women not to have their abortions. Since 1988, these "rescue missions" have resulted in thousands of arrests and a number of convictions leading to stiff fines and/or jail sentences. They have also gained massive publicity for the pro-life movement. As a result, during its brief history Operation Rescue has become probably the country's most notorious pro-life organization, and Randall Terry, its founder, is now a national figure.

Despite lawsuits, trials, fines, and imprisonment, including an antitrust suit filed by the National Organization for Women and charges and convictions under the federal Racketeer Influenced and Corrupt Organizations (RICO) law, Operation Rescue continues to carry out its mission, with more than 450 "rescues" to date. OR also has its own publishing affiliate, Rescue Education and Publishing (REAP).

PUBLICATIONS (published and distributed through REAP): *Operation Rescue* and *Accessory to Murder,* books by Randall Terry; *To Rescue the Children,* a "nuts and bolts, practical manual on starting a Christ-centered, pro-life activist ministry"; *Rescue Report,* monthly newsletter; plus various brochures, books, manuals, tracts, and videotapes and audiotapes. Write or call for a complete list: REAP, Box 2035, Binghamton, NY 13902, (607) 772-6750.

Planned Parenthood Federation of America
810 Seventh Avenue
New York, NY 10019
(212) 541-7800

Planned Parenthood (PPFA) is the largest and best known organization dedicated to "[assuring] access to family planning information and services for all who want and need them." This includes both direct provision of services and educational and other activities aimed at increasing support and access to reproductive health services, including legal, safe, affordable abortion. On the local level, Planned Parenthood affiliates provide a range of reproductive health services, including contraceptive instruction and materials, infertility screening and counseling, voluntary sterilization, testing for sexually transmitted diseases, parenthood decision-making counseling, pregnancy testing and counseling, and abortion and adoption referrals. Local affiliates also offer educational programs that are aided by national leadership and programming support. These include:

Presentations on reproductive health issues for schools, churches, and community groups

Programs for teenagers and parents "designed to enhance sexuality learning within the family"

Workshops and training seminars for teachers, physicians, nurses, social workers, and other health professionals

Additionally, PPFA is involved in a wide range of programs at the local, state, and national levels aimed at increasing access to reproductive health services; reducing pregnancy and birth rates among American teenagers; increasing the American public's understanding of and comfort with sexuality; and ensuring the widest possible choice of safe and effective fertility management for American women and men, including access to reliable contraception and medically safe, affordable abortion. Activities include:

Building networks with other community and national groups

Advertising, media, and public education campaigns, including the "Keep Abortion Safe and Legal" campaign implemented in the wake of the 1989 *Webster* decision

Organizing and participating in public rallies and demonstrations

Engaging in litigation to "protect individuals from restrictive legislation," as well as providing amicus curiae briefs in relevant Supreme Court cases

Providing technical assistance and background information to other organizations, the medical community, the media, religious and community leaders, health and civil rights groups, and concerned individuals on such topics as contraceptive options and the French "abortion pill," RU 486

Providing educational information to the public and elected officials and policymakers

Monitoring affiliate research projects in areas like high-risk sexual behavior, sterilization, and other topics

Working with affiliates to expand the scope and volume of medical services, particularly to under-served low-income, adolescent, and minority populations

Through its international division, Family Planning International Assistance (FPIA), PPFA also provides family planning services abroad. (FPIA, which is funded primarily through the U.S. Agency for International Development [AID], is prohibited under the Reagan and Bush administrations' "Mexico City policy" from any involvement with abortion, including provision of abortion services or information or attempts to change restrictive abortion laws.) PPFA is a founding member of the International Planned Parenthood Federation, which comprises family planning associations in 125 countries.

PUBLICATIONS: *Current Literature in Family Planning,* monthly collection of abstracts of books and journal articles; *LINKLine,* bimonthly newsletter on sexuality, reproductive health, and family planning; *Echoes from the Past* and *70 Years of Family Planning in America,* books on the history of Planned Parenthood; *Nine Reasons Why Abortions Are Legal* and *Five Ways To Prevent Abortion (and One Way That Won't),* booklets; plus books, curriculum guides, booklets, pamphlets, posters, videos, gifts, novelties, and other items on reproductive health, sexuality, and related topics. Call or write for catalog.

The Population Council
One Dag Hammarskjold Plaza
New York, NY 10017
(212) 644-1692;
FAX (212) 755-6052

Established in 1952, the Population Council is an international, nonprofit organization that pursues social and health science programs and research relevant to developing countries and that conducts biomedical research aimed at developing and improving contraceptive technology. A particular emphasis is on research into male reproductive physiology, with the goal of developing safe and effective contraceptives for use by men. An important focus for the council is the reduction and treatment of unsafe abortion. Current programs include:

Investigation into RU 486, with acceptability studies being planned for developing countries where abortion is legal but inaccessible to most women

A research program for the prevention of unsafe induced abortion and its adverse consequences in Latin America and the Caribbean

Projects designed to analyze and document the magnitude of social and health problems associated with incomplete and septic abortions in Sub-Saharan Africa, including programs in Kenya and Zaire

The council also provides advice and technical assistance to governments, international agencies, and nongovernmental organizations and disseminates information on population issues through publications, conferences, seminars, and workshops.

PUBLICATIONS: *Population and Development Review,* quarterly journal; *Studies in Family Planning,* bimonthly journal; plus books, working papers, pamphlet series, newsletters, and computer software. Call or write for catalog.

Presbyterians Pro-Life

Research, Education and Care, Inc.
P.O. Box 19290
Minneapolis, MN 55419
(612) 861-5346;
FAX (612) 861-5513

Presbyterians Pro-Life (PPL) is an organization of lay and clergy members of the Presbyterian Church who are opposed to the official church position that abortion "can . . . be considered a responsible choice within a Christian ethical framework," believing that this position contradicts biblical teaching and represents a departure from Christian heritage. Members of PPL are committed to "protecting the right to life of every human being from the moment of conception to the moment of natural death. . . . This leads us to stand against abortion, infanticide, euthanasia and any other practice which would devalue human life." PPL members work to strengthen the family and provide alternatives to abortion through their local chapters and the national organization, as well as working through church channels to change the church's stand on abortion.

PUBLICATIONS: *Presbyterians Pro-Life News,* newsletter; plus a variety of brochures, pamphlets, papers, study materials, audiotapes and videotapes, and books. Call or write for list.

Pro-Life Action League

6160 N. Cicero Avenue
Chicago, IL 60646
(312) 777-2900; FAX (312) 777-3061;
24-hour action line (312) 777-2525

The Pro-Life Action League (PLAL) is one of the country's most visible and confrontational activist groups. Working to "[save] babies' lives through non-violent direct action," league volunteers participate in such activities as "sidewalk counseling," picketing, and "rescue missions" at abortion clinics, as well as directly confront politicians and organizations that support legal abortion. By putting into practice the methods described by founder and director Joseph Scheidler in his book *Closed: 99 Ways To Stop Abortion,* PLAL claims to have closed 8 clinics in Chicago and nearly 100 around the country. Other activities include conducting seminars, workshops, and conferences; lecturing to student groups; and helping pro-life activists to develop effective local programs. PLAL also operates a 24-hour hotline to keep pro-life activists informed about abortion-related events and to suggest concrete actions they can take to stop abortion.

PUBLICATIONS: *Pro-Life Action News,* quarterly newsletter; *Closed: 99 Ways To Stop Abortion,* handbook by Joseph Scheidler; *Meet the Abortion Providers,* videotapes and audiotapes featuring testimony by former abortion assistants, clinic owners, and doctors.

Prolife Nonviolent Action Project
P.O. Box 2193
Gaithersburg, MD 20879
(301) 774-4043

The Prolife Nonviolent Action Project (PNAP) was founded in 1977 "to promote direct action to protect our brothers and sisters from abortion, to unleash a dynamic of peace and reconciliation within families, [and] to challenge and invigorate the moribund right to life establishment" through nonviolent demonstrations aimed at preventing women from having abortions. Since 1988, PNAP has conducted an annual "Rachel's Rescue" on January 22, the anniversary of the *Roe v. Wade* Supreme Court decision, at abortion clinics in the Washington, D.C., area. Rachel's Rescue was the "first national rescue led by women who have suffered abortion"; in 1990, a number of men affected by abortion also participated. These and other "parents of aborted children" serve as spokespersons for the group. PNAP also serves as an information and referral group.

PUBLICATIONS: *Nonviolence Is an Adverb* and *No Cheap Solutions,* booklets by John Cavanaugh O'Keefe; *She Trespasses Too?* transcript from a trial of nine pro-lifers in Baltimore; *In Need of Defense,* a trial transcript in which the three defendants spoke on behalf of the "victims of abortion" rather than themselves; plus videotapes of sit-ins and "rescues."

Religious Coalition for Abortion Rights (RCAR)
100 Maryland Avenue, NE, Suite 307
Washington, DC 20002
(202) 543-7032; FAX (202) 543-7820; legislative hotline (202) 543-0224

The Religious Coalition for Abortion Rights was formed in 1973 by 10 denominations and faith groups as a response to efforts to overturn the *Roe v. Wade* Supreme Court decision legalizing abortion. As of 1990, the coalition included 35 Protestant, Jewish, and other faith groups "committed to the preservation of religious liberty as it pertains to reproductive freedom." Members hold widely varying viewpoints as to when abortion is morally justified: "It is exactly this plurality of beliefs which leads us to the conviction that the abortion decision must remain with the individual, to be made in conjunction with family, clergy and doctors and free from government interference." RCAR's fourfold purpose includes:

Educating the public on the diversity of views on abortion within the religious community and the threats posed to religious liberty by "anti-choice" legislation

Mobilizing the religious community to safeguard the legal option of abortion and to oppose legislation that would limit accessibility of abortion services

Communicating the message of religious liberty in the pro-choice movement

Involving all women of color as decisionmakers in the reproductive choice movement and addressing reproductive health care concerns from the unique perspective of women of color

RCAR works to achieve these goals through four programs: communications, legislative influence, women of color partnership (see below), and affiliates. RCAR has 24 state affiliates and area units, with active groups in more than 30 states. Affiliate activities include clergy counseling for women facing unplanned pregnancies and Operation Respect, which "provides a peaceful, religious presence at often violent 'Operation Rescues.'" RCAR also sponsors a nationwide Clergy for Choice network, which includes more than 4,000 clergy members representing every state and virtually every denomination, and the Voices for Choice Network, a congregationally based action network.

The Women of Color Partnership Program (WCPP), created by RCAR in 1985, serves as a vehicle through which African-American, Latin-American, Asian-Pacific American, Native American, and other women of color can become involved as decisionmakers in the reproductive choice movement. The WCPP works to:

Broaden the agenda of the abortion rights movement to encompass a full range of reproductive health issues, including family planning, birth control, teen pregnancy, prenatal care, child care, and medical abuses against women of color

Promote the education of women of color regarding reproductive health care options

Build a partnership and agenda among all women of color that incorporates political and social organizations and individual faith perspectives

Expand the pro-choice movement to reflect the diverse needs, views, and aspirations of women of color and their families

Ensure that no one is denied access to comprehensive reproductive health care options

PUBLICATIONS: *RCAR Options,* quarterly newsletter; *Dispatch,* update on legislative activity; *Abortion and the Holocaust: Twisting the Language,* booklet; plus affiliate-produced publications and videos.

Seamless Garment Network
c/o Rose Evans, Secretary
P.O. Box 210056
San Francisco, CA 95121-0056
(716) 288-6146 (Carol Crossed)

The Seamless Garment Network (SGN) is an informal network of individuals and organizations devoted to promoting a "consistent ethic of reverence for life." The consistent ethic links issues perceived as life-threatening—including war, abortion, poverty, the arms race, the death penalty, and euthanasia—and challenges groups and individuals working on some or all of these issues to "maintain a cooperative spirit of peace, reconciliation and respect in protecting the unprotected." SGN also supports social justice, pro-life feminism, human rights, and rights for the disabled.

PUBLICATIONS: *Harmony*, bimonthly, nondenominational journal with coverage of consistent ethic news and events plus writing on peace, justice, and life issues; *Consistent Ethic Resource Directory*, including organizations, speakers, books, and periodicals; plus a video.

United States Coalition for Life (USCL)
P.O. Box 315
Export, PA 15632
(412) 327-7379

The United States Coalition for Life was founded in 1972 as a pro-life "think-tank" to deal with "all right-to-life issues including population control, sex education, abortion, euthanasia, and federal funding of anti-life projects." The organization is particularly concerned with population issues, sex education, and "eugenic abortion." The USCL's major goals are to ban classroom sex education, "the gateway to abortion"; to secure a universal ban on abortion and euthanasia; to support pro-life-oriented genetic research; and to end government funding for family planning programs in the United States and abroad. USCL serves primarily as an information clearinghouse, researching and documenting policies, legislation, and events related to its focal issues.

PUBLICATIONS: *The Pro-Life Reporter*, quarterly newsletter; plus various white papers, reports, and booklets.

Value of Life Committee, Inc. (VOLCOM)
637 Cambridge Street
Brighton, MA 02135
(617) 787-4400

The Value of Life Committee is one of the oldest pro-life organizations in the country; it was incorporated in 1970 to "affirm in the public domain the sacredness and inherent value of all human life from conception to natural death and to protect the lives of unborn children by literary research, publication and service." VOLCOM has occasionally published in newspapers such as the *New York Times* and the *Wall Street Journal* statements signed by "distinguished individuals" on issues such as the "humanity of the unborn" and fetal pain. VOLCOM also provides amicus curiae briefs in pro-life-related court cases, as well as testimony before state and national legislatures. VOLCOM maintains an extensive library and serves as a resource center on the "life issues, abortion, infanticide, fetal research, euthanasia and medical ethical areas," responding to requests from students, scholars, writers, legislators, and others. Additionally, individual members have published books and articles and lectured on abortion, in vitro fertilization, fetal research, and euthanasia.

PUBLICATIONS: "When Did Your Life Begin?" brochure.

Victims of Choice
P.O. Box 6268
Vacaville, CA 95696-6268
(707) 448-6015

Victims of Choice (VOC) is a Christian organization that provides assistance and training for counselors working with women suffering from "post-abortion syndrome" (PAS), as well as free counseling for women in the Vacaville area. In addition to training PAS counselors and providing materials for churches, crisis pregnancy centers, and other pro-life organizations, VOC is currently establishing a national referral system for PAS counselors. The organization also works to educate the public on the negative effects of abortion, through press conferences and speeches at rallies and church meetings as well as through testimony before local, state, and national legislatures. VOC also sponsors an annual national Memorial Day of Mourning, in which "aborted women" take part in a march and funeral.

PUBLICATIONS: *Post Abortion Syndrome: A Therapy Model for Crisis Intervention*, a manual for counselors; "Post Abortion Counselor Training," video; audiotape series on abortion recovery training; PAS information packet; plus various brochures, bumper stickers, and buttons.

Voters for Choice/Friends of Family Planning
2000 P Street, NW, Suite 515
Washington, DC 20036
(202) 822-6640

Voters for Choice is an independent, bipartisan political action committee (PAC) founded in 1979 to serve as an umbrella PAC and the electoral arm for the pro-choice community. Its primary purpose is to provide financial support and technical expertise to candidates running for public office who support choice in areas of reproductive health, including the right to legal, safe, affordable abortion. Activities include fundraising, providing campaign advice, phone banks, and media training for candidates.

PUBLICATIONS: *The Winning Campaign,* quarterly newsletter; *Winning with Choice: A Guide to Message and Strategy,* handbook for candidates, plus video.

Women Exploited by Abortion (WEBA)
National Headquarters
24823 Nogal Street
Moreno Valley, CA 92388
(714) 924-4164

Women Exploited by Abortion, founded in 1982, is a nonprofit, nondenominational Christian organization for "women who have had an abortion and now realize it was the wrong decision." In addition to ministering to women who have had abortions through individual counseling and support groups, WEBA works to prevent abortions by "educating women on the trauma of abortion" and to provide "a forum for aborted women to share their experiences through counseling other women who have had the same experience." WEBA currently has chapters in most of the 50 states and some foreign countries. Membership is $10.00 per year; associate memberships are also available for those who have not personally experienced abortion but "who want to help."

PUBLICATIONS: "Before You Make the Decision," "Joy Comes in the Mourning," "Surviving Abortion: Help for the Aborted Woman," brochures.

Women's Legal Defense Fund (WLDF)
2000 P Street, NW, Suite 400
Washington, DC 20036
(202) 887-0364

Founded in 1971, the Women's Legal Defense Fund works to promote women's rights—including the right to legal, safe, affordable abortion—and to shape public policies that support women and their families. WLDF provides technical assistance to activists and state and federal policymakers and participates in targeted litigation to challenge gender discrimination, as well as providing amicus curiae briefs in court cases related to issues of women's equality, including abortion-related cases. It also works to educate the public about the human and social costs of gender discrimination through the publication of guides, policy papers, and posters on such issues as family and medical leaves, affirmative action, sexual harassment, wage discrimination, child support, domestic violence, and reproductive freedom. Regarding abortion rights, WLDF is conducting a public education campaign aimed at "help[ing] the public understand the unbreakable connection between reproductive freedom and a woman's ability to participate fully and equally in this country's economy . . . and the necessity of ensuring that our diverse society does not allow one set of beliefs to dictate the fundamentally private decision of whether or not to terminate a pregnancy."

PUBLICATIONS: *WLDF News,* quarterly newsletter; plus various policy papers, handbooks, brochures, and posters.

Zero Population Growth
1400 16th Street, NW, Suite 320
Washington, DC 20036
(202) 332-2200

Zero Population Growth (ZPG) is a nonprofit membership organization advocating worldwide population stabilization, based on the belief that "the survival and well-being of planet Earth and all of its inhabitants depends on a sustainable balance of people, resources and the environment." To promote its goal, ZPG conducts public education and citizen action efforts to build support for domestic and international family planning and other key population issues, including:

Universal availability of family planning services

Development of safer and more effective contraceptives

Legal, educational, and social equality for women

Improvement of infant and child survival rates

Breaking the cycle of poverty

PUBLICATIONS: *Pro-Choice Action Kit,* information for working to support legal, safe, affordable abortion; "Abortion in America," brochure; "The Supreme Court and Reproductive Rights," brochure; plus a variety of books, booklets, fact sheets, teaching aids, posters, t-shirts, and pins.

5

Selected Print Resources

Bibliographies

Abortion Bibliography. New York: Whitson Publishing Company, 1970– LC 72-78877.

Appearing serially each fall, *Abortion Bibliography* is an attempt at a comprehensive world bibliography on abortion and related subjects. The 1984 edition, for example, includes article citations from over 600 English- and non-English-language journals, as well as dissertations, gleaned from more than 50 indexes and collections of abstracts. Articles are listed both by title and according to subject; the more than 120 subject headings include such topics as abortion in specific countries, abortion statistics, abortion techniques, abortion and economics, birth control attitudes, family planning research, and sterilization. A separate section lists books, government publications, and monographs. An author index is also included. As of 1990, issues of the bibliography were available through 1986.

Centers for Disease Control. **Division of Reproductive Health Publications Related to Abortion: 1980–Present.** Atlanta, GA: Division of Reproductive Health Center for Health Promotion and Education, Centers for Disease Control, 1988.

This is a non-annotated listing of abortion-related papers, articles, and book chapters produced by researchers at the CDC since 1980. Each listing includes the author, title, and publication (book or journal issue) where the paper or article appeared. Available on request from the Centers for Disease Control, Atlanta, GA 30333.

National Right to Life Committee. **Selected Bibliography.** Updated periodically.

This non-annotated bibliography lists more than 70 books, most of them recent publications, although a few date back to the early 1970s. The majority are about abortion and/or the pro-life movement, although a number of selections are included under the headings of medical ethics, euthanasia, infanticide, population, and post-abortion healing. The books are written primarily from an anti-abortion perspective, with the exception of some selections that have been included because they are "so revealing of how pro-abortionists think and operate that [they are] very much worth reading." Available from the National Right to Life Committee, 419 7th Street, NW, Suite 500, Washington, DC 20004-2293, (202) 626-8800.

Nordquist, Joan. **Contemporary Social Issues: A Bibliographic Series: No. 9, Reproductive Rights.** Santa Cruz, CA: Reference and Research Services (511 Lincoln Street, Santa Cruz, CA 95060), 1988. ISBN 0-937855-17-0; ISSN 0887-3569.

This slender bibliography contains non-annotated listings of books and articles on a variety of issues related to reproductive rights. The section on abortion is divided into three subcategories: "Legal and Ethical Concerns," "Minors and Abortion," and "The Pro-life and Pro-choice Movements." Relevant entries may also be found under the sections on fetal rights and paternal rights. Nearly all of the listings were published in 1981 or later, with the majority bearing copyright dates of 1984 or later. Other than that, there are no clear criteria for selection, and no commentary by the compiler is included, other than an occasional notation as to whether a particular book or article is pro-life or pro-choice. A listing of organizations is included in the back of the book.

Winter, Eugenia B. **Psychological and Medical Aspects of Induced Abortion: A Selective, Annotated Bibliography, 1970–1986.** Westport, CT: Greenwood Press, 1988. Indexes. ISSN 0742-6941, No. 7.

This useful volume is number 7 in the publisher's series of Bibliographies and Indexes in Women's Studies. It contains 500 listings, primarily books and artiles, although a few audiovisual items are also included. The items selected are "either classics in the field or representational of the kinds of writing being published on the subjects of interest." Most of the materials were originally published in English, although some translated works were deemed "too significant in terms of their influence on the field to leave out." The bibliography is divided into 10 broad subject areas: abortion (general), abortion clinics, abortion decision, abortion techniques (general), abortion techniques (specific), counseling, morbidity and mortality, abortion effects on subsequent pregnancy, psychological effects, and psychosocial aspects. Also included are author, title, and subject indexes and a review of the literature. The brief

(25–75 words), mostly non-evaluative annotations are essentially content summaries.

Anthologies

Baird, Robert M., and Stuart E. Rosenbaum, eds. **The Ethics of Abortion.** Buffalo, NY: Prometheus Books, 1989. 172p. ISBN 0-87975-521-0.

The essays in this collection were chosen to represent the most prominent and influential positions around the issue of whether "the current practice of allowing women to choose for themselves how to deal with unwanted pregnancies [is] a fundamental violation of the core of Western moral, religious, social or intellectual traditions . . . [or falls] comfortably and justifiably within the Western custom of respecting individual autonomy." The book opens with an excerpt from the majority opinion by Justice Blackmun in the 1973 *Roe v. Wade* decision, followed by a section from Justice White's dissent in that decision, and closes with portions of written opinions from the fragmented *Webster* decision more than 16 years later. In between are 11 essays, most of them by philosophers who have written extensively on abortion and related issues. Included is the 1972 Judith Jarvis Thompson essay "In Defense of Abortion," along with writings by Michael Tooley, Mary Anne Warren, Jane English, Charles Hartshorne, Joan Callahan, Richard Selzer, Paul Ramsey, Harry Gensler, and Sidney Callahan, and the text of a 1987 sermon by Baptist minister Roger Paynter.

Burtchaell, James Tunstead, ed. **Abortion Parley.** New York: Andrews and McMeel, Inc., 1980. 352p. ISBN 0-8362-3600-9.

In October 1979, the University of Notre Dame convened a National Conference on Abortion in the hopes of having an "open and honorable discussion" that would "clarify the issue, . . . establish the facts, and . . . elevate the discussion from inflammatory rhetoric on both sides to more sober and reasoned positions." About 75 persons attended the conference, including representatives from both pro-life and pro-choice organizations, abortion providers, clergy, law professors, executives, and "ordinary citizens." This anthology consists of 12 papers presented at the conference, covering such diverse topics as a statistical profile of individuals likely to take a position at one or the other extreme of the debate; the myths and realities of adoption as an alternative; public policy aspects of abortion, including public funding; psychological characteristics of women at risk for unplanned pregnancy; and a critique of Christian arguments against abortion. Well written and free of polemic, the papers provide a valuable contribution toward clarifying issues involved in the debate.

Butler, J. Douglas, and David F. Walbert, eds. **Abortion, Medicine and the Law.** 3d ed. New York: Facts on File, 1986. 795p. Index. ISBN 0-8160-1198-2.

This hefty but useful volume is the latest to grow out of a special issue of Case Western Reserve University's *Law Review* published in 1966, for which the editors commissioned a series of essays on abortion. The essays were published in book form under the title *Abortion and the Law* in 1967. A second series appeared in 1973 under the title *Abortion, Society and the Law.* The current volume retains 2 articles from the previous edition—an essay on abortion-related ethical issues by Daniel Callahan and a historical article by Alan Guttmacher (updated by Irwin Kaiser)—plus 15 new essays covering various legal, medical, and ethical aspects of abortion. These range from an overview of right-to-life efforts in Congress by Senator Bob Packwood to anti-abortion essays by then president Ronald Reagan and Professor (now Judge) John Noonan. Following the essays are three appendices that offer access to information not easily available elsewhere. The first contains the text of the Supreme Court decisions on *Roe v. Wade* and its companion case, *Doe v. Bolton;* the second contains the complete text of testimony and discussion from the 1981 Senate debate over the Human Life Bill; and the third contains the text of Senate hearings on the Human Life Amendment from 1983, as well as a breakdown of Senate voting on the amendment. A valuable resource for those concerned with the legal and political aspects of the ongoing abortion debate.

Callahan, Sidney, and Daniel Callahan, eds. **Abortion: Understanding Differences.** New York: Plenum Press, 1984. 338p. Index. ISBN 0-306-41640-9.

Daniel Callahan, a philosopher with a special interest in biomedical ethics, and his wife, Sidney, a psychology professor, have studied, discussed, and written about abortion for nearly 30 years—from opposing sides. In creating the project that resulted in this volume, they sought to "illuminate, enrich, and deepen the dialogue on abortion" by exploring the links between people's feelings about abortion and their "broader, more encompassing world views and life commitments." The 12 contributors—all women with the exception of Daniel Callahan—represent such diverse fields as sociology, psychiatry, theology, political science, and philosophy and are about equally divided between pro-life and pro-choice viewpoints. In the opening chapter, Mary Ann Lammana discusses the "middle course" steered by most Americans with respect to abortion. This is followed by Kristin Luker's discussion of her research on the world views of pro-life and pro-choice activists. In the remaining papers contributors explore their views on abortion within the context of their values and views on such fundamental issues as the role of the family, children and child-rearing, women and feminism, and social and cultural life. Each essay is followed by a commentary written by a participant representing the opposite point of view, thus establishing a "dialogue." Throughout, the authors display empathy and respect for each other's positions, while providing thoughtful and articulate defenses of their own views.

Hilgiers, Thomas W., M.D., Dennis J. Horan, and David Mall, eds. **New Perspectives on Human Abortion.** Frederick, MD: University Publications of America, 1981. 504p. Index. ISBN 0-89093-379-0.

Contributors to this anthology include professionals representing a range of fields and specialties, including pediatrics, nuclear medicine, obstetrics and gynecology, psychology, philosophy, theology, and ethics. Part I addresses medical aspects of abortion, including characteristics of the fetus and fetal development, mongoloidism (Down's syndrome), abortion-related mortality, short- and long-term complications of abortion, psychiatric effects of abortion, a model for estimating the number of criminal abortions, and sexual assault and pregnancy. Part II concerns legal aspects of abortion, including abortion and midwifery, the experience of pain by the unborn, the Supreme Court and abortion funding, religion and abortion, the West German abortion decision and the European Commission on Human Rights, and abortion and the law. Part III contains essays addressing various social and philosophical aspects of abortion. The majority, though not all, of the selections argue against abortion. The articles and essays are uniformly well written, carefully thought out, and thoroughly documented and present ample food for thought.

Hodgson, Jane E. **Abortion and Sterilization: Medical and Social Aspects.** London: Academic Press and Orlando, FL: Grune & Stratton, 1981. 594p. Index. ISBN 0-12-792030-7 (Academic Press); 0-8089-1344-1 (Grune & Stratton).

Originally developed as a textbook, this anthology has been widely used by legal as well as medical professionals and by students, instructors, and researchers. In addition to providing teaching material on the growing and controversial field of fertility control, the book was intended to "legitimate abortion and sterilization for the sake of those who need and seek the service" and to "present the best techniques, in the proper medical perspective, as well as the social and political history, epidemiology and public health aspects." Accordingly, contributions were sought from leaders in the field from around the world. The American contributors include Henry P. David, Christopher Tietze, Roy Lucas, Willard Cates, David Grimes, Malcolm Potts, and Jane Hodgson, who also edited the volume. The 23 papers cover a variety of topics, including abortion policies; the epidemiology of induced abortion; abortion law; abortions for teenagers; abortion morbidity and mortality; abortion and mental health; delayed complications of induced abortion; abortion and contraception in relation to family planning services; the provision and organization of abortion and sterilization services in the United States; and detailed, illustrated discussions of abortion and sterilization techniques. Though currently out of print, this useful volume is still available through legal and medical libraries.

Jung, Patricia Beattie, and Thomas A. Shannon, eds. **Abortion and Catholicism: The American Debate.** New York: Crossroad, 1988. 331p. ISBN 0-8245-0884-X.

This anthology was collected with the view that "only open, honest, and respectful dialogue" will help to resolve the abortion debate within the Catholic community. The editors sought to avoid articles that represented radical perspectives or "purely ideological or authoritarian pronouncements," instead focusing on "the middle ground—where the arguments are both more responsible, more complex, and often not that far apart." As a result, the articles are refreshingly free of the polemic that often characterizes arguments about abortion; rather, they are thoughtful—often painfully so—and thought-provoking. The book is divided into three parts, each focusing on one aspect of the debate: moral, political, and ecclesiastic. Part I includes defenses of the prohibition of abortion and discussions on the moral status of the fetus, as well as different feminist approaches to the issue. Part II contains articles addressing religion, morality, and public policy, and Part III addresses two aspects of the ecclesiastic debate: the implications of moral consistency and dissent within the Church. The contributors include several archbishops; a number of professors of theology, philosophy, ethics, and religion; a magazine editor; an author and lecturer; a law student; and one elected official, Governor Mario Cuomo of New York.

Melton, Gary B., ed. **Adolescent Abortion: Psychological and Legal Issues.** Lincoln: University of Nebraska Press, 1986. 152p. Author and subject indexes. ISBN 0-8032-3094-X.

This volume was produced by a committee sponsored by several divisions of the American Psychological Association, which was formed to review psychological issues involved in the Supreme Court's analysis of adolescent abortion policy and to provide guidelines for researchers and for psychologists who counsel minors regarding abortion. It provides a psycho-legal analysis of adolescent abortion, supported by four background papers that examine the epidemiological context of adolescent abortion, the psychological issues involved in abortion for adolescents, the consequences of adolescent abortion and child-bearing, and legal and ethical issues involved in counseling pregnant adolescents. The authors suggest that many assumptions about psychological issues in adolescent abortion policy are not supported by available research, nor does the research justify special provisions for minors' consent to abortion.

Sachdev, Paul, ed. **International Handbook on Abortion.** Westport, CT: Greenwood Press, 1988. 520p. ISBN 0-313-23463-9.

This is a one-volume compendium on abortion policies and practices in 33 countries. An introduction surveying international trends is followed by 33 chapters on individual countries, grouped according to region: Africa, Asia, Eastern and Western Europe, the Nordic countries, Latin America and the Caribbean, North and South America, and the Middle East. Each chapter was written by a public health specialist and includes detailed information on:

The historical development of abortion policy

The roles of the medical profession, news media, religious and women's organizations, and other pressure groups in legislative enactments

Attitudes over time of the medical community and the public toward abortion practices

Demographic data on women seeking abortions, including incidence, age, parity, marital status, gestation period, pre- and post-abortion contraceptive use, and repeat abortions

Abortions among special groups such as teenagers and minorities

The impact of abortion on fertility behavior and on family planning policy and programs

Data on illegal abortion, including incidence, complications, and morbidity

Abortion research

Many chapters contain supplementary statistical tables and references. This rigorously objective book contains a wealth of useful data for comparing national policies and trends on abortion throughout the world.

—————, ed. **Perspectives on Abortion.** Metuchen, NJ: Scarecrow Press, 1985. 281p. Name and subject indexes. ISBN 0-8108-1708-X.

This collection of 19 original essays is meant as a sourcebook for researchers; service providers in the health care, social work, and related fields; and teachers. The contributors represent such areas as sociology, obstetrics and gynecology, family planning, social work, health, social medicine, population studies, philosophy, and theology; among them are James Mohr, Malcolm Potts, and Christopher Tietze. The scholarly, carefully documented, and generally objective essays are based on empirical research and address abortion primarily as a political and social issue rather than a moral one. The book is divided into four thematic sections. Part I deals with the bases of the conflict over abortion in U.S. society, discussing it in terms of its historical origins, religious and sociopolitical contexts, and moral perspectives and suggesting possibilities for a compromise solution acceptable to most Americans. Part II concerns women who seek abortions—who they are, how they make their decisions, and the consequences of those decisions, including psychological and emotional effects, morbidity and mortality, trends in repeat abortions, and effects on future family goals. Part III examines how attitudes toward abortion are shaped over time and how they affect both the provision and the use of abortion services. Part IV addresses problem pregnancy counseling, particularly the lack of empirically based information on such counseling services; the importance of both pre- and post-abortion counseling; and the difficulty of conducting research on problem pregnancy counseling.

Szumski, Bonnie, ed. **Abortion: Opposing Viewpoints.** St. Paul, MN: Greenhaven Press, 1986. 214p. Index, bibliographies. ISBN 0-89908-380-3 (cloth); 0-89908-355-2 (paper).

This book is one of the Opposing Viewpoints series, whose purpose is to encourage critical thinking by helping readers learn to evaluate sources of information, separate fact from opinion, identify stereotypes, and recognize ethnocentrism. This volume contains more than 30 articles, essays, and excerpts representing conflicting points of view on several questions: When does life begin? Should abortion remain a personal choice? Is abortion immoral? Can abortion be justified? Should abortion remain legal? Are extremist tactics justified in the abortion debate? A number of prominent voices from both sides of the abortion debate (and a few from in between) are represented, including Kristin Luker, Joseph Scheidler, Kathleen McDonnell, Cardinal John O'Connor, Daniel Maguire, and James Burtchaell, as well as more general thinkers like columnist Ellen Goodman and essayist Barbara Ehrenreich. Each selection is preceded by questions to consider while reading the article, and each chapter concludes with a related activity aimed at helping the development of critical thinking skills and a periodical bibliography. Included are a list of abortion rights and anti-abortion organizations and a brief annotated book bibliography. An excellent volume for encouraging thought and discussion, especially among young people, and for gaining an overview of the diversity of thought on abortion.

Walsh, Mary Roth, ed. **Psychology of Women: Ongoing Debates.** New Haven, CT: Yale University Press, 1987. 484p. Indexes. ISBN 0-300-03965-4 (cloth); 0-300-03966-2 (paper).

This anthology includes two previously published articles on the psychological effects of abortion: "Psychological Reaction to Legalized Abortion" (Osofsky and Osofsky, 1972) and "Women's Responses to Abortion" (Lodl, McGettigan, and Bucy, 1985). Although the editor introduces the articles as representing opposing viewpoints, both actually reach a similar conclusion, specifically that the reaction experienced by the majority of women is relief and that only a small percentage of women experience lasting negative effects. The second article does, however, discuss factors related to negative responses and emphasizes the need for effective post-abortion counseling to help those women who do experience psychological problems. The volume also includes Carol Gilligan's original article "In a Different Voice" (1977), which contains an analysis of the thought processes of women deciding whether to have abortions.

Books and Monographs

Abortion—General

Benderly, Beryl Lieff. **Thinking about Abortion: An Essential Handbook for the Woman Who Wants To Come to Terms with What Abortion Means in Her Life.** Garden City, NY: Doubleday, 1984. 204p. Index, bibliography. ISBN 0-385-27757-1.

Meticulously researched and clearly written, this compact book addresses the social, medical, emotional, and moral aspects of unwanted pregnancy and the alternatives for dealing with it. The author does not pull any punches; her descriptions of abortion techniques and the experience itself are blunt and explicit, and her essay on the moral questions raised by abortion is both succinct and powerful. Without giving any answers, and without claiming the process is anything but difficult, Benderly explores the implications of what it means to choose whether to have an abortion and to take full responsibility for that choice. This is a valuable book.

Frohock, Fred M. **Abortion: A Case Study in Law and Morals.** Westport, CT: Greenwood Press, 1983. 226p. Index, bibliography. ISBN 0-313-23953-3.

This well-written and often engaging book attempts to step outside of the emotional atmosphere surrounding abortion and to engage in rational discourse, in order to discover "how morals and the law can be fitted together to represent a rational abortion practice." Frohock, a professor of political science, begins by examining the various justifications for state enforcement of morals as they relate to abortion, the moral arguments for and against abortion, the legal issues related to abortion, and the realities of abortion practice since *Roe v. Wade.* He then explores possible resolutions of the conflict, arriving at what he sees as the most agreeable moral, legal, and practical resolution for all involved. As part of his research, Frohock interviewed activists on both sides of the debate, and he quotes liberally from the interviews to weave a "dialogue" of pro-choice and pro-life arguments throughout the book. Each chapter includes suggestions for further reading. Also included is a bibliography divided into subject areas, including general studies, ethical issues, statistical studies, the politics of abortion, attitudes toward abortion, law and morals, legal issues, and case law on abortions and other moral issues.

Gardner, Joy. **A Difficult Decision: A Compassionate Book about Abortion.** Trumansburg, NY: The Crossing Press, 1986. 115p. Bibliography.

Joy Gardner is a counselor and holistic healer who specializes in loss and death issues. After finding that many of her clients bore emotional scars from abortions, some of which had occurred decades earlier, she developed a workshop called "Abortion—Healing the Wounds." This book, which might be described as a New Age handbook on abortion, discusses methods she uses to help women and couples overcome problems associated with abortions, including emotional release exercises, in-depth counseling, stress control, nutrition, herbs, visualization, and color therapy. While she supports the right to legal, safe abortion, Gardner also addresses the problems of women who would prefer to give birth but lack the resources to do so. She offers guidelines for making clear decisions about whether to have an abortion or to have the child and either raise it or give it up for adoption, offering full support for whatever decision is made. A special section addresses the feelings and experiences of men involved in an unexpected pregnancy; another describes fetal development up to 25 weeks LMP. While some might be put off by the New Age approach, many readers will find this book supportive and helpful, whether they are dealing with a current pregnancy or a past abortion.

Howe, Louise Kapp. **Moments on Maple Avenue: The Reality of Abortion.** New York: Macmillan, 1984. 209p. Bibliography. $13.95. ISBN 0-002-555170-1.

This is a sensitively written, "you-are-there" account of an "ordinary day" in an abortion clinic in White Plains, New York. Through her observations of and conversations with the clinic's staff and patients, as well as with the boyfriends, husbands, parents, and women friends who accompanied some of the patients, the author brings the abortion debate down to an intensely personal level that leaves little room for polemic or absolute answers on either side. She concludes by suggesting some societal changes that must take place if the number of abortions is to be reduced and women are to have real choices as to when and with whom they will bear children.

McDonnell, Kathleen. **Not an Easy Choice.** Boston: South End Press, 1984. 157p. Index, bibliography. ISBN 0-89608-265-5 (cloth); 0-89608-264-4 (paper).

Kathleen McDonnell is a Canadian feminist who was moved to reevaluate the feminist position on abortion by the birth of her daughter, which "gave the idea of the fetus in the womb a new concreteness." The result is this thoughtful and provocative book, which dares to risk "splitting the women's movement and giving ammunition to our enemies" by discussing aspects of abortion that many feminists have been too fearful to address: the grief, sense of loss, and ambivalence experienced by many, if not most women who undergo abortions, and abortion's moral dimension, which continues to trouble the "great middle ground of people" who nonetheless support the right to choose. McDonnell acknowledges that the right-to-life movement, to its benefit, openly discusses these and other bioethical issues: "Their solutions are for the most part wrong-headed and simplistic, but they are asking what is to many minds the right question: is life of value in itself? For it is not much of a leap from that abstract question to: 'is *my* life of any value?'" Through her exploration, McDonnell comes full circle to a renewed conviction that women must have access to legal, safe, and affordable abortion, as part of "reclaiming our reproduction [by] embracing it, celebrating it as the joyous miracle that it is, while at the same time affirming that it is not the totality of our existence, that we have needs, visions and potentials as broad and varied as the rest of humanity."

Rodman, Hyman, Betty Sarvis, and Joy Bonar. **The Abortion Question.** New York: Columbia University Press, 1987. 223p. Index, bibliography. ISBN 0-231-05332-0.

The Abortion Question is a dispassionate, balanced, and thorough examination of the moral, medical, emotional, social, and legal issues surrounding abortion. Rodman and Sarvis's earlier book *The Abortion Controversy,* published shortly after the 1973 Supreme Court *Roe v. Wade* decision, was widely praised for its even-handed analysis of the complex issues surrounding the debate. This latest work retains that balance and also manages to say a great deal within a short space. Though meticulously researched, it is not cloaked in scholarly language; instead it is straightforward, clear, and highly readable. Beginning with a succinct historical overview, the authors explore the rise of the abortion controversy; the social and cultural dynamics of fertility control; the central issues in the moral debate; the medical, pyschosocial, and emotional aspects of abortion; the developments leading up to *Roe v. Wade;* the legal controversy since 1973; and attitudes about abortion. They note that arguments about abortion "may be framed in rational and objective terms, but the conclusions are typically linked to subjective beliefs and values." In a final chapter, "Where Do We Go from Here?" the authors examine possible solutions to the controversy, finally predicting the adoption of an approach that, while it may not please either of the polar groups, will eventually "be accepted as reasonable and relatively noncontroversial public policy."

Terkel, Susan Neiburg. **Abortion: Facing the Issues.** New York: Franklin Watts, 1988. 160p. Index, bibliography. ISBN 0-531-10565-2.

This is a remarkably balanced and succinct summary of what abortion involves and the issues surrounding it. Susan Terkel has a degree in child development and family relationships from Cornell University and has written several books for children, including one on sexual abuse (with Janice Rench). In her preface, she states that she has tried to write an "objective, *passionate* book about abortion" (italics hers). Because her work has garnered criticism from both the pro-life and pro-choice camps, with each insisting that she favors the other, she feels she has succeeded—as indeed she has. Within this short volume, Terkel surveys the history of abortion laws in the United States, explains the *Roe v. Wade* decision and its impact, describes how abortions are performed, looks at the abortion industry, discusses who has abortions and why, explores public opinion regarding abortion, and examines the politics of abortion and the public controversy that surrounds it, including the moral issues involved—all the while displaying sympathy and compassion for different points of view and the lives and emotions involved. Clearly written and carefully researched, this book serves as an excellent overview of the abortion issue. Particularly recommended for young people.

Tietze, Christopher, and Stanley K. Henshaw. **Induced Abortion: A World Review, 1986.** New York: Alan Guttmacher Institute, 1986. 143p. ISBN 0-939253-05-4.

This is the sixth edition of the "abortion fact book," which Christopher Tietze created in 1973. Although Tietze died recently, the work he pioneered has been carried on by co-author Stanley Henshaw; an update of *Induced Abortion: A World Review* was published in the March/April 1990 edition of *Family Planning Perspectives*. This book contains a wealth of carefully documented statistical and factual information on abortion laws, policies, and practices, as well as its social and medical aspects, throughout the world and is one of the most cited sources in the field. Included is information on abortion laws and policies in different regions; the incidence of abortion; demographic and social characteristics of women obtaining abortions; periods of gestation; descriptions of and statistics on various abortion procedures; sterilization; abortion complications and sequelae; abortion mortality; abortion and contraception; repeat abortions; abortion service delivery; and the effects of abortion policy on mortality, morbidity, legal and illegal abortion, fertility, and children. Much of the information is presented in useful tabular and graphic form. An important resource.

Tribe, Laurence H. **Abortion: The Clash of Absolutes.** New York: W. W. Norton and Company, 1990. 270p. Index. $19.95. ISBN 0-393-02845-3.

Laurence Tribe is a respected authority on constitutional law and a Harvard law professor who has presented 19 cases to the Supreme Court, at least 13 of them successfully. In this far-ranging and provocative book, Tribe explores the complicated historical, social, cultural, political, and legal issues surrounding the abortion debate and lays the framework for a "negotiated peace" that can end the bitter conflict between pro-choice and pro-life, or, as Tribe puts it, between "liberty" and "life." Writing with crystal clarity, logic, and respect for the truth that exists on both sides of the debate, Tribe addresses the arguments for and against legal abortion, especially those that pit the rights of fetuses against the rights of pregnant women. He discusses the constitutional "rightness" of *Roe v. Wade,* examines in detail the potential implications of overturning that landmark decision, and outlines the repercussions of possible compromises. Finally, he asks readers to look at the deeper values underlying their feelings and opinions about abortion and to recognize that "what is at stake is not really the absolute in whose name the battle has been fought." Such honesty, he says, may enable us finally to "get beyond our once intractable dispute about the question of abortion." This book is must reading for anyone interested in the abortion debate and its wider ramifications.

Wharton, Mandy. **Understanding Social Issues: Abortion.** New York: Gloucester Press, 1989. 62p. Index, further readings. ISBN 0-531-17189-2.

This book, which was originally published in Britain, has been somewhat revised for a U.S. audience. Written for young adults, it presents historical, global, and social perspectives on abortion. Although openly favoring legal abortion, Wharton endeavors to present the ambiguities surrounding the issue, particularly with respect to fetal development and fetal rights. The book is thus relatively balanced. It is not, however, particularly well written, and young readers may find parts of it more confusing than enlightening. Also, some of the facts are inaccurate—the founders of NARAL, for example, might be surprised to learn that their organization dates back to 1932. Wharton also states that the World Health Organization (WHO) estimates the number of deaths from illegal abortions at 200,000 annually; the actual WHO estimate is a range—from 115,000 to 204,000. The intent of this book is admirable; unfortunately it falls somewhat short of its goal.

Willke, John C., and Mrs. J. C. Willke. **The Handbook on Abortion.** Cincinnati, OH: Hiltz Publishing Co., 1971. 169p.

This compact book has been called the "bible" of the pro-life movement. In question-and-answer form, it addresses the issues of when life begins, fetal development, abortion techniques, and arguments for abortion such as rape, incest, a woman's right to control her body, and the population explosion. It then offers advice and information on alternatives to abortion, "the words we use," and resources for working against abortion. *The Handbook on Abortion* is perhaps most famous for being the first publication to use dramatic color pictures of aborted fetuses—pictures that have since proliferated on posters, pamphlets, and protest signs and that have come to symbolize the movement. Also included is a short story dramatizing a society that enforces euthanasia for those over 50 who are no longer "useful"—a scenario that Willke and others claim will be one result of continued tolerance of abortion. Since the handbook's publication, the Willkes have become two of the movement's most visible and active spokespersons. Dr. Willke is the past president of the National Right to Life Committee.

Wilt, Judith. **Abortion, Choice, and Contemporary Fiction: The Armageddon of the Maternal Instinct.** Chicago: University of Chicago Press, 1990. 183p. Index. ISBN 0-226-90158-0.

The built-in drama of abortion makes it a powerful plot device for exploring complex issues of psyche and relationships. In this book, Boston College English professor Judith Wilt examines the role of abortion in a number of modern novels by such writers as John Barth, Margaret Atwood, Joan Didion, Marge Piercy, William Faulkner, Alice Walker, Mary Gordon, John Irving, Ernest Hemingway, Toni Morrison, and others. Underlying the literary analyses is Wilt's exploration of the "profound psychocultural shock" created as maternity, once regarded as instinctual, becomes a matter of conscious choice.

In an opening chapter, Wilt discusses the ways in which stories, both real and fictional, shape perceptions and emotions about abortion: "Debate about abortion may begin with reasons, proceed to statistics, but it always comes down, really, to stories." After discussing several "true stories" about abortion, Wilt proceeds to explore her theme in relationship to various novelists' treatment of abortion and the issues that surround it—issues of gender inequality, racial and sexual oppression, fears of change and abandonment, empowerment and disempowerment, and the choice of whether to allow "potentiality" to become real. Though extremely academic, this unusual and interesting book has the additional advantage of pointing the way to a rich and varied reading list of abortion-related fiction.

Abortion Activists and Activist Movements

Faux, Marian. **Crusaders: Voices from the Abortion Front.** New York: Birch Lane Press, published by Carol Publishing Group, 1990. 289p. Index. ISBN 1-55972-020-4.

In her second book about abortion, freelance writer Marian Faux profiles six individuals who are deeply embroiled in the controversy: Frank Sussman, the St. Louis, Missouri, lawyer who has made abortion the focus of his extensive pro bono work and who presented the pro-choice argument in the 1989 Supreme Court hearings on *Webster v. Reproductive Health Services;* B. J. Isaacson-Jones and the other women who work at Reproductive Health Services, a clinic in St. Louis; Randall Terry, the politically ambitious, charismatic leader of Operation Rescue; Moira Bentson, a poor, single mother who serves as a "foot soldier" in Operation Rescue's battle against abortion; Vernice Miller, a black pro-choice activist and the developmental director for the Center for Constitutional Rights in New York City, who has worked hard to get women of color involved—and heard—in the abortion debate; and Frances Kissling, head of Catholics for a Free Choice and one of the few activists who believes that the abortion issue can be satisfactorily resolved. Based on extensive personal interviews as well as outside research, the portraits are vivid and interesting, though clearly colored by the author's pro-choice views.

Paige, Connie. **The Right-to-Lifers: Who They Are, How They Operate, Where They Get Their Money.** New York: Summit Books, 1983. 286p. Index. ISBN 0-671-43180-3.

The Right-to-Lifers is a detailed look at the pro-life movement—its roots; its growth and development through the early 1980s; its strategies and tactics; its politics; and its key players, supporters, and allies, from the Catholic Church hierarchy to the organizers of the New Right. Paige, an investigative journalist, shares few, if any, beliefs with her subjects, and she does not hesitate to expose their foibles and gaffes, while at the same time giving them credit for their considerable skill and accomplishments. Rich in anecdotes, quotations, and descriptions of people and events, this book paints a vivid portrait that feminists, liberals, and abortion rights supporters are likely to find both disturbing and reassuring, since it will reinforce their beliefs about their opponents. Those it portrays and their allies, on the other hand, will probably find it biased and condescending.

Scheidler, Joseph M. **Closed: 99 Ways To Stop Abortion.** Westchester, IL: Good News Publishers, 1985. 350p. Index. $9.95. ISBN 0-89107-346-9.

Closed is a classic handbook of political activism, written by one of the country's most prominent, visible, and vocal opponents of abortion. The 99 brief "chapters" in this book offer practical, detailed guidance that would prove useful to almost anyone with a cause. The tactics—all ostensibly legal—range from "sidewalk counseling" of abortion patients to infiltrating "enemy" organizations. Included is a chapter titled "Why Violence Won't Work." Although Scheidler's language may alarm and anger his opponents and those with less radical convictions, people on both sides would agree that his advice has proven extremely effective.

The Ethics of Abortion

Burtchaell, James Tunstead. **Rachel Weeping and Other Essays on Abortion.** New York: Andrews and McMeel, Inc., 1982. 383p. Index. ISBN 0-8362-3602-5.

James Burtchaell is a Catholic priest and former university provost at Notre Dame who has written at length on abortion. This collection of essays holds firmly to the official Catholic Church view that the embryo is fully human from the moment of conception and that abortion is therefore murder. In one lengthy essay, Father Burtchaell draws parallels between abortion, the slaughter of Jews in Nazi Germany, and the depersonalization of American black slaves. In another, "What Is a Child Worth?" he extends the debate to infanticide and euthanasia. In yet another, he reflects on what he sees as a lack of character among women who choose to abort: "Story after story [tells] how unborn young lives have been the wastage of an incoherence, disaffiliation, self-indulgence, and repugnance for truth that afflicts their parents." Well written and carefully researched, *Rachel Weeping* is an eloquent, if wordy, presentation of the classic arguments against abortion.

Grobstein, Clifford. **Science and the Unborn: Choosing Human Futures.** New York: Basic Books, 1988. 207p. Index. ISBN 0-465-07295-X.

Embryologist Clifford Grobstein is professor emeritus in biological science and public policy at the University of California, San Diego, and a member of the Ethics Committee of the American Fertility Society. In this book he seeks "to dispel the darkness of the womb and to illuminate what is within," in an attempt to stimulate the development of public policies that address the status of the unborn with respect to such issues as abortion, in vitro fertilization, and medical research. Within the context of human development from fertilization to birth and beyond, he discusses the progressive development of individuality—genetic, developmental, functional, behavioral, psychic, and social. He then explores the issues and considerations underlying the status of the unborn at each stage of development—pre-embryo, embryo, and fetus. In conclusion, he calls for a concerted effort to address the questions of status of the unborn. Both scientific and philosophical, and totally free of polemic, this book is a valuable addition to the literature and a persuasive call for a national commitment to seek a consensus on issues that can only become more complex and troubling as time goes on.

Harrison, Beverly Wildung. **Our Right To Choose: Toward a New Ethic of Abortion.** Boston: Beacon Press, 1983. 334p. Index. ISBN 0-8070-1508-3 (cloth); 0-8070-1509-1 (paper).

Beverly Wildung Harrison is a Christian theologian and ethicist. In *Our Right To Choose,* she examines the ethics of abortion within the context of the attitudes of Western culture in general and Christianity in particular toward women, medicine, religion, and the law. Most discussions of abortion ethics center around the moral status of the fetus, but, Harrison argues, the reasoning behind such arguments is intrinsically sexist. Instead, "the well-being of a woman and the value of her life plan must always be recognized as of intrinsic value in any appeal to intrinsic value in a moral analysis of abortion." Placing the abortion controversy within the broader context of procreative choice, Harrison examines the theologies behind the moral debate and presents a new view of Christian teaching on abortion, arguing that the latter has been distorted by patriarchal ideology and ignorance of newer methodologies of social and cultural history. She proposes a liberal theological and feminist perspective on procreative choice and abortion, finally challenging "those who support both procreative choice for women and respect for fetal life [to work] together to simultaneously reduce the necessity of frequent resort to abortion and to enhance women's well-being in society." This is a bold, passionate, and often difficult work, a classic in the field.

History

Keller, Allan. **Scandalous Lady: The Life and Times of Madame Restell, New York's Most Notorious Abortionist.** New York: Atheneum, 1981. 191p. ISBN 0-689-11213-0.

This is a lively biography of the most famous—or infamous—abortionist of the nineteenth century, Anna Lohman, better known as Madame Restell. Restell had a thriving abortion practice in New York City for more than three decades, until she was finally brought down in 1878 by the anti-obscenity crusader Anthony Comstock. Comstock used his favorite trick of posing as a poor, desperate father to fool Restell into offering him "medicine" for his pregnant wife, whereupon he and his vice squad raided her house. Restell, whose income was rumored to be in excess of $1 million a year, escaped justice and accomplished a dramatic exit by slitting her own throat in her bathtub the night before the trial. Keller, a newspaper reporter, writer, editor, and columnist who served for 23 years on the faculty of the Graduate School of Journalism at Columbia University, unearthed an abundance of detail that enriches this vivid portrayal of one of the more notorious episodes in abortion history. The work includes illustrations.

Lader, Lawrence. **Abortion II: Making the Revolution.** Boston: Beacon Press, 1973. 242p. Index, bibliography. ISBN 0-8070-2180-6.

Abortion II is the inside story of the early abortion rights movement, told by Lawrence Lader, an author and activist whose crusade for abortion rights stretches back almost 30 years. His first book on the subject, titled simply *Abortion,* was published in 1966. With it, Lader launched a public campaign in which he realized he had "perilously few allies." Only two small groups had made any kind of organized protest against restrictive abortion laws: the Association for the Study of Abortion, a New York group made up mostly of doctors and lawyers; and, in California, the Society for Humane Abortion, which was "little more than a loyal band of partisans drawn to an incandescent rebel named Patricia Maginnis." Lader describes the growth of the abortion rights movement from this handful of protesters and lawbreakers—including clergy members and others who participated in referral services, as well as doctors who provided abortions at the risk of their careers and their freedom— to a series of judicial challenges, legislative debates, and mass protests that eventually shifted attitudes and finally laws about abortion. Though Lader can hardly be called objective, *Abortion II* stands as a classic and thorough account of the people and the events involved in the struggle for legalized abortion.

Messer, Ellen, and Kathryn E. May. **Back Rooms: Voices from the Illegal Abortion Era.** New York: St. Martin's Press, 1988. 224p. ISBN 0-312-01732-4.

This is an "oral history"—a collection of interviews about people's experiences with abortion prior to *Roe v. Wade.* Most of the brief stories are told by women who had abortions, or who wanted abortions and could not obtain them, during what the authors call the "dark years" when abortion was illegal. The women's current ages range from late 30s to mid-80s; their stories include descriptions of abortions conducted without anesthetic in filthy apartments by leering "doctors," of shotgun marriages ending in divorce, or of handing infants over for adoption. One or two were pregnant as a result of rape, some were "good girls" who "made a mistake," others were married and felt for various reasons that they could not add another child to their families. Also included are interviews with a psychiatrist who helped women qualify for therapeutic abortions, a doctor who performed a few carefully disguised illegal abortions, and abortion rights activists Bill Baird, Lawrence Lader, and Reverend Robert Hare.

Mohr, James. **Abortion in America: The Origins and Evolution of National Policy.** New York: Oxford University Press, 1978. 331p. Index. ISBN 0-19-502249-1.

This is the classic historical study on abortion and abortion policy in the United States. Mohr, a history professor, traces the roots of current attitudes and policies toward abortion through a detailed historical picture of abortion as it evolved through the nineteenth century. In 1800, abortion was a legal and accepted, if not openly acknowledged, practice. By mid-century, it had become increasingly common, particularly among married, native-born, Protestant women, and abortion practitioners and producers of abortifacients advertised openly in the everyday press and even in religious journals. By 1900, thanks in large part to the concerted efforts of the newly formed American Medical Association, abortion had been outlawed virtually throughout the United States. Mohr provides a fascinating and impartial analysis of the unique social, legal, and historical factors that led to this turnaround. Perhaps the most cited book in abortion literature, *Abortion in America* provides essential background for understanding present abortion policies, practice, and conflict.

Nathanson, Bernard. **Aborting America.** New York: Doubleday, 1979. 320p. Index, bibliography. ISBN 0-385-14461-X.

Bernard Nathanson, an obstetrician and gynecologist, is one of abortion's most visible and vocal opponents. In the late 1960s and early 1970s, however, he was a staunch advocate of legalized abortion and was in fact a co-founder of the National Association to Repeal Abortion Laws (now the National Abortion Rights Action League). This book chronicles his early experiences with abortion, including his stint as director of the Center for Reproductive and Sexual Health ("the largest abortion clinic in the world"), his political involvement, and his gradual realization that his feelings about abortion had undergone a dramatic change. In the latter part of the book, Dr. Nathanson conducts a broader examination of the issues surrounding abortion. He critiques the "specious" arguments for and against abortion, discusses fetal development, and explores some of the philosophical, medical, and legal questions surrounding the issue. Finally he suggests that it may soon be possible to transplant an unwanted fetus out of one womb and into another, or into some sort of artificial uterus—raising, but not answering, the question of what would be done with all those unaborted babies. This is a classic in the field, interesting both for its historical content and for its unique—and provocative—perspective.

Olasky, Marvin. **The Press and Abortion: 1838–1988.** Hillsdale, NJ: Lawrence Erlbaum Associates, 1988. 200p. Index. ISBN 0-8058-0199-5 (cloth); 0-8058-0485-4 (paper).

This book traces the history of abortion in the United States as it has been portrayed in the print media, with the emphasis on coverage by "broad-based, general interest print media," rather than that by religious, political, or special interest magazines and newsletters. From the early advertisements by Madame Restell to the current controversy over fetal tissue transplants, the book presents an array of articles, editorials, and advertisements gleaned from newspapers and news magazines—primarily New York based—as well as excerpts from a few popular books. Over the 150-year period, the author notes, attitudes toward abortion as expressed in the media have gone through a number of shifts. Restell and other abortionists used the press to promote abortion and build a lucrative business, but in the later part of the nineteenth century papers such as the *New York Times* and the *National Police Gazette* "helped to turn the tide" against abortion. Coverage waned in the first part of this century, but since the 1960s, Olasky alleges, the press has shown an increasing bias in favor of abortion, in response to "the strategies of masters of abortion public relations." Despite its obvious bias, this book is an interesting and thorough account of the media's role in shaping attitudes and arguments about abortion since the 1850s.

Medical and Legal Aspects of Abortion

Boston Women's Health Book Collective. **The New Our Bodies, Ourselves.** Revised ed. New York: Simon and Schuster, 1984. 352p. ISBN 0-671-22145-0.

Abortion is the topic of Chapter 16 of this well-known and highly acclaimed volume on women's health and self-care. The chapter packs a great deal of information and commentary into a relatively brief number of pages. It discusses both the physical and emotional aspects of abortion, including deciding whether to have an abortion, abortion techniques, finding and choosing an abortion facility, risks and complications, and what actually happens during an abortion. Included are firsthand accounts by women who have had abortions, as well as a brief resource list of organizations, readings, and films.

Drucker, Dan. **Abortion Decisions of the Supreme Court, 1973 through 1989: A Comprehensive Review with Historical Commentary.** Jefferson, NC: McFarland & Company, Inc. (P.O. Box 611, Jefferson, NC 28640), 1990. 206p. Index. ISBN 0-89950-459-0.

This slim volume offers clear and precise summations of Supreme Court cases dealing with abortion (with the somewhat puzzling exception of the 1980 *Harris v. McRae* case), from *Roe v. Wade* through the 1989 *Webster* decision. For each case, Drucker includes the disputed law in its entirety, followed by discussions of each contested provision and lower court rulings. These in turn are followed by paraphrased versions of the Court's opinion and the concurring and dissenting opinions, which retain the originals' "substance, tone and memorable diction." Each chapter ends with a brief summary of the Court's decision. The book also includes a brief historical overview of abortion, a description of the Supreme Court itself, a chapter on the "new era" of conservatism on the Court, and a short review of pending cases (which have since been decided). This invaluable reference work clearly shows the changing tone of the Supreme Court as it moves further away from the right-to-privacy precept of *Roe v. Wade* and toward upholding states' interest in the protection of fetuses as potential citizens.

Faux, Marian. **Roe v. Wade: The Untold Story of the Landmark Supreme Court Decision That Made Abortion Legal.** New York: Macmillan, 1988. 370p. Index, bibliography. ISBN 0-02-537151-7.

This book focuses on the events and the people behind the landmark *Roe v. Wade* decision: Linda Coffee and Sarah Weddington, two women fresh out of law school and looking to make their mark on the world; Norma McCorvey, alias "Jane Roe," an itinerant young Texan who "had a naive enthusiasm that occasionally made her a too willing party for the wrong opportunity and sometimes . . . for the right one"—in this case, acting as the plaintiff for a suit challenging Texas's restrictive abortion laws; John Tolle, the trial lawyer who defended Dallas County's right to enforce the laws; Jay Floyd, who defended the law's constitutionality on behalf of the state; and a host of characters— judges, lawyers, feminists, activists, and others—who played parts in the case. Much of Faux's book is based on interviews with the principals (with the exception of McCorvey, who would not agree to be interviewed unless she was paid), personal observations, and Dallas and New York newspaper accounts of the period. Despite occasional factual errors, Faux has produced a vivid and often dramatic account not only of the events leading to the decision but also of the social and legal contexts in which they took place.

Glendon, Mary Ann. **Abortion and Divorce in Western Law.** Cambridge, MA: Harvard University Press, 1987. 197p. Index. ISBN 0-674-00160-5.

Mary Ann Glendon is a Harvard Law School professor who has written extensively on family law, particularly from the perspective of comparative law, which compares how laws in different societies shape and are shaped by those societies. In this book, she compares abortion and divorce laws in the United States, Canada, and 18 Western European countries. Pointing to other nations that have achieved legal compromise in the face of fierce national debates over abortion, she offers suggestions for using foreign models to find both the substance and the expression of laws that combine compassion for unwillingly pregnant women with "affirmation of life." She argues that, in taking abortion regulation away from the states, the Supreme Court halted a process that would eventually have brought about compromise legislation in most states. If the issue were returned to the states today, "it . . . seems likely that a very few states might return to strict abortion laws, a few more would endorse early abortion on demand, and the great majority would move to a position . . . reflecting popular sentiment that early abortions should be treated more leniently, but that all abortion is a serious matter." Glendon's compromise proposals are not likely to please activists on either side but may find a receptive audience among the many Americans who find themselves caught in the middle of the current polar debate.

Hern, Warren. **Abortion Practice.** Philadelphia: J. B. Lippincott, 1984. 340p. Index. ISBN 0-397-50607-4.

Warren Hern is a physician, anthropologist, and epidemiologist who owns and operates an abortion clinic in Boulder, Colorado. A pioneer who has been responsible for a number of innovations in abortion practice, Dr. Hern is also an activist who has worked diligently to preserve abortion rights and to help make abortion both safe and available. Designed as a textbook for practitioners, *Abortion Practice* is a comprehensive treatment of all aspects of providing abortion services, including public health aspects of abortion, counseling, operative procedures and techniques, day-to-day clinic operation and management, management of complications, legal aspects of abortion practice, long-term risks of abortion, and the role of the abortion provider in the community. Abortion, Dr. Hern writes, "takes place in a context of public controversy and private anguish. . . . A commitment to provide this kind of care in an excellent fashion is more than a decision to practice a certain medical specialty or participate in a certain kind of health care for women. It is a commitment to the expansion of choice." Written for the most part in clear, nontechnical language, this book offers thorough, practical, and detailed advice for counselors, nurses, and other clinic personnel as well as for physicians. This book has recently been revised.

Imber, Jonathan B. **Abortion and the Private Practice of Medicine.** New Haven, CT: Yale University Press, 1986. 164p. Index, bibliography. ISBN 0-300-03554-3.

This well-written book examines abortion from the perspective of physicians in private practice. Sociologist Imber begins by looking at the history of abortion from a medical perspective. He then examines the medical profession's "search for its proper role" with respect to abortion, a role that "depends on far more than an ethics of choice." Imber spent 2 years observing and interviewing the 26 obstetrician-gynecologists practicing in "Daleton," a medium-size city whose lack of an abortion clinic forces doctors to decide whether, when, and how to provide abortions to their patients. Looking at characteristics that may affect the doctors' choices, Imber examines their reasons for refusing or agreeing to perform abortions and the feelings and opinions underlying those reasons. What he finds is a "haunting ambivalence," with many doctors approving of women's right to choose abortion but reluctant to perform abortions themselves. This ambivalence, along with a moral legacy of opposition to abortion, is an important factor in the failure of the medical profession to accommodate to legal abortion. "As long as abortion continues to occupy a controversial place in American life," Imber concludes, "its acceptance and discouragement will go hand in hand. This is its cultural legacy and the doctor's dilemma."

Noonan, John T., Jr. **A Private Choice: Abortion in America in the Seventies.** New York: Free Press (Macmillan Publishing Co.), 1979. 244p. Indexes. ISBN 0-02-923160-4.

Lawyer, professor, and historian John Noonan, now a federal judge, has written extensively about both contraception and abortion. In this book, made up of 21 "inquiries" on various aspects of the Supreme Court–granted liberty to abortion, he challenges the constitutional basis of that liberty. He describes what he perceives as the negative effects of *Roe v. Wade* and related decisions on other laws relating to marriage and the family, as well as on the traditional view of homicide. The liberty to abort, he asserts, has no foundation in the Constitution, and the decisions establishing it were based on serious errors in history, medicine, constitutional law, political psychology, and biology. Further, the liberty is destructive to the structure of the family, oppressive to the poor, and in violation of the ethic of Western medicine "from Hippocrates to the present." It divides the country and "encourages the coercion of conscience." It has "fostered a sinister and Orwellian reshaping of our language," has led to the use of unborn children and dying infants for experiments, and has caused a high loss of human life. There must, Noonan concludes, "be a limit to a liberty so mistaken in its foundations, so far-reaching in its malignant consequences, and so deadly in its exercise."

Rubin, Eva. **Abortion, Politics and the Courts.** Revised ed. Westport, CT: Greenwood Press, 1987. 254p. Indexes, bibliography. ISBN 0-313-25614-4.

Eva Rubin is a professor of political science and public administration who has also written on the Supreme Court and the American family. In this book, she examines the use of litigation as an avenue for effecting changes in public policy—specifically, the campaign by women's organizations to use the courts to overturn state criminal abortion laws. She also attempts to "assess the impact of [*Roe v. Wade*] to see what we can learn about the consequences, intended and unintended" of Supreme Court "megadecisions" that cause "indirect changes across a broad spectrum of activities: political, governmental, medical, social, religious, moral, organizational." In clear, understandable language, Rubin explains the background of abortion law reform and early litigation efforts; the backstage negotiations and reasoning behind *Roe*, especially the concepts of trimester and viability; the political battles that followed the decision; and the state legislative response and corresponding judicial responses to new laws through 1985. Although she agrees with many critics that the Court took a legislative role in the *Roe* decision, she interprets that role differently: "the decisionmaking . . . is often legislative in that it is prospective and affirmative, rather than historical and negative." The Court's reasoning in *Roe* may have seemed inadequate, she proposes, because it failed to reconcile the doctrines of liberty and privacy with the real constitutional principle at issue in the case—"gender equality, the proposition that only with the right to accept or reject responsibilities for procreation could women choose to play roles as free, autonomous, participating citizens in a democratic system on an equal basis with men." The work includes a detailed chronology of abortion-related legal, political, and judicial events from 1980 to 1986.

Psychological and Health Aspects of Abortion

Adler, Nancy E., Henry P. David, Brenda N. Major, Susan H. Roth, Nancy F. Russo, and Gail E. Wyatt. **"Psychological Responses after Abortion."** American Psychological Association, 1990. Published in *Science*, April 6, 1990: 41–44.

This report, which gained considerable public attention when it was published in *Science* magazine, is based on an in-depth review of 19 studies "with the most rigorous research designs" that met the following criteria: (1) they were empirical and based on a definable sample; (2) they were conducted in the United States; and (3) they studied women who had undergone abortions under legal and nonrestrictive conditions. Although each study had its own limitations and shortcomings, "the diversity of methods used provides strength in drawing general conclusions." Overall the studies consistently found that negative responses following abortion were relatively rare and that in most instances psychological distress decreased after abortion. The studies also found that women who want "personally meaningful" pregnancies, who lack support from their parents or partners for the abortion, who have abortions in the second trimester, or who feel more conflict or uncertainty about the abortion decision are more likely to experience emotional stress following the abortion. The report goes on to cite weaknesses and gaps found across studies that "provide challenges for further research," focusing on problems of representativeness, lack of baseline data, lack of long-term studies, and the need for studies that "separate the experience of abortion from the characteristics of women seeking abortion and from the context of resolving an unwanted pregnancy." The report concludes that, although "case studies have established that some women experience severe distress or psychopathology after abortion and require sympathetic care . . . the development of significant psychological problems related to abortion is [in the words of former Surgeon General C. Everett Koop] 'minuscule from a public health perspective.'"

American Psychological Association. **Testimony on the Psychological Sequelae of Abortion.** Paper presented to the Office of the U.S. Surgeon General, December 2, 1987. 39p. Bibliography. May be obtained from the American Psychological Association, 1200 Seventeenth Street, NW, Washington, DC 20036.

Over the last 20 years, American Psychological Association (APA) members have conducted research on the psychological sequelae of abortion and have published several comprehensive reviews of the literature; this testimony represents their consensus views. Given the large numbers of women who have had abortions, the report states, "if there are widespread, severe psychological sequelae of abortion, we would expect them to be readily detectable." However, "because there is no reporting system in place to track the number of visits of patients for post-abortion psychological sequelae, no statistics with known measurement error are possible." The report discusses the problems with existing research, including (among others) inadequate methodology, researcher bias, lack of consensus in defining psychological sequelae and in selecting comparison groups, lack of standardization in data collection methods, lack of pre-abortion comparison data, small sample size, and the fact that "studies of women's response to abortion do not all examine the same event or medical procedure." Given these limitations, the majority of studies indicate that although "at some level, abortion is a stressful experience for all women . . . psychological sequelae are usually mild and tend to diminish rapidly over time without adversely affecting general functioning." The report cites apparent risk factors for negative abortion sequelae and concludes with a recommendation for a theoretically sound, multivariate approach to investigating post-abortion psychological reactions. An extensive bibliography of journal articles is included.

Committee on Government Operations, 101st Congress. **The Federal Role in Determining the Medical and Psychological Impact of Abortion on Women.** Washington, DC: U.S. Government Printing Office, 1989. 30p. House Report 101-392.

In 1987, President Ronald Reagan directed Surgeon General C. Everett Koop to prepare a comprehensive report on the health effects of abortion on women. The report was prepared in 1988, but the surgeon general decided in January 1989 not to release it. Consequently, the Subcommittee on Human Resources and Intergovernmental Relations of the House Committee on Government Operations conducted an oversight investigation of the surgeon general's report. This report is a summary of the committee's findings. Both the former president's and the surgeon general's opposition to abortion are well known, and abortion rights groups interpreted Koop's refusal to release the report as evidence that its findings did not favor the anti-abortion point of view. The congressional report would tend to back this assumption, citing discrepancies between the report and Koop's letter to the president as well as testimony from various experts and information from the report itself. In a strongly worded dissent, however, six representatives assert that the report paints "a misleading and inaccurate picture of the abortion issues" presented before the subcommittee and that it has an "unambiguous proabortion bias" that fails "to acknowledge the health effects on the pre-born child."

Francke, Linda Bird. **The Ambivalence of Abortion.** New York: Random House, 1978. 261p. Index. ISBN 0-394-41080-7.

This oft-cited book consists primarily of the personal stories of individuals who have been involved in abortions—not only the women themselves, but also their husbands, lovers, and parents. In their own words, people describe how an abortion—whether pending, just over, or years in the past—has affected their lives and their relationships. Of all ages and from all walks of life, the storytellers run the gamut of emotions, from anger to regret to relief. The book is divided into chapters according to whose story is being told: single women, married women, men, couples, teenagers, and parents, plus a chapter on women who had abortions 30, 40, or even 50 years ago. This work is a classic in the field.

Reardon, David C. **Aborted Women: Silent No More.** Chicago: Loyola University Press, 1987. 373p. Index. ISBN 0-8294-0578-X.

This book purports to be an objective, research-based report on the physical and psychological effects of abortion, based on answers to a questionnaire sent to about 250 members of Women Exploited by Abortion (WEBA). (It is worth noting that the author never states how many women actually responded to the questionnaire—all results are shown in percentages rather than numbers.) Although Reardon goes to some pains to explain that the respondents are representative of all women who have had abortions, based on factors such as age, marital status, and socioeconomic background, the self-selected nature of the survey group and the small sample size fatally flaw the results. Nevertheless, the book offers a well-written, sympathetic, and thought-provoking portrait of women who consider themselves victims of abortion. Most of the respondents report they were pressured into having abortions; they cite such after-effects as severe depression, alcoholism, drug abuse, and physical abuse. Additionally, many of the women felt that the treatment they received in abortion clinics was cold, uncaring, and coercive. The foreword is by Nancyjo Mann, founder of WEBA.

Rogers, James L., George B. Stoms, and James L. Phifer. **"Psychological Impact of Abortion: Methodological and Outcomes Summary of Empirical Research between 1966 and 1988."** Published in *Health Care for Women International,* 10 (1989): 347–376.

This review of articles on the psychological impact of abortion published in English between January 1966 and April 1988 was undertaken in an endeavor to provide policymakers and clinicians with "a reliable method [for deciding] how much confidence to place in statements seemingly supported by quantitative references from this literature." Only articles that reported original empirical data were included; articles "motivated only by theoretical, philosophical or moral considerations" and those that presented case studies of patients in clinical practice were excluded. Out of 280 articles located that dealt with psychological sequelae of abortion, only 76 met the review criteria. Of these, 31 were defined as prospective studies (subject measurement first occurred prior to abortion) and 32 as retrospective studies (subject measurement first occurred after abortion), while 13 were comparison studies that compared a post-abortion group with a group of women who had given birth. The bulk of the report consists of tables that summarize data from the articles to provide a synopsis of study demographics, methodological limitations, and gross statistical features (such as sample size, attrition rate, type of outcome measured, and outcome incidence). Also included is a table of definitions of methodological limitations, such as contradictions, interviewer bias, lack of baseline comparison, small sample size, and unclear criteria. The report conclusion notes that outcome incidence and methodological profiles vary substantially across the studies and that "Both advocates and opponents of abortion can prove their points by judiciously referencing only articles supporting their political agenda." A list of investigations summarized is included.

Shostak, Arthur B., and Gary McLouth. **Men and Abortion: Lessons, Losses, and Love.** New York: Praeger, 1984. 333p. Index. ISBN 0-03-063641-8.

This poignant and insightful book addresses a gaping hole in the literature on abortion—its impact on men, the "co-conceivers" who are mostly ignored in what is often perceived to be solely a women's issue. Using questionnaires completed by 1,000 "waiting room men" and a small number of interviews, including several with male abortion counselors, the authors explore the thoughts, behavior, and emotions of men who were, willingly or unwillingly, abortion participants. The study reveals that many men, rather than being unfeeling villains who get women pregnant and then abandon them emotionally, in fact are deeply and permanently affected by the experience of abortion. It also shows the importance of involving men in both pre- and post-abortion counseling and offers suggestions for "[helping] men *and* women make the best of an experience which tries them as few others may in their lifetimes."

Weber, Linda. **Healing the Pain of Abortion: An Exploration of the Psychology of Women.** Unpublished Master's thesis, Vermont College of Norwich University, 1990. 126p. Bibliography.

Linda Weber has been involved in abortion counseling for more than 20 years, including long-term post-abortion therapy. This paper, which was written for a master's thesis, is currently being expanded into book form. Weber looks at women's experience of abortion within the psychological, social, and historical context of a patriarchal, "fundamentally anti-woman" culture, which condemns women for being sexual and attempts to control them by limiting their identity to the institution (as opposed to the relationship) of motherhood. "An unintended, unwanted or crisis pregnancy is a crisis of a woman's sexuality and identity. It is a sexual crisis." In exploring the arguments against abortion, she notes the tendency to view the developing fetus in isolation, as somehow separate from the woman herself—"To abstract the fetus from the woman within whom it exists is to distort and demean." Further, many people oppose abortion because of doubts about their own intrinsic worth: "The assertion that every woman should want every pregnancy is actually an expression of the fears so many people carry about being unwanted or unloved." Ultimately, Weber concludes, abortion, while painful, is an opportunity for a woman to develop as an individual—to discover the truth and power of her own feminine identity. An appendix of drawings by women who have had abortions is included.

Zimmerman, Mary K. **Passage through Abortion.** New York: Praeger, 1977. 222p. Index, bibliography. ISBN 0-03-029816-4.

In this book, Dr. Zimmerman, a sociologist with a particular interest in women and health, examines women's abortion experiences within the context of their relationships to "significant others" and to society in general. In a study that began soon after the 1973 Court decision legalizing abortion, Zimmerman conducted in-depth interviews with 40 women, about 6 weeks after each had had an abortion. She found, among other things, that the ways in which the women experienced their abortions, and how well they assimilated the experience, were strongly affected by their relative "affiliation" or "disaffiliation." Those women with secure relationships, a sense of direction, and well-defined societal roles fared much better than women whose social ties were tenuous. Zimmerman also found that, despite the legality of abortion, virtually all of the women regarded abortion as a deviant and nonmoral act and disapproved of it—even after having had abortions themselves. To retain their concepts of themselves as moral persons, therefore, the women attempted to deny responsibility for their abortions, saying that they had been "forced" by circumstances to abort. It is important to note that this study, while valuable, is now some 15 years old; it would be interesting to see it repeated in the context of the current social climate.

Social and Political Aspects of Abortion

Condit, Celeste Michelle. **Decoding Abortion Rhetoric: Communicating Social Change.** Champaign, IL: University of Illinois Press, January 1990. 236p. Index. LC 89-33469. ISBN 0-252-01647-5.

This difficult but fascinating book explores the impact of rhetoric ("the use of language to persuade") on social change and vice versa through a detailed examination of changes in attitudes, policies, and perceptions about abortion since 1960, as revealed through public discourse. "Explanations of the path through which America has arrived at its current abortion laws, practices, and understandings must include the study of discursive forces, because only through public discourse can material realities be expressed and ideas materialized." Through in-depth analyses of the language and imagery of books, articles, speeches, media coverage, court decisions, laws, "educational" and political campaigns, and television programming, Condit shows how elements of both the pro-life and pro-choice viewpoints have been assimilated into public views and practices concerning abortion. Combining rigorous scholarship with the attitude that "studying meaning-laden human activities requires not detachment from competing sides but full empathetic enagagement with all positions," *Decoding Abortion Rhetoric* is a valuable addition to the literature on abortion.

David, Henry P., Zdenek Dytrych, Zdenek Matejcek, and Vratislav Schuller. **Born Unwanted: Development Effects of Denied Abortion.** New York: Springer Publishing Co., 1988. 143p. Index, bibliography. ISBN 0-8261-6080-8.

The abortion debate as it is currently framed focuses primarily on either the fetus or the pregnant woman, while psychological studies have dealt primarily with the effects of abortion on the women who have them. Another body of work exists, however, that deals with the psychological and social repercussions for children whose mothers, at least initially, did not want them to be born. This international anthology presents detailed examinations of several longitudinal studies of children born from unplanned, unwanted pregnancies, including the oft-cited Swedish study by Forssman and Thuwe of children born to women denied abortions between 1939 and 1942. The findings consistently show that such "unwanted" children are at a developmental disadvantage—they do less well in school, are more likely to have mental health problems, are more likely to get into trouble with the law, and are less likely to be satisfied with their lives as adults than "wanted" children. The authors go to some pains to clarify both the methodologies used and the weaknesses in each study and to explain the concepts of "wantedness" and "unwantedness" as viewed in the research. Clearly written, well organized, and thoroughly documented, this slim volume helps to fill a significant gap in the literature on abortion.

Davis, Nanette J. **From Crime to Choice: The Transformation of Abortion in America.** Westport, CT: Greenwood Press, 1985. 290p. Index. ISBN 0-313-24929-6.

In this far-ranging and complex work, sociologist Davis analyzes the evolution of abortion from criminal act to legal option within the broader context of social transformation. She examines the slow, nonlinear process of change in abortion attitudes, laws, policies, and practices since the nineteenth century, from granting "exceptions" to the laws, through gradual liberalization, toward full legality. Abortion, she writes, has yet to evolve into a woman-centered procedure that benefits women themselves rather than the doctors and clinics that provide abortion services. Further, the "medicalization" of abortion has made the medical profession, rather than the church, family, or state, the primary agent for regulating abortion. Davis's discussion places abortion and the struggle for a "free, rational and just reproductive policy" at the center of a feminist vision of the transition from patriarchal control to a society in which neither responsibilities nor choices are constricted by gender. "In the framing of a moral outlook that proceeds from women's needs and experiences, the human values that women have historically been assigned to preserve expand out of the confines of private life and become the organizing principles of society. Such a gender-free society does not obliterate differences, but opens up to each person the fullest expression of both masculine and feminine attributes."

Devereux, George. **A Study of Abortion in Primitive Societies.** New York: International Universities Press, 1976. 414p. Index, bibliography. ISBN 0-8236-6245-4.

This oft-cited book was first published in 1955, when abortion was a topic rarely spoken of or discussed in public forums. Devereux's primary focus, however, was not abortion itself but a desire to link the "social and psychological sciences" by performing a comparative study that linked cultural studies with an in-depth psychoanalytical approach to understanding human behavior. In Part I, Devereux examines data on abortion as practiced by some 400 primitive tribes, as well as the practices of 20 historical and modern nations. He looks at a variety of factors, including conscious and unconscious motivation for abortion; alternatives to abortion; frequency and timing of abortion; techniques and physical consequences of abortion; attitudes toward and treatment of aborted fetuses; abortionists; attitudes toward abortion; and social action, including penalties and nonpunitive measures taken toward abortionists and women who aborted. Part II takes a psychoanalytic approach, discussing such factors as "trauma and unconscious motivation in abortion," "the flight from parenthood," and abortion as "castration of the father." Also included are descriptions of abortion as practiced by each of the tribes studied and tables comparing the occurrence of various abortion-related traits among the tribes. Whether or not one agrees with its heavily Freudian interpretations, the book presents a fascinating array of comparative information on the motives, methods, and attitudes regarding abortion in so-called primitive societies, some of which provide remarkable parallels with our own.

Francome, Colin. **Abortion Freedom: A Worldwide Movement.** London: George Allen & Unwin, 1984. 241p. Index, bibliography. ISBN 0-04-179001-4.

Colin Francome is a British sociologist who has done extensive research and writing on abortion, birth control, and teenage pregnancy. This book examines recent widespread changes in abortion laws, policy, and practice—in the 15 years preceding the book's publication, more than 40 countries liberalized their laws. Francome examines the ideas and strategies of the forces promoting and opposing legal abortion, focusing particularly on Britain, other European countries, and the United States. From early debates over birth control, through legalization of abortion, to the debates following such legalization, Francome follows the course of the legal and political battles over abortion as they have been waged in different nations. He concludes that birth control education and availability has the best potential for reducing the number of both legal and illegal abortions and notes that, although "developments in rights of control of fertility will obviously not solve the deep economic and social problems facing the world . . . they will give people greater control over their lives and more opportunity to have the number of children they want and at a time of life when they are best able to care for them."

Ginsburg, Faye D. **Contested Lives.** Berkeley: University of California Press, 1989. 315p. Index, bibliography. ISBN 0-520-06492-5.

This is an anthropological case study of the response of a middle-American community (Fargo, ND) to the opening of the state's first abortion clinic within its borders. Within the context of a local conflict between pro-choice and pro-life activists, Ginsburg explores the much larger cultural drama of women's social movements in the United States. In her analysis of life stories of the Fargo activists, Ginsburg found that, though the women represent polar opposites in their stances on abortion, their involvement grew out of a shared belief that something is very wrong in the way U.S. society treats women and families: "Whether pro-life or pro-choice, activists express their motivation for social action as a desire to alter the meaning and circumstances of pro-creation in order to make conditions better for the next generation. In other words, they are concerned, as female activists, with their role in reproducing the culture, but in terms different from the present." The fact that the two sides have distinctly contrasting views of what it means to "make things better" is at the heart of the abortion debate. This is a difficult but fascinating work.

Jaffe, Frederick S., Barbara L. Lindheim, and Philip R. Lee. **Abortion Politics: Private Morality and Public Policy.** New York: McGraw-Hill, 1981. 216p. Index. ISBN 0-07-032189-2.

This is an examination and analysis of public policy on abortion from the 1973 *Roe v. Wade* decision through the late 1970s. The book does not attempt to assess the rightness or wrongness of abortion, but asserts that, since women have throughout history sought abortions and will continue to seek them whether they are legal or not, all women should have access to legal, safe abortion services. The authors present various findings on the social, emotional, demographic, and health benefits of legal abortion and note the failure of the U.S. health care system to respond adequately to the Supreme Court's decision as of the late 1970s. They also draw strong parallels between the battle over abortion and earlier battles over contraception, which is still opposed by the Catholic Church and a number of anti-abortion groups. Though somewhat dated now, this book provides valuable in-depth historical and political analyses of public policies and private practice in the area of abortion services and birth control.

Joffe, Carol. **Regulating Sexuality: The Experiences of Family Planning Workers.** Philadelphia: University of Pennsylvania Press, 1987. 208p. ISBN 0-87722-423-4.

This book is based on a sociological tradition of studying conflicts in social policy by examining the experience of "front-line" workers—those in service bureaucracies who interact directly with the public. In the case of abortion and birth control services, these are the counselors, doctors, nurses, and other staff members who work at family planning and abortion clinics. Although much of this book is dedicated to the ways in which such workers directly and indirectly influence ("regulate," in Joffe's terms) sexuality in the United States, the chapters dealing with abortion counseling provide an interesting portrait of people who are involved with abortion on a daily, or at least weekly, basis. Abortion work qualifies as what Everett Hughes described as "dirty work"—"it can be physically disgusting; it can be symbolically degrading; it can involve morally dubious activity. Yet, under certain circumstances, such work can also take on a heroic or 'charismatic' character." Although their work was often difficult and emotionally draining, and although they found abortion morally troubling, the counselors perceived their jobs as satisfying and important, and all but 1 of the approximately 75 counselors involved believed firmly that abortion must remain a legal option.

Luker, Kristin. **Abortion and the Politics of Motherhood.** Berkeley: University of California Press, 1984. 324p. Index, bibliography. ISBN 0-520-04314-6.

This is an unusually balanced and compassionate study of how the practice of and attitudes toward abortion in the United States have changed over the nineteenth and twentieth centuries. Much of the book is based on lengthy, in-depth interviews with activists on both sides of the issue. Luker, a sociologist who has spent much of her career studying abortion, concludes that pro-choice and pro-life activists (as opposed to the general population) hold diametrically opposed world views that affect their attitudes on a wide range of issues, most notably the roles of women and men in the family and in society. Thus, for both sides, the abortion conflict is a win-lose situation that allows little room for compromise. Luker sees little chance that the debate will be resolved any time in the foreseeable future.

————. **Taking Chances: Abortion and the Decision Not To Contracept.** Berkeley: University of California Press, 1975. 207p. Index. ISBN 0-520-02872-4.

Although some women seek abortions as a result of contraceptive failure, many more seek abortions because of a failure to use contraception at all or to use it effectively. These women are often stereotyped as irresponsible, disturbed, or neurotic. Luker, however, examined women's own reasons for not using contraception despite having access to contraceptives and the skills to use them. She conducted a study of 500 women seen at an abortion clinic in California in the early 1970s, when the state's relatively liberal law made abortions fairly easy to obtain. Fifty women also participated in a series of in-depth interviews, along with 10 women who obtained abortions from a private physician. Luker places contraceptive risk-taking inside a social and cultural context of complex relationships, going well beyond the simplistic psychological explanations usually given for women's "irresponsible" risk-taking behavior. She concludes that women's decisions about contraception are part of an ongoing process and are based on weighing perceived costs and benefits of contraception against the perceived risks of pregnancy—percep-tions that do not necessarily coincide with those of family planning and abortion practitioners.

Petchesky, Rosalind. **Abortion and Woman's Choice: The State, Sexuality, and Reproductive Freedom.** Boston: Northeastern University Press, 1984, 1990. 412p. Index. ISBN 1-55553-075-3 (1990 edition).

This is an updated edition of what is perhaps the most comprehensive and well-known feminist work on abortion. In her far-ranging, thoroughly researched, and well-written analysis, Petchesky seeks to determine: (1) why abortion has become so controversial politically and socially, (2) what are the historical developments and social and cultural conditions that have led to increases in abortions and the development of state policies and moral ideologies related to abortion, (3) how these conditions and policies affect the changing position and consciousness of women, and (4) what are the elements of a feminist vision of abortion and its relation to the total conditions of women's reproductive freedom. A "feminist morality of abortion," she writes, "would [address] the issues that 'right-to-lifers' raise in human, social terms and [move] well beyond them." It would "contain within it the possibility of transcending and transforming the existing sexual division of labor *at the same time* as it recognizes women's specific situation in reproduction. Ultimately, this means rejecting 'maternal thinking' as a gender-specific practice while persistently defending abortion as a gender-specific need."

Periodicals

Most of the organizations listed in Chapter 4 publish quarterly newsletters. Many also publish journals or other periodicals. The following are periodicals that either have wide circulation independent of organization membership or that are not associated with an organization.

Bernadell Technical Bulletin
P.O. Box 1897
New York, NY 10011
Bimonthly. Free—write to be placed on mailing list.

The *Bernadell Technical Bulletin* is a newsletter published by abortion-provider-turned-abortion-opponent Dr. Bernard Nathanson and his wife, Adelle. The newsletter consists of abstracts and reviews of articles published in the medical literature concerning abortion and other "life issues." Each abstract or review is followed by commentary written by Dr. Nathanson that interprets the articles in terms that are "easily understandable by the reader" and that strongly supports the pro-life point of view.

Family Planning Perspectives
111 Fifth Avenue
New York, NY 10003
Bimonthly. $38/year for institutions; $28/year for individuals; $34/year for subscription agencies.

Established in 1968, *Family Planning Perspectives* is a professional journal published by the Alan Guttmacher Institute, an independent nonprofit research institute that has become a leading source of abortion statistics and information. The journal contains in-depth, peer-reviewed articles by medical and social science professionals, scholars, and researchers on new research, policy positions, and other topics related to reproductive health services in the United States. Highly regarded in the field, *Family Planning Perspectives* features frequent articles on various medical, social, and legal aspects of abortion, along with other topics such as teenage pregnancy and sexuality, prenatal and maternity care, sex education, unintended pregnancy, infertility, sexually transmitted disease, birth control, and abortion. Three monthly departments, "Update," "Special Report," and "Digest," report on new developments in areas of special interest. Back issues are available for $8 a copy.

Human Life Review
Human Life Foundation, Inc.
150 E. 35th Street
New York, NY 10016
Quarterly. $20/year in the U.S.; $25/year in Canada and other foreign countries.

Established in 1975, *Human Life Review* is a journal dealing primarily with abortion and related issues from a pro-life point of view. Some of the articles and essays are original; others have been reprinted from newspapers and other periodicals in an attempt to "bring our readers the best of what has appeared elsewhere, if we think it belongs in our 'permanent record' of the Abortion War and related battles." Recent contributors include such luminaries as Nat Hentoff, Patrick Buchanan, William F. Buckley, Jr., and Malcolm Muggeridge. Sample articles include "Feminism and Abortion," by Martha Bayles; "Bioethics and the Holocaust," by Richard Neuhaus; "Rape and Abortion," by Mary Meehan; and "The Lie of Prochoice," by James Bowman. The summer 1990 issue also featured the full text of Cardinal John O'Connor's statement, "Questions and Answers on Abortion," which includes pastoral suggestions on "how every person can incorporate concern for the unborn into his or her daily life." Back issues are available at $4 a copy; also available are library-bound volumes for previous years, including a full 15-year set for $700. Also available in microform.

Subscriber-Based News Service

The Abortion Report
282 N. Washington Street
Falls Church, VA 22046
(703) 237-5130;
FAX (703) 237-5149

The Abortion Report is a daily (Monday–Friday) briefing of abortion-related political, judicial, and legislative events occurring around the country. Established in 1989 following the *Webster* decision, *The Abortion Report* draws on a nationwide network of information sources, including local newspapers, activists, journalists, researchers, elected officials, and others. Included in each report is a "Spotlight Story" focusing on a particular event; examples from 1990 include a question-and-answer press meeting with Louisiana Governor Buddy Roemer following his veto of that state's restrictive abortion laws, a report on the AFL-CIO board's decision to stay neutral on abortion, and a discussion among Massachusetts gubernatorial candidates on the Supreme Court nomination of Judge David Souter. Each issue also includes "State Reports," on court actions, demonstrations, polls, etc.; "Legislative Outlook," on current legislative actions in the states; "National Briefing," on events of national scope; "Insider Commentary," interviews with politicians, activists, scholars, and other individuals; and coverage of upcoming state and national political races. The report averages 9–12 pages per day. Items are brief, to the point, nonpartisan, and wholly factual, making this a valuable source of up-to-the-minute information for journalists, researchers, and activist organizations. Three methods of delivery are offered: downloading to computer via modem, FAX, and mail, although mail delivery is discouraged because of the timeliness of the information. Cost varies according to type of subscription; call or write for details.

6

Selected Nonprint Resources

Computer Database Search Service

The Abortion Report
282 N. Washington Street
Falls Church, VA 22046
(703) 237-5130; FAX (703) 237-5149

The publishers of *The Abortion Report* (see Chapter 5) maintain a database that contains all information previously published in the report. A full-time staff person is available to search the database for information on any topic related to abortion; a full printout will then be delivered, faxed, or mailed to the inquirer. Subscribers to *The Abortion Report* receive a discount for database search services.

Films and Videocassettes

New videos on abortion are being produced at a tremendous rate; therefore, it was not possible to make this section comprehensive. Following are some of the better known and frequently shown selections. The accompanying annotations are intended to evaluate the films less in terms of content than in terms of presentation: production, writing, and (if applicable) acting quality; and effectiveness in getting their messages across.

A Better Way
Type:	Videocassette
Length:	30 min.
Date:	1986
Cost:	Purchase $39.95, rental $5/week through NRL Educational Trust Fund
Sources:	Boone Productions, Inc. 2600 West Olive, Suite 930 Burbank, CA 91505 (818) 841-6565

National Right to Life Educational Trust Fund
419 7th Street, NW, Suite 500
Washington, DC 20004-2293
(202) 626-8809

Host Pat Boone talks with people who have chosen alternatives to abortion in this upbeat yet low-key film. Included are an 18-year-old mother of a 3-year-old, along with her parents and the child's father; a woman who was raped in her own home and her now 22-year-old daughter; an obstetrician who works to match unwanted babies with caring parents; a couple who have adopted three "special needs" children, including a boy who suffered severe abuse and two girls with Down's syndrome; a woman who became pregnant at age 40 and had her son, now a 16-year-old law school graduate, against her doctor's advice; and the mother and the therapist of a cerebral palsy victim who died at age 31. Boone reads a passage written by the young man before his death in which he eloquently states his opposition to abortion, while affirming that it is a "question of personal morals." What to do about a "crisis pregnancy," Boone concludes, is "a matter of personal choice," but "once those choices are made, they're final." And, he adds, with the thousands of parents wanting to adopt, "there is no such thing as an unwanted child." Boone is a relaxed and congenial host, and his interviewees are warm and attractive people. This film's nonjudgmental and positive tone has a great deal to do with its success in promoting its message.

Abortion: For Survival
Type:	16 mm film, videocassette
Length:	30 min.
Date:	1989
Cost:	Purchase $29.95 ea. for 1–9, $19.95 ea. for 10–29, $14.95 ea. for 30 +, $39.95 for both in combination with Abortion Denied: Shattering Young Women's Lives, plus 10% shipping/handling (video); rental $250/week (film)
Sources:	Feminist Majority Foundation 1600 Wilson Boulevard, Suite 704 Arlington, VA 22209 (703) 522-2214

8105 W. 3rd Street, Suite 1
Los Angeles, CA 90048
(213) 651-0495
186 South Street
Boston, MA 02111
(617) 695-9688

The primary message of this well-produced video is that making abortion illegal causes women to die. Citing international evidence that criminalizing abortion does not cause the rates of abortion to decrease, *Abortion: For Survival* argues forcefully not only for keeping abortion legal in the United States, but also for changing U.S. funding policies that restrict family planning programs in other countries and that even in some cases prohibit treating women for the effects of botched abortions. The video, which includes footage of a suction abortion and interviews with social scientists, medical professionals, population experts, and Third World government officials, also addresses such issues as the decline of contraceptive research in the United States, the plight of unwanted and abandoned children, and the effects of uncontrolled population growth in the world's poorest countries. An accompanying booklet contains statistical information cited in the video, which was produced by a coalition of abortion rights advocates.

Abortion: Past, Present and Future

Type: Videocassette
Length: 18 min.
Date: 1989
Cost: Purchase $75, rental $50
Source: Educational Video Center
60 E.13th Street, 4th Floor
New York, NY 10003
(212) 254-2848

This brief video was researched, filmed, and edited by a group of teenagers in New York City. Much of the video consists of interviews with passersby, who are asked, "What do you think of abortion?" "Do you know anyone who has had an abortion?" "Do you think abortion should be illegal?" "What do you think would happen if abortion were illegal?" More in-depth interviews feature two women who describe their abortion experiences ("How did you feel when you had the abortion?")—one of which took place in 1946—and two clergymen, one a Catholic priest who reiterates the Church's stand against abortion, the other a black Baptist minister who asserts that choice is a God-given right and one that must be supported. Also included is footage of both abortion rights and anti-abortion demonstrators. The filmmakers provide some background information, but for the most part they let their subjects speak for themselves. Other than the audio, which sometimes makes the speakers difficult to understand, the production quality is quite acceptable. What makes this video outstanding, however, is the open-minded, nonbiased way in which the filmmakers approached their subject and the wide range of viewpoints they were able to include. These qualities make the video an excellent starting point for discussion, particularly for high school classes and various youth groups. Also included is a teacher's guide with questions and activity suggestions designed "to motivate students to read, write, discuss and ultimately act responsibly when confronted with the issue of abortion."

Abortion: Stories from North and South

Type: 16mm film, videocassette
Length: 55 min.
Date: 1984
Cost: Purchase $895 (film), $595 (video); rental $100
Source: The Cinema Guild
             1697 Broadway
             New York, NY 10019
             (212) 246-5522

This film was produced by Studio D, a special mostly female unit of the Canadian Film Board that was founded in 1974 to create films from the perspective and experience of women. Explaining that each year throughout the world 30 million to 50 million women have abortions, more than half of them illegally, and that more than 84,000 of these women die as a result of abortion complications, *Abortion* presents personal stories, interviews, and case studies from six countries—Ireland, Canada, Peru, Colombia, Japan, and Thailand. These stories—of desperation, resourcefulness, and, sometimes, tragedy— provide vivid documentation of the film's central premise: abortion is, and always has been, a fact of human existence. "Only the laws and conditions under which abortions are performed vary from place to place, and time to time." In Peru, women who survive abortion complications are taken by "abortion police" straight from hospitals to jails where they, and their children with them, will serve sentences of two to three years. In Thailand, a village abortionist massages her pregnant daughter's belly in an unsuccessful attempt to dislodge the placenta and cause a miscarriage. In Japan, women who have had abortions bury the fetuses in expensive crypts meant to capture the unborns' drifting souls. This visually beautiful film has a detached, unemotional, "just-the-facts" tone, but its content packs an emotional wallop. *Abortion* won the grand prize at the 1985 Golden Gate Awards film and video competition of the San Francisco International Film Festival and received first place in the Contemporary Social Issues category from the National Council on Family Relations 17th Annual Film Awards Competition.

Abortion Denied: Shattering Young Women's Lives

Type: 16 mm film, videocassette
Length: 30 min.
Date: 1990

Cost:	Purchase $29.95 ea. for 1–9, $19.95 ea. for 10–29, $14.95 ea. for 30 +, $39.95 for both in combination with Abortion: For Survival, plus 10% shipping/handling (video); rental $250/week (film)
Sources:	Feminist Majority Foundation 1600 Wilson Boulevard, Suite 704 Arlington, VA 22209 (703) 522-2214
	8105 W. 3rd Street, Suite 1 Los Angeles, CA 90048 (213) 651-0495
	186 South Street Boston, MA 02111 (617) 695-9688

This half-hour-long video addresses the impact of recent Supreme Court decisions upholding parental consent laws in Ohio and Minnesota. Currently 34 states have passed parental notification or consent laws; court action has blocked laws in 20 states, but they are enforced in 14. Such laws, the film argues passionately, do not increase family closeness and support parental involvement. Rather, they force young women to resort to desperate measures to avoid exposure of their pregnancies and to obtain abortions. The film focuses on the case of Becky Bell, an Indiana high school student who, according to her friends, could not bear to disappoint her parents by telling them she was pregnant. Because state law required their permission before she could have a legal abortion, Becky had an illegal abortion and later died from complications. Her parents, Karen and Bill Bell, have since become ardent spokespersons against parental notification and consent laws. Most of the film consists of testimony, often poignant, from persons who discuss their own experiences to support their argument that parental notification/consent laws are dangerous, discriminatory, unrealistic, and punitive. Included are the Bells, friends of Becky Bell, young women who have been affected by laws in other states, plus judges, doctors, legislators, and lobbyists. A synopsis/discussion guide is included.

The Answer

Type:	16mm film, ¾″ broadcast tape, videocassette
Length:	12 min.
Date:	1987
Cost:	Purchase $198 (film), $49.95 (¾″), $23.90 (video); discounts for quantities of ten or more.
Source:	Bernadell, Inc. P.O. Box 1897 Old Chelsea Station New York, NY 10011 (212) 463-7000

This film, which was produced in response to criticisms of Bernard Nathanson's *The Silent Scream,* consists of voluntary testimony from Jay Kelinson, the doctor who performed the abortion documented in that film. Seated at a desk, Dr. Kelinson answers an unseen questioner as if he were indeed giving testimony at a legal trial. Yes, says the 38-year-old obstetrician/gynecologist, he learned to do abortions as a medical resident; no, there was no discussion of ethics in the lessons. From 1979 to 1982, he performed perhaps 10,000 abortions, working in 3 or 4 different clinics, and during that time he noticed "personality changes" in himself. No, he is not pro-life; in fact, he still does abortions "for medical reasons," though since seeing (during editing) the film used in *The Silent Scream* he no longer performs them "on demand." Kelinson goes on to say that he himself made the ultrasound tape used in the film, that there was no manipulation of the tape or its speed, and that there is "no doubt in my mind that there was some perception of impending doom" and that the fetus did indeed pull away from his instruments as claimed in the film. As Kelinson points out, he has "nothing to gain" by making this film, which, although it does indicate the veracity of the ultrasound tape made during the abortion itself, does not answer many of the other criticisms made of *The Silent Scream* (see also *Planned Parenthood's Response to The Silent Scream, The Silent Scream,* and *The Silent Scream: Responding to Critics,* this chapter).

Are You Listening: People Who Have Struggled with Abortion
Type: Videocassette, audiocassette
Length: About 29 min.
Date: 1984
Cost: Purchase $300 (video), $30 (audio); rental $50

Are You Listening: Women Who Have Had an Abortion
Type: 16mm film, videocassette, audiocassette
Length: About 28 min.
Date: 1972
Cost: Purchase $450 (film), $300 (video), $30 (audio); rental $65 (film), $50 (video)

Are You Listening: Women Who Have Not Had an Abortion
Type: 16mm film, videocassette, audiocassette
Length: About 28 min.
Date: 1977
Cost: Purchase $450 (film), $300 (video), $30 (audio); rental $65 (film), $50 (video)

Source: Martha Stuart Communications
147 W. 22nd Street
New York, NY 10011
(212) 255-2718; Cable: Listening NY; Telex: 508937 Stuart

These three videos, produced with the aid of the Ford Foundation, span a period of 12 years. *Women Who Have Had an Abortion,* produced in 1972, and

Women Who Have Not Had an Abortion, produced 5 years later, feature informal discussions among groups of women of different ages, races, and marital status. One group is made up of women who, faced with an unwanted pregnancy, chose to have abortions; the other group is made up of women who chose to carry their pregnancies to term. The third film, *People Who Have Struggled with Abortion,* was produced in 1984. It also features an informal discussion, this time among a group of men and women from widely varying backgrounds, including a doctor, a rabbi, a counselor, a nurse, a legislator, a nun, a black activist, and others, all of whom have struggled with abortion in some way. In each of these films, people talk candidly about their experiences with abortion, their beliefs about its rightness or wrongness, the politics associated with it, and their feelings about whether it should be legal and available. As one man points out, people on both sides of the debate have a tendency to view each other as "the worst people in the world"—mainly because in looking at their opponents, they see what they are afraid to see in themselves. These films are an attempt to cut through the polemic and show, as Martha Stuart remarks, that "it's not that simple." Although interesting separately, the films are best viewed together, so that viewers can clearly see both the contrasts and the similarities among people who have struggled with the same issue, but who have emerged with different, and very individual, answers.

Assignment: Life

Type: Videocassette
Length: 52 min.
Date: 1980
Cost: Purchase $29.95
Source: American Portrait Films International
503 E. 200th Street
P.O. Box 19266
Cleveland, OH 44119
(216) 531-8331; (216) 531-5228; (800) 736-4567;
FAX (216) 531-8355

This "docudrama" about a fictional journalist's exploration of the abortion issue made its debut at the 1980 convention of the National Right to Life Committee. "Ann Sommers," a writer for the "Daily Press," is assigned to do a story on abortion and to cover both sides of the debate. Although she initially feels that abortion should be a woman's personal decision, Ms. Sommers comes to believe that abortion is, indeed, murder. During the course of the film, she interviews a doctor who owns and operates a chain of family planning clinics, an administrator for the Birth Control Institute, several women who have had abortions as well as several who have chosen to have and keep their babies, a former prostitute and topless dancer who nearly died from abortion complications, the parents of an adopted child, the mother of a baby born at 23 weeks gestation, a lab technician who processed fetuses from abortions, and a number of well-known anti-abortion activists, including John and Barbara Willke, Bernard Nathanson, James Dobson, Representatives Henry

Hyde and William Dannemeyer, Don Smith of Crusade for Life, and Cardinal Manning, the archbishop of Los Angeles. She also witnesses, along with the audience, a suction and a saline abortion and attends a right-to-life rally in Washington, D.C. The viewer is left wondering why, if she is supposed to be covering both sides of the issue, Ms. Sommers gives such lopsided attention to people on the anti-abortion side of the debate. This lack of balance diminishes the film's effectiveness. A study guide is included.

Eclipse of Reason

Type: 16mm film, ¾" broadcast tape, videocassette
Length: 27 min.
Date: 1987
Cost: Purchase $309 (film), $85.90 (¾"), $44.90 (video); discounts for quantities of ten or more.
Source: Bernadell, Inc.
             P.O. Box 1897
             Old Chelsea Station
             New York, NY 10011
             (212) 463-7000

Like its predecessor, *The Silent Scream, Eclipse of Reason* aims for and achieves maximum emotional impact. The film features graphic footage of the dilatation and evacuation abortion of a 20-week-old fetus, interspersed with interviews with several former abortion providers and two women who suffered physical and psychological damage as a result of their abortions. The film is intended to supplement *The Silent Scream,* which showed an early abortion, by showing an abortion late in the second trimester (when fewer than 1 percent of all abortions are performed). Introduced by Charlton Heston and hosted by Bernard Nathanson, the former abortion provider who has become one of the anti-abortion movement's most vocal activists, *Eclipse of Reason* uses a fetoscope to show the fetus in utero before and during the abortion procedure. A step-by-step guide for presenters is provided, including a script of introductory remarks. Not for the faint-hearted.

Girl on the Edge of Town

Type: 16mm film, videocassette
Length: About 30 min.
Date: 1980
Cost: Purchase $85 (video),
             call or write for rental cost
Source: Paulist Productions
             P.O. Box 1057
             Pacific Palisades, CA 90272
             (213) 454-0688

This film, which is aimed primarily at teenagers, demonstrates the power of a good story well told to make a point without preaching or exhorting. Gina and her boyfriend Wayne get "carried away" one night, and inevitably she discovers she is pregnant. Gina and her parents live on the edge of town; her father hauls wood and does odd jobs, and her mother runs a fruit stand. Her mother is harsh and bitter, and when Gina tells her mother the news she finds out why—her parents married because they "had to," and they have been struggling ever since. Her mother urges her to have an abortion and save herself from the same fate. Wayne raises the money, but in the clinic Gina changes her mind, because, "if my mother had done it, there wouldn't be any me." The two plan to marry, but then Wayne gets the news that his navy scholarship has come through—and he is required to remain single until he graduates. How Gina makes, and accepts responsibility for, her final decision, becoming stronger and more mature as a result, and how she finally triumphs make for an engrossing and audience-involving story. The characters in this film are multidimensional, and they act and talk like real people. The result is far more effective than other films that work much harder at getting their message across. Included is a study guide with excellent thought- and discussion-provoking questions.

Greater than Gold

Type: 16mm film, videocassette
Length: 63 min.
Date: 1983
Cost: Purchase $590 + $10 shipping (film—must be special ordered), $69 + $2 shipping (video); rental $69 + $10 shipping (film)
Source: Evangelical Films
            1750 Northwest Highway
            Garland, TX 75041
            (800) 527-4014; (214) 270-6675

This openly evangelistic film, which is intended largely for a teenage audience, attempts to portray the negative effects of abortion on two people, a father and a daughter. The father, a widower recently converted to Christianity, opposes abortion and believes it is murder; his stance finally costs him his job as chief of staff at a large urban hospital. Daughter B. J., pregnant and confused, has an abortion to preserve her chances for a college scholarship; grief- and guilt-stricken, she tries to kill herself. In the end, the two are reconciled through their faith and love for one another. This could have been a powerful film. Unfortunately, the story has been badly manipulated in the effort to prove a point. Several of the events portrayed are implausible at best—a woman who has had a legal abortion, in a hospital, collapsing in a dingy city alley; an abortion clinic nurse handing an obviously distraught teenager a full vial of barbiturates; the girl's sudden "miraculous" revival after her apparent death from the drug overdose. With the exception of the two protagonists, who are believable and whose relationship is well portrayed, the characters tend to be one-dimensional and to speak in cliches, especially the teacher who urges B. J. to have the abortion and the hospital's director. A near-miss.

Holy Terror

Type: 16mm film, videocassette
Length: 58 min.
Date: 1984
Cost: Purchase $895 (film), $595 (video); rental $100
Source: The Cinema Guild
1697 Broadway
New York, NY 10019
(212) 246-5522

This is a fascinating inside look at the radical elements of the anti-abortion movement who seek to stop abortion by any means possible, including violence. With a minimum of narration, the film offers footage of activists praying, meeting, demonstrating, confronting clinic workers and women seeking abortions, testifying in congressional hearings, being loaded into paddy wagons, and rallying in a prison yard. At a mock Nuremberg trial held in a hotel ballroom, the jury convicts the defendants (represented by papier mache heads)—"the Feminists," "the Courts," "the Doctors," "the Lawyers," "the Providers," "the Celebrities," and "the Politicians"—of "crimes against humanity." At a right-to-life convention, attendees display name tags decorated with tiny sticks of "dynamite" and the phrase "Have a blast." At an abortion clinic, protesters lock arms to block the entrance and yell at a frightened and dismayed teenager as clinic workers attempt to comfort her. Interspersed with these often-dramatic moments are statements by clergymen, politicians, pro-life and pro-choice leaders, and abortion clinic staff members, as well as scenes of clinics destroyed by bombs or fire. Although the filmmaker is an abortion rights supporter, the film is subject to multiple interpretations—pro-choice advocates will find it horrifying, while pro-life activists may very well be cheering. This film received a blue ribbon from the American Film & Video Festival and a Certificate of Merit from the Chicago Film Festival, and it was named the Nonprint Editors' Choice by *Booklist* magazine.

No Alibis

Type: Videocassette
Length: 38 min.
Date: 1986
Cost: Purchase $39.95, rental $5/week through
NRL Educational Trust Fund
Sources: Boone Productions, Inc.
2600 W. Olive, Suite 930
Burbank, CA 91505
(818) 841-6565

National Right to Life Educational Trust Fund
419 7th Street, NW, Suite 500
Washington, DC 20004-2293
(202) 626-8809

The jacket for this video calls it "a fast-paced drama on abortion designed especially for teenage audiences." The design incorporates an MTV-style rock video—which includes images of apparent Nazi soldiers shooting down the musicians—interwoven with the linked stories of three people: a television journalist whose assignment to do a story on abortion coincides with her dismayed discovery that she is pregnant; a high school teacher who takes his crusade against abortion into the classroom; and a pregnant student who was one on a long list of conquests by an arrogant jock. These stories could indeed provide high drama—but they, and the message they attempt to promote, are trivialized by the presentation, which is awful. Some of the characters spill over into caricature, particularly the doctor/owner of the abortion clinic, a leering, cigar-smoking sleaze who lives in a palatial mansion complete with a foreign maid and a wife and friends who prattle on about animal rights while he says with a sneer that he "leaves the moral and ethical problems [about abortion] to theologians." The high school students preach at each other obnoxiously, and the teacher uses a class "discussion" as a forum to ram his views down students' throats. The slick production, vivid imagery, and catchy music are not enough to compensate for the poor quality of the writing.

Operation Rescue

Type: Videocassette
Length: 30 min.
Date: 1988
Cost: Purchase $19.95
Source: American Portrait Films International
             503 E. 200th Street
             P.O. Box 19266
             Cleveland, OH 44119
             (216) 531-8331; (216) 531-5228;
             (800) 736-4567;
             FAX (216) 531-8355

This film pays tribute to the radical organization that has received considerable media attention for its use of civil disobedience in its campaign to stop abortion—a campaign that the film leaves no doubt is indeed a holy crusade. Footage of demonstrations and "rescues" is interspersed with pictures of fetuses or unborn children (depending on your perspective), both post-abortion and in utero, and abundant biblical quotations. Randall Terry, Operation Rescue's founder and leader, exhorts his followers to repent of their apathy and atone for their "blood guilt" by doing whatever is necessary to stop the "legalized child-killing" and save the nation, which is "increasingly staggering under the weight of God's judgment." When man's law and God's law conflict, he says, Christians must act to change man's law, not from a position of judgment but from a "platform of repentance." *Operation Rescue* provides a vivid portrait of the passion and purpose behind the pro-life movement; whether it inspires or dismays will depend on the audience's point of view.

Our Right to Abortion

Type: Videocassette, ¾″ or VHS
Length: 28 min.
Date: 1986
Cost: Purchase $250 (¾″), $195 (VHS), discounts available to pro-choice activist groups; rental $60
Source: Women Make Movies
225 Lafayette Street, Suite 212
New York, NY 10012
(212) 925-0606; FAX (212) 925-2052

This video aims to inspire viewers to join the struggle to keep abortion both safe and legal in the face of continuing legislative and judicial challenges. It opens and closes with footage of the March 9, 1986, rally for reproductive rights in Washington, D.C., and features such prominent spokespersons as Gloria Steinem, Eleanor Smeal, and Karen DeCrow, along with the powerful vocals of singer/songwriter Holly Near. Also included are interviews with both advocates and opponents of legal abortion, among them several New York State legislators and the respective directors of the Syracuse chapters of the National Right to Life Committee and Planned Parenthood, as well as women who discuss their own abortions and a doctor who describes women who come to him saying, "I don't believe in this, I really don't believe in this—but I don't want this pregnancy." Although it breaks no new ground, the film is well produced, and it shows respect for all of its subjects, including those who express opposing points of view.

Personal Decisions

Type: 16mm film, videocassette
Length: 30 min.
Date: 1985
Cost: Purchase $395 (film), $295 (video); rental $50
Source: The Cinema Guild
1697 Broadway
New York, NY 10019
(212) 246-5522

Personal Decisions presents the stories of seven women who chose to have abortions at particular times in their lives: a woman who in 1954 became pregnant as a result of a brutal rape; a 16-year-old girl who took two weeks to decide, with the full support of her parents, that she was not ready to have a child; a couple looking forward to the birth of their second child who chose abortion after amniocentesis showed a severe defect in the fetus; an obstetrician and mother of four who became pregnant during medical school as a result of contraceptive failure; an immigrant mother of three whose fourth pregnancy threatened her plan to leave her abusive husband; a single teenage mother of two who became pregnant just as she had completed her high school degree and was about to enroll in a job training program; and a woman whose best friend was beaten to death by her father when he discovered she was pregnant and who, 40 years later, supports her daughter's decision to have an abortion despite her own strong Catholic beliefs. Interspersed with these stories are segments of an interview with Dr. Kenneth Edelin, an obstetrician and gynecologist who at one time was convicted as a result of performing an abortion (the conviction was subsequently overturned). The women and their families and partners represent a wide range of socioeconomic, cultural, and religious backgrounds; they are frank and open as they discuss their decisions, which they feel were both intensely personal and right for them. The film is well produced and the stories are sensitively portrayed; nevertheless, it would be more balanced if it had included women who chose not to abort as well as those who did.

Planned Parenthood's Response to The Silent Scream

Type: Videocassette
Length: 24 min.
Date: 1985
Cost: Arrange for viewing or rental through local Planned Parenthood affiliates—see white pages or Yellow Pages for affiliate nearest you

This film was produced by Planned Parenthood of Seattle as a rebuttal to *The Silent Scream*, which it says presents only one dimension of abortion, with "deliberate distortions of film and fact." Several stories of women who have had abortions are presented, along with testimony from specialists in the areas of pediatrics, neonatology, embryology, obstetrics and gynecology, family medicine, ultrasound, and medical ethics. They list the "five most alarming inaccuracies" in the film, including inaccurate statement of fetal age; use of a plastic model of different gestational age; use of different cameras for the ultrasound imagery, beginning with a sophisticated camera and changing to one that shows less detail; alterations in film speed; and the description of the fetus's sense of danger and attempts to avoid it, which could not occur at this gestational age because the brain is too undeveloped to sense danger or pain or to perform purposeful movements. The doctors also criticize the terminology used in the film, such as "rip apart," "tear," and "crushed," as manipulative. Other criticisms include a lack of sympathy for the woman or others involved and the implication that "everything will be fine" if every pregnant woman carries her pregnancy to term. This film is simply produced, with no music or special effects. The interviewees are direct and straightforward and use nontechnical language to present their case. *The Silent Scream*, they say, will not change a woman's decision to have an abortion; it will simply cause her to feel more guilt about doing so (see also *The Answer, The Silent Scream,* and *The Silent Scream: Responding to Critics,* this chapter).

Pro-Life Doctors Speak Out

Type: Videocassette
Length: 17 min.

Date: 1986
Cost: Purchase $19.95
Source: American Portrait Films International
             503 E. 200th Street
             P.O. Box 19266
             Cleveland, OH 44119
             (216) 531-8331; (216) 531-5228; (800) 736-4567;
             FAX (216) 531-8355

This brief video is Volume 1 of the Pro-Life Video Library produced by American Portrait Films. Other titles in the series are *Death on Demand: An Abortionist's Day, The Miracle of Ultrasound,* and *Living Experiments.* In this film, three pro-life physicians offer their "medical viewpoints on abortion" and the "fascinating truth about what science has to say about abortion." Dr. John Willke, author of *Handbook on Abortion* and past president of the National Right to Life Committee, states that the difference between an adult human and a fertilized egg is only a matter of age and "place of residence"—the egg is "unique, alive, growing" and "nothing will be added to it but nutrition." In a later segment, Willke describes the various methods of abortion and "frightening" long-term effects such as increased chance of miscarriage and postnatal death in subsequent pregnancies. Former surgeon general C. Everett Koop cites the case of test-tube babies to support his statement that life begins at conception and decries the "embarrassment" of late-term abortions. Dr. Bernard Nathanson, the former abortionist, explains that the inability to grow babies outside the bodies of women is only a limitation of technology and that within five to ten years "unborn humans may never know the inside of a mother's uterus." Women, says Nathanson, are the "ultimate victims of abortion," and unplanned pregnancy is a "wrenching social problem" that should be solved by social means. In conclusion, Willke says that neither churches nor philosophy will solve the question of when life begins; rather, doctors will, based on scientific knowledge.

Roe vs. Wade
Type: Videocassette
Length: 92 min.
Date: 1989
Source: Rental available at many video rental stores

This Emmy Award–winning, made-for-TV movie stars Holly Hunter as Ellen Russell, a substitute for real-life plaintiff Norma McCorvey, and Amy Madigan as Sarah Weddington, the Texas attorney who successfully argued the *Roe v. Wade* case in front of the Supreme Court. The movie is loosely based on the events leading up to the now-famous 1973 decision legalizing abortion. Ellie Russell, an itinerant, poor Texas woman who has reluctantly agreed to let her own mother raise her young daughter because she is unable to, discovers that she is pregnant. In the course of her unsuccessful attempts to gain an abortion, she meets Linda Coffee and Sarah Weddington, two fresh-out-of-law-school attorneys who have been searching for a plaintiff to challenge the constitutionality of Texas's strict abortion laws. Thinking that she might be able to win her abortion, Ellie agrees to participate as "Jane Roe"—only to learn that the case will take many months to wind its way through the courts. The movie then follows the separate stories of Ellie, who goes to stay with her father while she awaits the birth of the child she cannot afford to keep but cannot bear to give up, and Coffee and Weddington, who are moving the case ever closer to the ultimate forum, the Supreme Court. An important minor character is Jay Floyd, the attorney who is given the task of arguing for the state and who finds himself increasingly convinced that abortion is in fact murder and that "children's lives are depending on me." The movie is satisfyingly dramatic, although the dialogue suffers from an occasional lapse into exposition and the writer has taken a fair amount of artistic license. The acting, particularly from Holly Hunter, is first rate, making this an entertaining and absorbing, if not precisely accurate, portrayal of a pivotal period in abortion history.

The Silent Scream

Type:	Videocassette
Length:	28 min.
Date:	1984
Cost:	Purchase $29.95
Source:	American Portrait Films International
	503 E. 200th Street
	P.O. Box 19266
	Cleveland, OH 44119
	(216) 531-8331; (216) 531-5228; (800) 736-4567;
	FAX (216) 531-8355

This is probably the most famous abortion film ever made; it is certainly the most controversial. Its release provoked a storm of outrage among abortion rights supporters and galvanized pro-life activists, who saw in it documentary proof of their claim that abortion is murder. *The Silent Scream* is artfully produced and written, making maximum use of music, emotional language, and props to deliver its message. Hosted by Dr. Bernard Nathanson, *The Silent Scream* begins by showing a high-resolution ultrasound exam of the fetus inside the belly of an obviously pregnant woman—though it is never stated, she is almost certainly not the same woman whose uterus is shown in the abortion segment of the film. Then Dr. Nathanson states that we are going to see an abortion "from the victim's viewpoint." After a discussion of fetal development and a description of the abortion procedure, both explained with the aid of plastic models, Dr. Nathanson appears seated in front of a large-screen television. As the ultrasound tape is shown, he uses a plastic model of a fetus and actual instruments to explain what is happening in the fuzzy pictures on the screen—now the baby is pulling away from the instruments inserted into the uterus, now the mouth is open in a "silent scream," now the forceps are being used to crush the head. He describes the "secret language" used by the abortionist and the anesthesiologist ("Did you get 'number one'?"—meaning the head) and talks about abortion clinics that are "franchised out like fast food." As the camera alternates between shots of grieving women and apparent discarded fetuses, he talks of victimized women who are sterilized and "castrated." "The destruction of a human being," he says, "is no solution to what is basically a social problem." Nathanson calls for a better solution that would have "decent regard for the overriding priority of human life" (see also *The Answer, Planned Parenthood's Response to The Silent Scream,* and *The Silent Scream: Responding to Critics,* this chapter).

The Silent Scream—Responding to Critics

Type: Videocassette
Length: 29 min.
Date: 1985
Cost: Purchase $15
Source: National Right to Life Educational Trust Fund
             419 7th Street, NW, Suite 500
             Washington, DC 20004-2293
             (202) 626-8809

In this video, Kay James of National Right to Life interviews Dr. Bernard Nathanson, the former abortionist turned anti-abortion activist, about his controversial 1984 film *The Silent Scream,* which critics claim contains inaccuracies and deliberate distortions. James questions Nathanson about each of the criticisms leveled at the film; whether his answers are satisfactory or not will probably depend on the audience's point of view. For example, in response to denials that a 12-week-old fetus can perceive pain, as is asserted in the film, Nathanson says that he was not claiming that "pain is recognized on a cognitive level" and that cortical development is not necessary for the perception of pain. Further, the point of the film was not that the fetus felt pain, but that viewers witnessed "the cold-blooded destruction of a living human being." Nathanson also delivers a scathing attack on the "high cash, low-visibility [abortion] industry," which he estimates takes in over a billion dollars annually, and decries the victimization of women who "have not been told the truth" prior to obtaining abortions. Nathanson, who attributes his change of mind to his experience in perinatology, concludes by saying that he is working on a new technology that will "finally decide the abortion issue"—probably a reference to *Eclipse of Reason,* reviewed above (see also *The Answer, Planned Parenthood's Response to The Silent Scream,* and *The Silent Scream,* this chapter).

So Many Voices: A Look at Abortion in America

Type: 16mm film, videocassette
Length: 30 min.
Date: 1982
Cost: Purchase $450, rental $50

Source: Phoenix Films and Video
468 Park Avenue S.
New York, NY 10016
Order #22169

Hosted by Ed Asner and Tammy Grimes, this film opens with a montage that nicely illustrates the poles of the abortion debate. "One in ten women has had an abortion," say the hosts, and they cite polls showing that the majority of Americans believe that abortion should be legal—but only in certain circumstances. Some of those circumstances are described by people who have experienced them directly—a couple whose first daughter was born with Tay-Sachs disease and who would not have risked a second child without the option of abortion; a rape victim; a police woman whose own mother died from an illegal abortion and who deals daily with unwanted children; a doctor who recalls a ward filled with women suffering complications from illegal abortions; a mother of 4 whose own mother died from an illegal abortion 51 years ago; a doctor who changed his mind after 30 years of opposition to abortion; a former president of the National Abortion Federation; a former anti-abortion volunteer who speaks positively of her decision to have an abortion and the experience that followed; and workers at an abortion clinic in Ft. Wayne, Indiana, that has been subjected to harassment and threats. Although it claims to look at both sides of the debate, this film comes down clearly on the side of "the right to make our own choices"—the anti-abortion viewpoint is represented primarily through segments of public speeches by anti-abortion leaders Mildred Jefferson and Carolyn Gerster.

Who Broke the Baby?

Type: Videocassette
Length: 28–30 min.
Date: 1987
Cost: Purchase $19.95
Source: American Portrait Films International
503 E. 200th Street
P.O. Box 19266
Cleveland, OH 44119
(216) 531-8331; (216) 531-5228; (800) 736-4567;
FAX (216) 531-8355

This visually attractive and well-produced film is aimed primarily at teenagers. It is based on the book of the same title; both were written by Jean Garton, a self-described former abortion activist who tried to have an illegal abortion in 1971 and who changed her mind after researching abortion slogans and finding that "they lied." The title comes from a question asked by Garton's son at age three, on seeing a picture of a dismembered fetus. As the film opens, the attractive young narrator explains that our minds are conditioned by "image-distortion and double-speak" to not think of the fetus as human. Like building contractors who avoid numbering the thirteenth floor to "avoid the reality of its existence," society has made "the unborn child . . . the thirteenth floor of the human family." The rest of the film is a brisk-paced examination of the best-known abortion rights slogans. The segment on "Every woman has a right to control her own body" compares the risks of sexual activity to the risks of driving. "Abortion," states the narrator, "is evidence of a body that has been out of control." In response to the claim that women will seek abortions even if they are illegal, she asks, "Should we legalize car theft and shoplifting" because some people will do them anyway? Saying that women have abortions because of "convenience, expediency, and economics," she concludes with a plea to viewers to "be the person who will help [a pregnant woman] want her baby to live."

With a Vengeance: The Fight for Reproductive Freedom

Type: 16mm film, videocassette
Length: 40 min.
Date: 1989
Cost: Purchase $600 (film), $225 (video), discounts available to pro-choice activist groups; rental $75
Source: Women Make Movies
             225 Lafayette Street, Suite 212
             New York, NY 10012
             (212) 925-0606;
             FAX (212) 925-2052

Filmmaker Lori Hiris has used some deceptively simple techniques to make a powerful film about the expansion of the abortion rights movement to a broader struggle for full reproductive freedom. Filmed completely in black-and-white, the film has a deliberately rough, old-fashioned feel that emphasizes its blend of past and present. Throughout, Hiris combines sound and pictures in unusual and provocative ways to juxtapose different periods and aspects of her subject. Interview segments intersect with cartoon drawings, still photos, footage of demonstrations and speeches, newspaper headlines, and printed words to reveal the historical, political, and personal underpinnings of the women's movement and its continuing struggle to win not only reproductive freedom but also freedom from racism, sexism, and poverty, along with full access to health care and support for having and raising children. No single voice tells the story. Instead we see and hear numerous women and men—old, young, black, white, Latina, Asian—from early abortion rights activists such as Patricia Maginnis, Lawrence Lader, and the Redstockings, to present-day leaders like Billye Avery and Flo Kennedy, to young college students concerned that a right they have grown up with may be taken away. This is a radical film that almost certainly will not win converts among those who oppose abortion. Abortion rights activists, however, will find it both an absorbing portrait of their history and an inspiration to continue their struggle.

Your Crisis Pregnancy

Type: Videocassette
Length: About 26 min.
Date: 1987
Cost: Purchase about $30, rental $5/week through
            NRL Educational Trust Fund
Sources: National Right to Life Educational Trust Fund
            419 7th Street, NW, Suite 500
            Washington, DC 20004
            (202) 626-8809

            American Portrait Films International
            503 E. 200th Street
            P.O. Box 19266
            Cleveland, OH 44119
            (216) 531-8331; (216) 531-5228; (800) 736-4567;
            FAX (216) 531-8355

Dr. James Dobson of Focus on the Family introduces this video, which is intended to be shown to pregnant women at pregnancy help centers, churches, and pro-life groups. The film includes interviews with four women who have "been through just what you're going through"—a single woman just beginning a promising career, a rape victim, a high school student, and a woman whose childhood was spent in a succession of foster homes. The interviews are the most effective portion of the film, since the women are obviously speaking the truth about their experience. The remainder of the film, however, hammers its message at the viewer, particularly in sections emphasizing the physical and psychological risks of abortion. An obstetrician says, "Please don't think we're trying to frighten you," but abortion might cause sterility and "every year a few women die." Dr. Susan Stanford, a specialist in "post-abortion syndrome," tells women that they *will* experience grief, guilt, and depression; that they may become suicidal if they decide to abort; and cites unidentified studies showing that women who have abortions are more likely to enter psychiatric hospitals. There is "definite scientific evidence," she says, without stating what the evidence consists of, "that you will be happier if you go through with the pregnancy." The film's conclusion assumes that the viewer has been convinced to carry her pregnancy to term and advises her to seek help immediately, whether she plans to keep the baby or put it up for adoption. Under the guise of helpfulness and concern, this film exerts considerable pressure on its hapless viewers.

Glossary

abortifacient A substance, such as an herbal mixture, used to cause abortion.

abortion Delivery or removal of a fetus before it becomes viable.

abortion, failed An abortion that does not successfully terminate a pregnancy.

abortion, incomplete An abortion in which a portion of the embryo or fetus remains in the uterus.

abortion, induced An abortion brought about by the use of drugs or by mechanical or surgical means.

abortion, spontaneous See miscarriage.

amniocentesis Introduction of a hollow needle into the uterine cavity to withdraw amniotic fluid or to inject a drug.

amniotic fluid Liquid within the membranous sac that surrounds the fetus within the uterus.

aspirator A device that removes material by suction.

caesarean section Removal of a baby from the uterus through an incision in the abdomen. Also spelled cesarean, cesarian.

cannula A tube that is inserted into the uterus and through which the contents of the uterus are withdrawn.

catheter   A hollow cylinder or tube placed into the vagina and threaded into the uterus, through which drugs are administered.

cervix   The neck or opening of the uterus, which extends down into the vagina.

conception   Alternatively defined as: 1) the moment at which an egg and a sperm come together to create a zygote and 2) the implantation of a fertilized ovum in the lining of the uterus.

contraception   The prevention of conception or impregnation through any of several methods; also called birth control.

contraindication   A reason for not using a procedure.

curette   An instrument used to scrape tissue from inside the uterus.

D & E abortion   Dilatation and evacuation. A procedure where the cervix is dilated, after which the fetus and pregnancy tissue are grasped with a forceps and removed from the uterus.

DIC (disseminated intravascular coagulation)   A condition that prevents blood from coagulating properly.

dilation   Stretching or enlarging the cervical opening. Also called dilatation.

dilators   Tapered metal or plastic rods of progressively larger diameters, which are inserted one at a time into the cervix to stretch the opening so that a cannula or other instruments may be inserted.

Down's syndrome   A genetic disease characterized by the presence of 47 chromosomes rather than the normal 46, which causes mental retardation and physical abnormalities.

echogram   See sonogram.

ectopic pregnancy   A pregnancy that occurs outside the uterus, most often in a Fallopian tube, and that can be fatal to the mother.

embolism   An obstruction in an artery caused by a blood clot, air bubble, or foreign material.

embryo   Technically, the term given to the fertilized zygote after it has attached to the wall of the uterus and through the eighth week of development.

ergonavine   A drug used to contract the uterus.

Fallopian tubes   The two tubes leading from the ovaries to the uterus. Each month an ovum passes from one ovary through the Fallopian tube to the uterus. The Fallopian tubes are where fertilization takes place.

fertilization   The union of a spermatozoon and ovum to form a zygote.

fetus Technically, the term given to the developing human organism from the end of the eighth week of development through the completion of pregnancy.

forceps An instrument used to grasp tissue.

gestation The period of a pregnancy from conception to birth.

gravida A pregnant woman.

HCG Human chorionic gonadotropin, a hormone produced during pregnancy.

hysterectomy Surgical removal of the uterus.

hysterotomy Technically, an incision into the uterus; also used to describe a method of abortion in which the fetus is removed from the uterus through an abdominal incision.

implantation Attachment of the fertilized egg to the lining of the uterus about one week after fertilization takes place.

infertility The inability to conceive and bear offspring.

instillation abortion An abortion accomplished by placing a chemical substance in the uterus that subsequently causes contractions, or labor, so that the fetus is expelled.

IUD Intrauterine device, a small metal or plastic object that is placed in the uterus to prevent implantation (see above) of the fertilized egg.

laceration A tearing of tissue.

laminaria The stem of a Japanese seaweed that, when inserted into the cervical os, causes the cervix to dilate over a period of several hours or overnight.

laparotomy An incision made through the abdominal wall.

lithotomy position The standard position for pelvic exams, pelvic surgery, or childbirth, in which a woman lies on her back with her knees bent and her legs apart.

LMP Last menstrual period. Length of pregnancy is usually calculated from the first day of the last menstrual period. In actuality, however, fertilization usually takes place in the middle of the menstrual cycle, so that length of pregnancy LMP is actually about two weeks more than the gestational age of the fetus.

menarche   The onset of menstruation at puberty.

menstrual extraction   Removal of the contents of the uterus by suction before pregnancy has been confirmed.

miscarriage   The expulsion of an embryo or fetus from the womb before it is sufficiently developed to survive.

molar pregnancy   An abnormal mass in the uterus that is often mistaken for a pregnancy in the early stages of gestation.

mucus   The material secreted by the cells lining the body cavities.

multigravida   A woman who has been pregnant more than once.

multipara   A woman who has given birth two or more times.

nulliparous   Never having given birth to a child.

oral contraceptive   A pill that contains hormones that simulate early pregnancy and prevent ovulation, thereby preventing pregnancy.

organogenesis   The origin and development of organs.

os   Opening (in this context the openings at either end of the cervix).

osmotic dilator   A compressed sponge containing a chemical that dilates the cervix by absorbing fluid from it and expanding.

ovary   The female reproductive gland that contains the ova, or unfertilized eggs.

oxytocin   A drug used to stimulate uterine contractions.

parity   Having given birth to one or more children; often used with a number to indicate how many times a woman has given birth (a multiple birth delivery is defined as a single parous experience).

perforation   An opening or tear in the uterine wall.

peritoneal cavity   The abdominal cavity containing the pelvic and abdominal organs.

peritonitis   Inflammation of the lining of the abdominal cavity, usually as a result of infection.

PID   Pelvic inflammatory disease, an inflammation involving the Fallopian tubes, ovaries, and peritoneum.

pituitary gland   The pea-size gland in the brain that secretes hormones that control the ovaries, testes, and adrenal and other glands.

placenta The organ that transmits nourishment from a woman's blood-stream to her fetus; also called afterbirth.

placenta previa A condition in which the placenta blocks the cervical canal during childbirth.

pregnancy test, radioreceptor A blood test that can detect very early pregnancy.

pregnancy test, urine slide A test performed on the urine to detect pregnancy.

primigravida A woman pregnant for the first time.

primipara A woman who has given birth to a child or children for the first time.

pro-choice A term used by those who support legal abortion to describe themselves.

pro-life A term used by persons opposed to abortion to describe themselves.

prostaglandin A fatty acid found in many body tissues and a substance used in some methods of abortion to stimulate uterine contractions.

psychotropic drugs Drugs used to relieve anxiety by affecting the brain.

quickening The first perception of fetal movement by a pregnant woman.

quinine A plant extraction used to treat malaria and sometimes used as an ineffective abortifacient.

retained tissue Tissue that remains in the uterus after an abortion.

Rh factor A substance found on the surface of red blood cells in individuals who are Rh-positive. Those who do not have the substance are called Rh-negative.

Rh-immune globulin A substance containing a specific amount of Rh antibodies, which protect against the Rh-positive red blood cells of an Rh-negative woman after an abortion, miscarriage, or childbirth.

right to life The belief that human beings have a right to live that begins at conception and ends at natural death.

rubella Also known as German measles. A viral infection that, if contracted in the first three months of pregnancy, can cause such defects as mental retardation, blindness, and/or deafness in the child.

saline A salt solution.

saline abortion A method in which amniotic fluid is withdrawn through a needle inserted into the amniotic sac and replaced with a saline solution, which causes the fetus to die and to be expelled by the uterus.

septic abortion An abortion associated with high fever (100 degrees or more) caused by uterine infection; may lead to septic shock and death.

septic shock A severe loss of blood pressure caused by certain infections. Usually accompanied by high fever, it is fatal unless treated promptly.

sickle-cell anemia A genetically transmitted disease of black and Mediterranean peoples that can cause disintegration of the red blood cells.

slippery slope An argument claiming that once society has taken the first step along a given path, it will inevitably go the rest of the way "down the slope." In the context of abortion, the slippery slope argument is used most often by those who believe that legal abortion will lead to such societal abuses as involuntary euthanasia and elimination of "defective" or "useless" people such as the physically or mentally disabled or the elderly. The argument is used less frequently by those who claim that criminalizing abortion will lead to a revival of restrictions on birth control and increased repression of women.

sonogram Also called echogram. An image or picture created by sound waves, similar to an X-ray.

sound An instrument used to measure the depth of the uterus.

speculum An instrument that is inserted into the vagina and opened so that the vaginal walls and cervix are visible.

sterilization Surgery to permanently end reproductive capacity.

suction curettage See vacuum aspiration.

Tay-Sachs disease A genetically transmitted disease of Ashkenazic Jews that causes mental retardation and early death.

tenaculum A grasping instrument used to hold the cervix in place during an abortion.

thalidomide A psychotropic drug that, if taken during pregnancy, can cause severe limb deformities in the fetus.

trimester One third of a full-term pregnancy (about 13 weeks).

ultrasound See sonogram.

urea A natural liver by-product that can be produced synthetically. Used in abortion in conjunction with other agents to induce uterine contractions.

uterus The hollow, muscular, pear-shaped organ in which the fertilized egg implants and grows into a fetus.

vacuum aspiration Evacuation of uterine contents by vacuum suction.

vacuum aspirator A hollow tube through which the contents of the uterus are removed in a suction abortion; also the suction machine to which the tube is attached.

vagina The canal that extends from the uterus to the vulva.

viability The point at which a fetus can survive outside the uterus, either with or without artificial life support.

vulva Vaginal lips.

womb See uterus.

zygote The fertilized egg before it implants itself in the uterine wall.

Index